# NEIGHBOUR DISPUTES

# NEIGHBOUR DISPUTES

A Complete Guide - How to deal with them, How to prevent them, How to survive them

What? You don't like my new hedge?

# PAUL BENEDEK

Visit the author's website at **www.neighbour-dispute.com**

Cover and book design by Paul and Berna Benedek

Printed in the United Kingdom-First Printing: December 2010

ISBN 978-1-4467-1734-9

# Disclaimer

The aim of this guide is to help you to avoid a neighbour dispute or to deal with one should you be unfortunate enough to be in that position. The advice given in this guide is not that of legal experts but is the personal views and experience of the author as a result of dealing with neighbour disputes, Solicitors, Barristers and mediators as well as the UK legal system for many years. Therefore where you have any doubt or need further advice it is strongly recommended that you take the appropriate counsel from a suitably qualified person who can assist you further. The Author accepts no liability for the advice or the consequences of any advice, commentary, discussions or recommendations given in this guide.

# Acknowledgement

*'This book is dedicated to my lovely wife'.*

# Contents

Disclaimer ........................................................................................ v

Acknowledgement ........................................................................ vii

Why you should Consider This guide and Take its Contents Very
Seriously ...................................................................................... xiii

**Chapter 1**

How to Avoid Disputes withYour Neighbour Before You
Buy! ................................................................................................1

Layer Three: Taking a Look at the General Area .............................3

Layer Two:Take a Look at Street or Avenue Level ...........................9

Layer One: Viewing the House ........................................................16

**Chapter 2**

Committing to Buy: What to Consider Before You Commit
to Buy............................................................................................27

Collecting and Receiving Data .........................................................30

Checks with the Land Registry ........................................................35

Maps................................................................................................41

Adverse Possession.........................................................................43

**Chapter 3**

After Exchanging the Contract- When You Move In ..........................53

**Chapter 4**

Dealing with Neighbours .................................................................61

Problems, Remedies and Their Prevention......................................65

**Chapter 5**

When You Have a Dispute ...............................................................85

How to Deal With the Issues and the Other Side ............................86

Actions to Take..................................................................................89

Instructing a Solicitor to Deal with Nuisance.................................94

Costs..................................................................................................96

Dealing with Incidents ...................................................................100

**Chapter 6**

When it All Goes Wrong and the Dispute Heads for Court! .........103

Pre-Action Protocols.......................................................................107

Personal Issues................................................................................111

Personal Issues Check List .............................................................115

**Chapter 7**

Possible Solutions to Disputes........................................................117

Mediation or Alternative Dispute Resolution................................119

When Not to Mediate.......................................................................120

**Chapter 8**

Preparing for the Court ...................................................................129

Land Registry...................................................................................141

Solicitors .........................................................................................143

Barristers .........................................................................................156

Contacting a Barrister .....................................................................157

Judges...............................................................................................165

**Chapter 9**

Court Process—Land Registry Adjudication and the
Adjudicator to Her Majesty's Land Registry..................................175

County Court Process ......................................................................180

Appeals Process ..............................................................................182

**Chapter 10**

Cost Assessment Process.................................................................189

**Chapter 11**

If All Else Fails and You do Not Win Your Case or Part of It ......201

Money, Financing Your Dispute ...................................................201

**Chapter 12**

Final Thoughts ...........................................................................211

**Appendix**

Useful Resources .........................................................................215

Before You Move In ....................................................................215

After You Move In .......................................................................215

When You Have Issues (The Law Regarding Problems) .............216

Forms and Documents .................................................................218

Adjudicator to Her Majesty's Land Registry ...............................218

Her Majesty's Courts Service ......................................................218

The Legal and Professional Regulators, Sources ..........................218

Complaints ..................................................................................221

# Why you should Consider This guide and Take its Contents Very Seriously

It is estimated that one in three people in the United Kingdom have some form of dispute with their neighbours and as a result there are a lot of court cases, and massive financial expenditure in this area. Whenever you buy or rent a property you have potential for a neighbour dispute. Seemingly innocent and inconsequential actions or even inaction may cause a dispute with your neighbour. If you have formally recorded a dispute, you have to declare it when you want to sell your home. This may make the sale of your house difficult and the likelihood is that you will have to discount the value to sell it.

A neighbour dispute is a time consuming, costly and nasty affair that will damage your life. Even if you are lucky enough to win your case, after much heartache, you will have lost a lot of opportunities and time in your life. To defend yourself you will have to spend tens of thousands of pounds, spend many hours writing correspondence, and you will go through endless days and nights bickering with your family and generally living in a state of stress. If you loose your case you will suffer all of the above, and will have lost tens of thousands of pounds in the process and you may have to pay for your neighbours legal fees as well. In any event you are a loser. Losses and anguish are avoidable if you steer the right path. The legal system in the UK is a lottery. If you can present a better case than your neighbour, you may win. However Judges are opinionated and the law is not clear cut so there are no guarantees of success! Ask yourself do you really want to gamble? You could lose everything you have worked for in life and a whole lot more!

In a no-nonsense format that cuts straight to the heart of the matter, this guide examines a whole series of disputes including boundary and land disputes, which are the most common form of neighbour disputes. It looks at ways to prevent them and offers practical advice to help you to minimise the substantial financial and emotional costs that you will incur should you be in the unfortunate position to deal with such disputes. The book also gives practical advice regarding the instruction of experts and Solicitors and makes recommendations of how you can minimise the risks of losing your dispute case in the court or tribunal, should it go that far. If you lose your case, this book also gives you advice on how to move on with your life and offers practical ways for raising money and for funding your dispute and its outcome.

# Chapter 1

## How to Avoid Disputes with Your Neighbour Before You Buy!

The seeds for a neighbour dispute are numerous and most disputes start long before a person moves into their new home. The majority of disputes are as a result of history and if you do not understand this, then is can lead you directly and unwittingly into a dispute. It is estimated that fifty percent of land is unregistered in the UK. When this statistic is considered along with other potential areas for dispute, the odds are initially not in your favour. Therefore the best way to avoid a dispute is to plan for avoidance and consider each and every contributing element to a potential neighbour dispute before you move into your home and by doing so, you can avoid one.

While choosing a property to live in, the location, the size and the condition of the property are not the only factors to consider. Most people search for properties to deal with specific needs and these needs may change over time. When you buy your first home for example, you may have only a limited budget so you will most likely try and buy the best home you can for your money. Perhaps your second home will be bigger than your first as you may wish to start a family. Most people look at only a few things around their home purchase and they very seldom consider the potential for any kind of dispute. This means that when a purchase is made, there could be inadvertent issues already there that could ruin your life and without their consideration, they will hit you very hard.

When the author was searching for his home he had specific requirements for the house he wanted to buy and he did not think about the many aspects and conditions that could cause a neighbour dispute. The character house the author purchased was in a very good part of the town, it was in a most influential area and it had many 'wow' factors as well as potential for future expansion. He now realises that he should have also looked at the purchase of his new home from the perspective of there being a possible dispute or of there being problems in the neighbourhood. This perspective will be summarised in three "layers" that should always be examined when you are looking to buy or rent a property. These "layers" should be looked at systematically and you start your home search from a good distance away from its location and you work your way in until you finally get to your proposed new home. The benefits of taking this "layered" approach is that you can discount a lot of factors that could cause you problems before you get to your new home. It allows for you to eliminate the purchase or rent of a property without emotional involvement and it also forces you to consider a wider number of aspects such as local infrastructure that may be important to you, yet you may not have contemplated.

The first layer is the most outer layer and it is here where you should start your search. This layer, "Layer three" is your local area, and it covers an area of a few miles around where you are proposing to live. The middle layer, "Layer two" is your local neighbourhood and "Layer one" is the consideration of direct neighbours in and around your proposed new home.

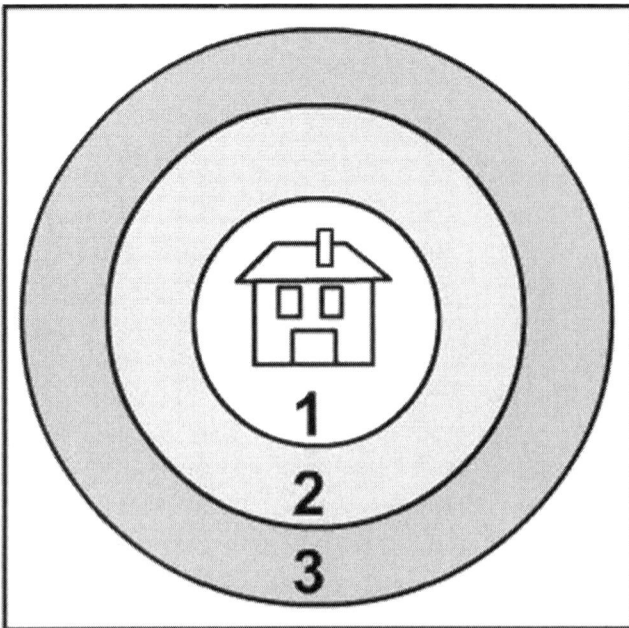

# Layer Three: Taking a Look at the General Area

Before you even look at the street or home where you are planning to live, look at the area around your proposed new home first. Consider a three mile radius to the area. If the area looks bad, rough, isolated, degenerated or has poor infrastructure you may wish to discount moving to this new area before you even see your proposed new home.

## Do You Know Where You Are Moving to? What is the Area Like?

If you are moving to a new area, even if it is just a short distance away from where you live now, do some research before you move. Even if you like your current local area and even if your proposed new home is a short distance away, you must always check the area again. The reason for this is that there are areas that are very good and just a few hundred metres away, there could be very bad areas. Similarly if you live in one part of an area, you may not know that there are issues in another part of it. For example you may live in a quiet street, yet the street where you are proposing to buy your house is built may be on the edge a major road, so noise could be an issue to you and if there are paths and alleyways, so could crime. When starting your search of layer three, first look on the internet to see what is in the news that relates to the area where you are proposing to live. Find the website of the local councils, both the parish and the town council. Surf to see if there are any community websites in the area, look at churches, clubs, pubs etc. You need to get an understanding of the community and what are important issues to the local council. When you start your search try and talk to the police in the area and see what their priorities and issues are. The local community support officer is a good person to talk to at the police station. They will really know what is going on from a crime perspective in their local patch. When searching, do not only consider the general area where you are proposing to live but look at the neighbouring and surrounding areas as well. Infrastructure is a key consideration in buying your home and if you have to travel through rough areas to go shopping, to visit friends or go to work, this can be disturbing and unpleasant, yet without considering it, you could purchase a home and will have to suffer the consequences. When considering the infrastructure also consider the state of the roads.

During summer they may be fine, however in winter they may be hard to drive due to snow or flooding. Make sure you find out about the roads that get blocked and the ones to avoid.

There are a number of national websites to help you find the information you need to examine an area in order to get an idea of what it is like, many of these sites give a good deal of detail and show relevant information to potential home buyers, from the good points to the bad ones and a few of these sites are listed in the appendix at the back of the document.

## Using Local Magazines, Radio and Newspapers to Help You

When researching at layer three, look in the local newspapers and magazines to see if there is any news about the area where you wish to live. Consider all news elements and ask a number of questions. For example is there any crime in the area? Is the crime petty theft or violent crime? Listen to the local radio station for local news and events. All of this information will let you determine if it is a safe area to live or whether there are problems of a more concerning or violent nature. For example in the area where the author lives, the crime is petty crime where opportunists break into cars or the main crime is the theft of agricultural tools and implements to order. The numbers of burglaries and violent crimes are very low around where he lives. There are very few youth problems, and the schools have excellent attendance records. It is worthwhile looking at the local schools to see how well they are doing in the national league tables for attendance as well as academic achievement. Absenteeism is something to watch out for where there are schools nearby as this could mean kids could be at home making a noise during the day or out creating issues instead of attending school. When considering your home and the area, also look at parish or town council updates in the papers, and find any planning applications in the area. These will show how the area is developing and will also give you an indication of any potential problems that could arise. For example, are the housing developments that are being proposed for build for affordable housing or are they permissions for more up market homes? Are buildings likely to be built that could bring problems? For example flats or apartment blocks that could take away light and make the surrounding area darker. If these are the types of buildings that are being developed, unless their build and design is undertaken tastefully, they could devalue the homes in the area as they could create opportunities for criminals to come and go with alley ways or areas to hide being created. Take a look at local businesses as well when undertaking your search. These companies also tell a story. What are their problems and issues? Are local businesses growing or declining? Is employment high or are there companies that are laying off people? Look at the types of business in the area as well. For example are there companies that need distribution? If so then you could see lorries and deliveries coming and going both day and night. This could create both noise and traffic problems.

## Walk the Ground!

After you have done your research, it is worth getting out and looking at the area on foot. If driving, make sure you park up and actually walk the whole area slowly yourself. You can miss important clues if you drive only. While walking you see greater detail and can hear things as well! Take a walk of the area on a number of occasions during different times of the day and on different days of the week. If you have the time, do it over a couple of months as each area changes during the seasons and at particular times of the year. For example visit during half term or during the summer holidays when there are more children around. Visit during the winter to see if the roads are clear or if they are blocked because the council no longer grits them on frosty nights.

## Pubs, Clubs and Shops

Go to the local shopping or recreation areas at different times of the day and night. Look at local pubs; are they nice quiet places to go for a break or are they rough drinking dens with straw on the floor and holes in the pool table? If they have beer gardens, are these maintained or roughly paved areas of grass with the leftovers from a few days drinking left lying around? Are the patrons respectable or are they loud at night? Do the pubs or local shops play loud music? Does this go on into the night? Go into the pubs and talk to people. If you buy someone a drink it is quite surprising how much information you can get about the area and the issues within it. Make sure you visit the area after closing hours as some pubs have a "lock in after hours" where they continue to sell beer and stay open very late into the night. If they do, this could be a bad sign as you can be disturbed at any time of night as the patrons come and go.

Go to the local shops. Look at the shop keepers. Are they respectable tradesman? Do they look like they could sell things to underage youths or children? Are there group of children or teenage yobs congregated around the shops or staying close to them? These are all signs of potential trouble. Ask the traders how business is, ask them how trade has changed over time, and what the local problems are. For example the author went to one shop in a seemingly respectable part of town. The shop was a hairdresser, and the author found out that the day before he visited, during a conversation with the barber that the jewellery shop next door had been robbed by armed criminals.

Are there local activity centres for youths or other members of the public? Most crime happens because of boredom and opportunity. If there are local clubs in the area and where there are activities for the younger generation, crime is generally reduced within this age group, and the older generation tend to be more socially respectable. Ask about local scouts, cadets and boys and girls brigades. Find out what the local sports, community and religious centres are doing to keep people occupied.

Are there any takeaway's, sandwich or fish and chip shops close to the area where you are proposing to live? If so these areas could be noisy. Noise could be an issue at weekends as well as litter if the council has not provided bins around these shops. Do these shops do home deliveries? Are they open twenty four hours a day? Make sure you go to these shopping areas on different days of the week where the wind has changed direction. Noise carries on the wind and if it is in the wrong direction you may not hear how noisy the place really is.

Look at local parking and the state of the street or the shopping centre in the area. Is it clean as well? Is it maintained or is it neglected? Is it busy or quiet? Are there rubbish bins provided to the shops and are they regularly emptied. Go to the back of the shops at different times of the day and week and see. Some shops do not have regular litter collections or alternatively they just pile waste up outside their back doors for days on end. This encourages the less pleasant forms of wild life and can present a health hazard.

## Playing fields, Parks and Footpaths

Are there any playing fields close to the area where you are proposing to live? Are there any local clubs that could create noise or issues at the weekends or mid-week? For example there is a playing field by the side of the authors' house. When he checked it out before he purchased his home, he saw only dog walkers and children playing there. He did not check the field at the weekend and when he moved in he found it used by three different football clubs at different times of the weekend. When balls from the weekly football matches came into his garden, he regularly saw people tramping down his hedge, and climbing over his wall to recover their ball. This led to friction with the clubs and one day some yob climbed over his fence and deliberately damaged his plants. When the author confronted him, the footballer got aggressive and started swearing and threatening violence at the author and was just itching for a fight.

Are there any public rights of way or footpaths close by each other near your new home? Are there any areas that are dark and that could hide unlawful activities? For example at one stage on the playing field the author found local youths drinking and messing around during the evening. The field had benches for seating and was not lit. It was ideal to hide drinking, and it was frequented by underage drinkers until the police took action and prevented it.

Another problem is that paths and rights of way allow for people to get away and hide quickly. Some paths and parks allow for people to simply melt away without being seen or heard. Criminals favour places like this as they can commit a crime and disappear quickly without being noticed or discovered. Make sure that any areas near your home are not places where criminals can appear and then disappear. If there are any areas like this, you may need to increase your home and personal security or you will need to be extra vigilant if you decide to live there. For example the author learned this lesson the hard way when he parked his car outside his flat on the edge of a park that had many exits and entrances. Sometime during the day someone smashed his car window and stole some tools that were in the back. When the car alarm went off, the author ran to his car but the thief had already disappeared into the park with the tools. It took less than two minutes for the thief to melt away and he was not spotted by the author or by anyone else in the park.

## Roads, Schools and Parking

Roads can become a problem and their traffic patterns can change depending on the time of day. Some roads can be quiet backwaters with little or no traffic passing; they are just used to access the houses on or at the end of them. Other roads can become very busy during the rush hours, at weekends or particularly during the school run. Dark or dimly lit roads can become ideal spots for fly tippers, car thieves or boy racers. Make sure you look at this matter closely as it can become a major source of irritation to you. For example at the end of the authors' road there is a school and the parents of the children going to this school are extremely inconsiderate if not outright rude. The author had an issue over several weeks where the main road to the school was blocked due to road works so the parents of the school children used the road in front of his house to take their children to school in the morning. The parents thought nothing of blocking the authors' driveway to chat with the other parents, thought little of complaining to him that the postman was in the way in the morning and thought nothing of driving over the grass lawn in front of his house. One day the author took delivery of a new fridge around the time of the school run, and because the lorry inconvenienced the parents of some of the children, he had several of them coming and knocking on the door complaining because the lorry was blocking the road and that the author should be taking deliveries after the school run and not inconveniencing them. Sex and travel was his response to these people!

Parking can also become a problem at certain times of the day or week. For example parents evening at the local school can cause major parking issues close by the authors' house as can any games played on the field by the local football club. It is worthwhile checking around to see what happens at different times of the year if you can. Also bear in mind future uses for underutilised areas around your home. Their usage could be changed with the council's permission to something that may cause a problem to you. Think about commercial buildings and fields as these could easily be redeveloped into something different or they could have permissions granted for a change of use that could be detrimental.

## Employment & Regeneration

What is the employment situation in the area where you are proposing to live? Is there high unemployment, seasonal employment or is the area prosperous? What is it like compared to how it was several years ago. Is investment high in the area? Is the area declining? Are the houses desirable there? These are all good indicators of the social conditions in the area. Are there any issues regarding local businesses? For example are they growing and expanding their operations or contracting and scaling back? Where the author now lives there were a lot of strawberry fields and orchards in the area. These are gradually going and the farms are closing or not operating like they used to, their buildings are now being let as storage or are being converted into houses. If you are proposing to live in a town or a nearby suburb, look at the number of shops, and commercial premises available for rent. Check signage to see if there are leases available. If there are lots of empty offices or units, the chances are that there is high unemployment in the area and standards could be low or drop as a result. Office and business unit holders are in business to make money and very often they will look to convert property rather than leave it empty or let it deteriorate over time. As the demand for affordable housing increases, many former offices or shops could be converted to cheap housing. This will impact any area where you are proposing to live as low wage earners will look to move into the area.

# Layer Two:Take a Look at Street or Avenue Level

There are lots of things going on at street level and these "indicators" are a good measure of whether you are likely to face problems if you buy a house in this street or avenue. Make sure you take the time and visit the street at different times of the day and on different days of the week during the year. Make sure you go and visit on foot and try and absorb everything around you. Take in the whole atmosphere, the smells, and the noises on the street or avenue as well as examining the local wildlife.

## The State of the Street or Avenue

When you walk down the street there are several areas to look out for. First check to see if the gardens in the neighbourhood are maintained and well kept. Look to see if there is litter in any of the gardens. Are there toys strewn around? Danger signs are ill kept gardens, broken walls or fences and rubbish. Toys everywhere could mean children and this will increase the potential for noise. If toys are just left lying in the garden or are on the street then this could show that the parents are not supervising their children, and this could add to problems if their children wander and as they grow up.

Every street has its nosy parker or busy body. Are they apparent when you walk by? Are there gatherings of people around on driveways, in garages or on their lawns or gardens? The chances are that if there are people gathered together during the day on a regular basis, then they could be there at night or at weekends, and noise could become an issue. Similarly if there are groups of people together, they could all be good friends or family members and the chances are that as a stranger you are unlikely to be made truly welcome in their area.

What does it sound like as you walk down the street? Can you hear the birds or do you hear music from televisions or radios? Is there a driveway with a collection of cars or motorbikes on or nearby? There is a strong probability that there is a local "mechanic" and he or she will likely rev his or her car or cars on a regular basis; or have lots of friends working late into the night or at weekends or holiday periods.

## Noise

Weekends and evenings are the best times to check for any noise or activity in the street as sound travels better in still air or at night.

Check out the houses or properties on each side of the house or flat that you're interested in buying or renting, look at the state of your immediate neighbours' home and of those living next door to them. Stop and listen for a while near each one. Is it noisy or quiet where you are standing? Are there thin walls in each house? Can you hear what's going on inside them?

Loud music can be a real issue and this is something you really need to think about. Sometimes people play their music too loud without thinking about it, others play it loud deliberately and do not care. Sometimes the music is loud because there are teenagers that live in the house who are unsupervised. Take a look carefully at the source of the noise if you hear loud music. If it is teenagers that are creating the noise, then the chances are that the noise will be a regular feature when their parents are away.

Keep your ears open for the next one hit wonder who thinks that he or she could be the next chart topper or television star. Amateur musicians can play their instruments loudly at awkward times of the day and many can also play badly, adding to the annoyance they cause with loud beats and overzealous drumming a regular feature.

# Parking

Cars can be a major nuisance at street level and people become very territorial in and around their homes. If there are many cars parked outside a particular house, they could be a hobby mechanic and so will work on their cars regularly and this may be disturbing, particularly if they have power tools, or if they listen to music whilst working. Other issues could be that they are repairing or selling these cars so you could see high numbers of visitors turning up and looking for bargains or other opportunities.

If the street or avenue is full of cars then this could also present issues to you or any visitors at busy times of the day and at weekends. If people are competing with each other for parking spaces, and if they have lived in the street for a long time it will be an immediate problem to you, even if you have a parking area directly outside your house. It is inevitable that someone will park outside your home and will block you in or prevent you from parking. If you have a visitor and they park in someone else's spot, then this will also cause friction. The author has even seen bad neighbours pour paint stripper onto cars that have parked in "their spot" without their permission. The police naturally do nothing about this when it is reported to them, as they are either not interested, not motivated or will make the excuse that they find it difficult to prove if there are no direct witnesses to a crime. Double parking is another general problem and it adds to the issues described above as both sides of the road are involved. Even where they do not completely block, access for larger vehicles such as rubbish removal trucks can be an issue. Very often the council will not make collections where they have no access. This means that if you are unlucky, then your rubbish may not be collected for a while. During the summer months this can be a real issue as the smell will increase and the potential for flies and vermin increases. This is a particular problem in high density urban areas.

## The Street or Avenues Appearance - Gardens

Do people take pride in their gardens or their outside home decor? Are their gardens maintained or is there rubbish or toys strewn around them? Well-kept gardens are a sign of pride as are nicely painted doors and windows, or other adornments, decoration or workmanship. If there are many well-kept gardens in the area, then the whole street is likely to be better maintained, as people will take pride in the neighbourhood.

If there is rubbish or toys strewn around, then the likelihood is that the owner will not take pride in the street as they have no pride in their own garden. If there are toys, then children could be an issue in the area. Does each garden have a high fence around them or are the gardens open? If they are open with lots of toys around, then the children will be both visible and the noises from their playing will not be screened. Similarly if there is a high fence around a garden, then this may warrant further investigation as it could be a security measure, and so could indicate that the local crime rate could be high.

## Houses

Houses say a lot about their owners. Are the houses in the street well-kept or are they shabby and not looked after? Like most streets you are likely see a mixture of well maintained or shabby houses where perhaps older neighbours are not able to spend the time or money in maintaining their homes like they used to. Look out for high fences, alarms and visible security deterrents. Crime could be an issue if there are many visible deterrents. Look for old cars, bikes and many cars around as these could be signs of teenagers, car mechanics or scrap dealers. Other things to look out for are if there are any problems around guttering, roofs or any part of the building fabric of your neighbouring homes as these could be signs that builders are needed for repairs and you may see them appear in the future along with trucks, noise and scaffolding. Although this in itself may not be an issue in the short term, noise, pollution and parking may be if builders do undertake any repairs and are around on a long term or regular basis.

## Lighting

Is the street or avenue well lit? Can you see clearly at night or is it dimly lit with lots of shadows? Opportunists notice this and so car crime, petty crime as well as the burglary of homes could be high in this area, or could increase as opportunists look for easy targets to take advantage of. Talk to the police and local people to see what is going on in the area.

## Street Access

What is access like at street level? Are there roads coming in and out around your home or is it located on a cul-de-sac? Are there side alley ways or streets that could hide people coming and going? Again this could be ideal for the opportunist criminal or for teenagers to come and go as they please without being detected.

Visit the area at night so you can to see the street lighting and the dark areas as the authors experience has shown that even though there may be light poles on a street, they may not come on at night, thus giving cover for any opportunist criminal or yob who wants to come and go unnoticed. Check to see the lighting on these side streets and on the adjoining roads as well as the main ones. Look at areas that are hidden and obscured at night. If they are on or near roads and footpaths, the chances are that they will hide people coming and going. Crime, if not currently an issue in these types of areas, could become an issue particularly in today's economic climate.

## Garages

Watch out for detached garages located across from people's houses as they could attract thieves or bad types. Take a look at them carefully to ensure that they have not been forced or damaged as this is a clear sign of crime. If you can see inside one or two of them then this is even better. Are they just for cars or are people storing goods to run businesses from inside of them? Are they clear or is there material inside that could construe a fire hazard? Take a visit to the garages in the evening or at night. Are they lit or are they dark? If they are dark, then it gives criminals perfect cover to try and steal from inside of the garage without drawing too much attention to themselves.

## Dogs & Mess

Some people think nothing of letting their pets foul the pavement or the grass by the side of the road. If there is a lot of mess in the area, it is a sure fire sign of trouble at a later date. It is not only unhygienic, it shows that the dog owners are inconsiderate and as most people tend not to wander too far from their homes, it could be a sign that you will hear barking, or there could be unattended dogs wandering or it could just be a poorly maintained environment.

## People - Your Potential New Neighbours

The biggest factor as to whether or not you will live in peace and quiet will be your neighbours. When looking for a new home, do not only think about your direct neighbours but your extended ones as well. When considering the neighbours; look at the immediate vicinity to your proposed new home, your chosen street or avenue as well as several streets away as people can drift. This is particularly true of teenagers or people with time on their hands. Also look for groups of people who appear to stick together in clans or look for smaller groups of people who gather at regular times during the day or week.

There will be a general atmosphere to the street and if you talk to people you can generally get a good feel of what the neighbourhood is like. For example when you talk to people are they interested in talking to you, and are they genuine, or are they reserved with what they say and suspicious of you? Are they quiet or loud and boisterous in their dealings with you?

Be on the lookout for people who have regular visitors at unusual hours. As an example the author once lived on a quiet cul de sac and one of the neighbours regularly had teenagers visiting. They were turning up at different times of the day, sometimes in the middle of the night. This went on for several months and then one day the police turned up and arrested the neighbour. The person concerned had been buying alcohol and had been selling it on to children and teenagers for profit. Although this is a real world but extreme example, regular visitors at odd hours could mean that there is some kind of activity going on. In the authors case it was illegal activity.

## The Older Generation

An area where there are mainly elderly residents sounds as though it would be quiet and idyllic, but some members of the older generation may be very 'set in their ways', and may object to your children playing in their own gardens, or to you doing things that are contrary to their firm beliefs, for example gardening on a Sunday. The authors'brother had an incident one day at his home where an elderly neighbour came round and complained that the lawn was being cut on a Sunday. In this elderly persons eyes Sundays were seen as a day of rest, and so work and the noise from a lawn mower was contrary to his religious and personal views. Needless to say that the authors brother had numerous other issues from this person over time as this persons beliefs were extreme in modern terms and contrary to the practicalities of modern life, especially of people like the authors' brother who works during the week and can only do gardening and house work at the weekend.

# Pets

Pets can be a real problem. Look out for dogs that are either wandering around or that are left unattended in people's gardens. They are a sure fire bet for some noise and hassle. Very often people are oblivious as to the noise that their pets make because they are used to it and so leaving them outside to howl or bark is nothing to them. Another problem the author has encountered is dogs roaming and getting themselves into problems due to their owners neglect. For example one of the authors' neighbours' regularly threw his dog out of his home in the morning and he let his dog do what it wanted to do, this included letting it go out under his fence and letting it wander the streets to look for food in neighbours dustbins.

Cats are another problem and this also needs to be considered when moving home. Cats are territorial and they leave scents to mark their "areas".If a cat has not been neutered it will regularly spray urine to mark its territory and if cats are wandering into your garden or driveway, the smell from their activities can be very unpleasant. Similarly cats have favourite spots that they use as a toilet. This again can be a problem particularly if you want to grow plants and vegetables or if you have small children. Cats are creatures of habit so it will be an on-going problem unless you do something about it.

People are very protective of their pets and even when they are a nuisance, they tend to give their pets the benefit of doubt. People also tend to let their pets get away with anything. This can be particularly aggravating and it is a potential area for a great deal of problems and anguish, as your neighbours will often see you at fault and not their pets as the problem.

# Houses for Sale or to Let

If there are a large number of houses for sale or for let in an area this could mean several things. Either people are on their way up and are cashing in on house price rises, or alternatively there could be an underlying negative trend around the health of the neighbourhood. In the latter case crime or problem neighbours could be the reason for so much sale or rental property being available. This will need to be researched carefully if it is the cause of so much movement as the house owners may not want to tell you there is a problem.

The other consideration with regard to houses for sale or to let is that the occupiers will change over time. This is may be an obvious statement, however in the case of the authors' last house his initial neighbours in one house nearby were nice and friendly and assisted whenever they could. When they sold their house and moved away to retire the author was left with a new neighbour who did not care for anyone apart from himself and was the cause of a great deal of anguish to the author from the moment he moved in. This person was selfish, arrogant and a thief. It only takes one or two people to go and for them to be replaced with people with a poor attitude or bad principles and the whole neighbourhood atmosphere and outlook will change for the worse.

One of the other experiences that comes from people moving around is that new people are treated differently sometimes by established neighbours, and again in the authors' case he found that he was made very welcome by two neighbours especially. These neighbours wanted to get involved with him from day one. It was not until several weeks after moving in to his new home that he found out that they were being friendly because they were touting for business. One was a landscaper who wanted to clear and plant the authors' garden and the other was a builder who wanted to remodel the authors' home. When the author said he was not interested, they went off in a huff and although did not create problems directly, they made the author feel unwelcome whenever possible until he moved out of that home several years later.

People have fads and follow fashion. As the new ones on the block you may find that people spend time to get to know you as this is generally what they do out of curiosity. Because someone is nice to you do not consider for one moment that this will continue in the future. The smallest thing can change peoples attitudes towards you, so consider the characters of the people you meet. Ask yourself do these people gossip or are they more reserved in their outlook? The authors advice is pick and choose people to talk to carefully as you can never really tell who is genuine or who has an agenda to follow.

# Layer One: Viewing the House

Before you visit your proposed new house there are a few considerations for you to think about. First and foremost, consider that the seller has a vested interest in selling their house. Whatever they say needs to be verified to the greater or lesser extent. Most people are honest and descent, however some people are not and appearances can be deceptive. It is difficult to tell the difference between these types of people and so you need to be wary.

The next consideration to take into account is that estate agents are paid on results. That is to say that if they sell a home they make their commission. No sale, no money. Again most estate agents are hardworking and honest people. This issue however is that sometimes commercial interests may prevail and the pressure for a quick sale from the house owner may see that important details that could help you avoid a neighbour dispute in the future could be overlooked. Most estate agents do not consider neighbour disputes in the sales process as they typically want to sell the house for their client and then move on to the next sale, therefore if you do not ask the right questions of the estate agent, they certainly will not tell you anything that could be detrimental to achieving their sale..

## A Foundation to Build Upon Before You Buy

If you have examined layers three and two and have found that the area and street are fine around where you are proposing to live and in line with your expectations, then your final layer to check is the house you propose to rent or buy. Bear in mind this is just an initial check and even though you may be excited about the visit, try and be objective when viewing. Given below are a number of questions to ask the sellers of the property you are viewing, or to ask the estate agent showing you the property on behalf of the sellers. If a home information pack or HIP is available, try and get a copy before you view the house.

If you are happy after the first visit make sure you go back again at a different time of the day. If you are limited in the time you have available to visit, make sure that you visit during an evening or even better try and get a weekend appointment as most of your prospective neighbours are likely to be back from work. If the owners of your prospective new home have children then they also could be home as could be other children in the neighbourhood. If your immediate neighbours are home, you can gauge quickly if noise, children or parking are going to be issues to you in the future.

Do not be afraid to ask the seller as many questions as you can. If the owner of the house cannot answer the questions you ask there and then, ask the sellers estate agent to get the answers for you. It is in everyone's interest to answer as much as possible as each party will want to sell to you. Remember this and do not be pressured into a decision on purchasing or letting without getting the answers to your questions. Do not be afraid to take your time in deciding and go back to the seller or his or her agent as often as you feel necessary in order to make you comfortable in your decision to buy or to let the property.

When you visit the property that you propose to buy or let, take a camera with you and take as many pictures as you can as you walk around. The best camera to use is a digital one with a large amount of memory. The reason why a digital camera is better is that if the images are downloaded to your computer they can be examined in more detail by zooming in on certain points with digital camera software. This will allow you to look at details that you may not have noticed during your walk around. The benefit of using a camera is that not only is this a useful exercise for avoiding any issues around a potential dispute, it can also serve as a memory jogger for the details of the property both before and after you buy or lease your new home. There are many details that need to be considered around a new home and these are often missed at first or lost over time. Pictures allow you to answer questions that you may think up long after your visit. The pictures may also record something that is vital in a legal defence if you get into a neighbour dispute at a later date.

As with any major decision or commitment, make sure that you are completely comfortable with what you are intending to do. If you have any doubts as to whether this purchase is the right decision to make, just do not be rushed, do not buy if you have any issues! People talk about having a sixth sense, or as one of the authors' friends says "a gut feeling". In most cases these feelings of doubt are correct. Never feel pressured into a decision and importantly do not be afraid to walk away from any deal, even if it costs you some money. If the home is not right for you, get away as fast as you can and do not worry about anything else. Instincts matter and count for a lot. If you lose some money in this it is not the end of the world. Consider that if the decision to buy or let is the wrong one and your purchase leads to a neighbour dispute, it can cost you tens of thousands to defend yourself and to challenge your neighbour in the dispute. Moreover a dispute will make your life miserable and so will erode your quality of life, and this is probably one of the things that a new home was meant to bring you.

# Questions to Ask the Owners When Viewing

- Why are the owners moving?

- How long have they lived at the house?

- How long have they lived in the area?

- What are their neighbours like?

- What do their neighbours do?

- Do their neighbours have any particular hobbies? If so what are these hobbies?

- Do their neighbours have any children? If so how young or how old are their children?

- How long have their neighbours lived there?

- Have they had any issues or problems with their neighbours? If so what were these problems or issues?

- Have they undertaken any building works while they lived at the house? If so what building works?

- Have their neighbours undertaken any building works while they have lived at the house? If so what were these building works?

- Who maintains the boundaries? Walk with the owners & let them show you.

- What happens if the boundary fence or hedge needs to be repaired or maintained? Who does the work?

- Where does the water come in to the property?

- Are there any external drainage / sewerage pipes on the property? If so where are they?

- When were the boundary fences last replaced? If they were replaced, who paid for them?

- Is the neighbourhood a peaceful one?

- Ask them about trees and plants in the garden, when were they planted?

- Have they had any issues over plants, such as overhanging tree branches on their property or on their neighbour's properties?

- Who owns the plants and trees etc. on the borders?

- What about parking? Is there any shared parking with the neighbour? If so have they had any issues?

- Is there any right of access, drainage or an easement on any part of the property? If so what are these rights and where are these easements?

- Are there any informal agreements in place with the neighbour?

- What about crime? Have there been any break ins or burglaries in the immediate neighbourhood?

- Are there any gangs of youths in the area that they know of?

- If they have heard of any crime, what was it? When did the crime or crimes occur?

- Do they get regular visitors trying to sell or influence them? For example Jehovah's Witnesses, doorstep merchants or people soliciting for work?

- What facilities are there in the area for children?

- What about local schools & children in the area?

- Are there any restrictive covenants associated with the property?

- Are there any local papers or newsletters such as parish council newsletters that they get?

- Is there a strong sense of community within the area?

## Observations That need to be Made

If there is a garden with the property, look at the garden from different places and different angles. For example look at the garden from the top floor or from the front of the house. Ask yourself is the garden secluded or can you see everything going on in it and around it?

Look to see if your neighbours' garden can be seen? If you can see their garden from the house then the chances are they can see your garden from their house as well, so your time outside may not be private as you can be seen.

Ask yourself what else can you see in the garden or from the garden?

Are there children's toys in the garden of your neighbours' property? If so then noise may be an issue when the children are home and the weather is fine.

Is your neighbours' garden well-tended and kept neat or is it strewn with rubbish and litter.

Do the neighbours have piles of leaves or branches in their gardens?

Is there any evidence of fires that have been started for the disposal of garden debris and are these signs of regular burning? Deeply scorched earth or very dull and black bins are signs of regular burning so look out for them.

Go out into the garden and listen for noise. Is it peaceful there or is there noise? What type of noise is it? Is it the birds or is it the sound of children or traffic? Ask yourself whether the noise is natural or whether it is unpleasant and difficult to live with.

Go back inside the house you are looking to buy and listen from the inside. Can you hear your neighbours' televisions through the wall? Can you hear cars driving outside? If you can hear noises inside, there is a strong chance you can be heard outside or can be heard through the wall by your neighbours'.

Put your ears close to the wall to hear better. Can you hear anything? If you can, again you can be heard on the other side of the wall by your neighbour.

Bang on the wall to see what the wall is made from. Is it solidly constructed? When banging does anyone bang on the wall back in return? If someone does bang back then the chances are that noise could be an issue in the future if you buy or rent the property.

Look for anything that could be a joint responsibility between you and your proposed new neighbour's. A shared driveway, fences, or a pathway leading to your house are all examples of things that could be a shared responsibility and these are most definitely worth further investigation as they are sure fire ways to disputes as people are territorial and may have a different view of how the responsibilities should be shared.

## Trees, Bushes and Hedges

Trees bushes and hedges are a major source of problems with neighbours and this is something worthwhile considering if you are buying or renting a property. If you have hedges, bushes and trees on your border you have to consider that they will grow bigger. As they grow larger, they can encroach on the boundary between you and your neighbour. If the branchesof the hedge or tree go over the boundary onto your neighbours' property you could have a maintenance issue ahead of you, as the branches will need to be trimmed and cut back on a regular basis, and your neighbour may not be keen for you to do this.

The other issue with trees, bushes and hedges are that as they grow they can take away a lot of light. There is legislation now in the UK around plants growing and blocking the light, however it is a difficult area in law and so is both costly to pursue and complex to solve. During the autumn trees also tend to shed theirleaves and this could also be a problem as a high leaf build up can damage a neighbours' lawn or a pond if there is one close by, thus leaving you with a bill to clean up and replace any damage created.

The best thing for you to do is to cut the trees, bushes and hedges right back as soon as you can and to ensure that they do not grow above a certain size. If the trees, hedges or bushes on the property you are proposing to buy are overgrown, request that they are cut hard back by the owner you are buying from or if letting, the landlord before you move in. If necessary request it as a part of your contract for purchase or rent.

## Fences and Walls

It is very important that you establish who is responsible for the boundary fences and walls around the property you are proposing to rent or buy. If you are buying, the Title Deeds to the property may not always provide this information. If you are renting, your landlord should tell you this. If it says in your deeds that you are to maintain the boundaries, then there is a very strong likelihood that you own the plants or fence on the border and that they are on your land. Although you must also be aware that this is not always the case and so will need to be verified. If your neighbour maintains the fences and walls on the boundary then the likelihood is that they are on his or her land. The significance is that these points at the boundary edge could be the physical extents of your property. Do not make the mistake of thinking that the property title plan defines the exact boundaries as this is not necessarily the case. You also need to be aware that if a historical precedent has been made with the boundaries, and your previous owners had agreed to this either directly or indirectly, or if a mistake has been made, your title extents and your boundaries on the ground may not correlate with each other and so this could lead directly to an adverse possession case or some other form of dispute. Make sure you know who does what on the borders around your home and verify where the boundary's lie as accurately as you can. This is an extreme area for problems as a few centimetres or inches of land can cost you thousands if it develops into a dispute with your neighbour.

## Rent or Buy?

It does not matter whether you are renting or buying a property. At the end of the day there are still issues that need to be considered regarding your neighbours and if you are to avoid any kind of conflict, these issues are better off being examined from the very beginning of your decision to either buy or rent a property. Renting does change some of the requirements regarding the potential for dispute. The key to prevention however will be to talk to the land lord or his agent and obtain a copy of their proposed contract for you to review and amend if necessary.

Within the rental contract there may be provisions that require you as the lease holder to maintain parts of the property. If this is a requirement within the contract, make sure that the requirements placed upon you are clearly understood and that your responsibilities are clearly defined. For example if you have to maintain the garden, then a clear indication of the properties extents, boundaries and a detail of what maintenance is required will need to be explained and agreed between you and your new landlord. If there are any omissions to this agreement or contract then this could lead to a conflict with either your land lord or a neighbour. If you have any doubts as to the implications of any terms or requirements, consult an expert before signing.

Even if you are renting a house however you should still go through the checklists recommended in this book. You will still have neighbours and the potential for a dispute. Do everything you can up front to avoid any dispute as it will save you personal anguish and money in the longer term.

## Viewing Flats or Apartments

Flats and apartments are different to houses, although many of the considerations for purchasing or renting a flat or apartment are the same as for houses. Consider the check list given above for use in flats or apartments. The checks for the garden will not be relevant unless there is a garden that comes with the flat or apartment, but the other checks most definitely are relevant to you so make sure you carry them out. If the flats or apartments have communal areas of gardens that are shared between you and others, look very closely at the rights of each owner and their rights of access to the communal areas or garden. Before you consider an offer from the landlord or before agreeing the lease agreement, spend time in the communal areas of garden at different times of the day and week to see how people behave in these shared areas.

## Close Living

Flats and apartment present their own challenges for living. These challenges range from noises to smells and from downright poor hygiene to bad personal administration from your neighbours. There are however many advantages to flats and apartments, but because they have elements that are communal by nature there can be areas that can cause problems with neighbours. This is particularly the case in rented flats or apartments in buildings where there are likely to be high numbers of passing tenants on short term leases.

## Bad Smells

The other consideration for living in flats or apartments is the emanation of bad smells from neighbouring areas. Go around each of the flats or apartments at meal times to see if there are any bad odours coming from them. For example the author moved into a flat in Nottingham without thinking about smells and found to his dismay that one neighbour loved home made curries and that the smell of them cooking lingered for hours in the flat and around the corridors afterwards.

Take a walk up and down the stairs in the flats or apartment and travel in each lift. Visit any communal area such as the rubbish bins or rubbish collection points. Look at each stairwell and at each flat. It is not uncommon to find that people have placed rubbish outside the doors of their flat, and that they have not bothered to take it to the rubbish points, so they leave it for days on end to create a smell or to attract vermin. In summer this can smell very strongly and can create pest problems. This is particularly the case in older and less well maintained flats.

Take a look at the proposed lease terms to the property and see if there are specific responsibilities for cleaning or clearing rubbish associated with the property. The author had an interesting neighbour problem once in a flat that was being rented where the obligation was on you as a renter to keep the stair and door areas in front of your flat clear of rubbish. The authors neighbour did not want to clear their own rubbish even though they were obliged to do so, every time they had any rubbish to dispose of, they placed it in front of the authors' door in the middle of the night. This was an on-going problem, and despite letters and pleas to the neighbour for them to stop and repeated complaints to the land lord, they refused to do so. The problem only stopped when the author took the law into his own hands and used a covert camera to take pictures of the neighbour in the act, and posted these pictures around the flats so everyone could see what the other neighbour was doing. Their activity stopped immediately they were exposed and they moved out several months later. The moral here is that sometimes the only way to solve your problem is to be harsh, otherwise life can be difficult. When considering any form of personal action however, do not break the law as it can create even more problems for you if you do so.

## Noise

The biggest issue around people living so close together is the potential for noise. In flats there are many different sources of noise that can be a point of conflict or irritation depending on where the flat is actually located within the building. For example a flat in the middle of a building could get noise from all sides and noise both from the top and bottom flats. Even though there are regulations around noise in buildings, insulation and soundproofing, the actual standards will vary from flat to flat depending on the age and quality of the building materials used in the construction of the flat. Visit the flat at different times of the day and on different days of the week to determine if noise is going to be a problem. Sit quietly in the flat and listen. If you can hear someone, they can also hear you. Make sure you do this at a busy time of day when others are likely to be home.

## Shared Parking

Any kind of shared or communal parking is a nightmare waiting to happen. Although in some cases you cannot avoid using shared parking, it is best if you can get your landlord to number each parking spot corresponding to the flat or apartment being rented. Even if they do this however, there are still issues sometimes. In many cases land lords may not be able to allocate a dedicated space to you. In this case try and seek alternatives to parking such as a rental garage that you can use exclusively yourself. If you do have a parking spot mentioned specifically in your lease, make sure that the landlord enforces any infringements of other flat owners parking on your space.

# Chapter 2

## Committing to Buy: What to Consider Before You Commit to Buy

Before you commit to buying your new house there are a number of important things to consider. From the very moment you have decided you are interested in buying and making an offer, and have looked at the other "layers" mentioned in Chapter 1, you need to carry out further surveys yourself during and after the conveyance process. Do not rely purely on your conveyance Solicitor to do all of the work as they will have limited knowledge about the property and the area where you are going to live, and so do not consider many points given in this book. These survey points could be indicators of potential issues around your boundary, and if you can clarify and resolve them at the time of the purchase of your new home you can avoid a boundary issue or other forms of disputes with your neighbour.

When the author bought his first house he had some romantic vision of living in the country and of enjoying and developing what he had bought into something really special. As it was the first house that he had ever owned he was keen, eager and excited. The author engaged with a London Solicitor who had been recommended to him as a conveyance expert for country homes. Naturally as an expert the author put his faith in the knowledge of this Solicitor and took the advice he was given. Sadly the authors' subsequent experiences after having suffered as a result of this Solicitors advice, has shown that anyone can invent themselves as an expert and unless you know what you are looking for, you are at the mercy of these so called experts. For the most part these false experts get away with it and leave you a legacy that if you are unlucky enough to hold, can ruin your dreams, damage your relationships and leave you with a massive bill. The authors' knowledge built by his experience and that of others is given below. He hopes it saves you from any future problems with your neighbours

# Research You Can Do Yourself Before You Buy

1.  Talk to the seller as often as you can and ask as many questions as you can of the seller. Some of the questions that you need to ask are listed in the checklist at the end of this section. Ask the questions as many times as you like and do not be put off by the purchasing or conveyance deadlines if the seller tries to impose these upon you to make the exchange of contracts sooner. In a small neighbourhood you may also meet people who can give you more information about the house and neighbours and it is also worthwhile approaching them to ask questions as well.

2.  Talk to the immediate neighbours. Get their point of view. Ask if you can look at the property that you propose to purchase or rent from their side and ask questions as to where they see the boundary lays. Their understanding may be different to that of the seller and this could be the first sign of problems. Consider your immediate neighbours'personalities. Can you get on with them in good times and bad? What do the other neighbours say about the neighbours who are moving? What do the other neighbours' say about your immediate neighbours', Refer to the checklist for more questions

3.  Consider the history of the property you are proposing to rent or purchase. This is very important and is an area that is very often overlooked by buyers or renters. For example, the authors'old house was once part of a farm and it was left as a gift to a previous owner. The previous owner had a lot of knowledge and information that would have been useful to the author should he ever have a dispute with his neighbour. If you get the opportunity, ask the current owner for any photographs they have of the house and key features. Ask them if they know anything of the history of the house. Find the previous owners to the current ones and ask them if they had any issues and if they have any photos or details that may be of use to you. The author took many photos of his house from day one and was able to quell some of the potential issues that could have developed with his neighbour before they started because of his possession of these pictures.

4.  Do not be bothered by time. Do not feel pressured by anyone. If the seller and estate agent are applying pressure on you to buy quickly then there is a reason for this. One of these very reasons could be why you should not buy. If the agent and the seller are genuine then they will wait a reasonable amount of time for you to be satisfied before they sell to you. Do not be afraid to walk away from the deal, even if you love the place, an impulsive buy without thorough research could lead to a boundary or neighbour dispute and it will seriously affect your life as well as your finances.

5.  Consider Ordnance Survey Maps. Look at the ordnance survey maps of your property and the surrounding area. Although in a town these maps may be of limited value, on an estate or in the country they can provide invaluable information. Look at both current and older revisions going back as far as you can, sometimes the earliest maps provide you with the most detail so if you can, go back a hundred years or so, then it is worthwhile doing so. Pay particular attention to key features that have been mapped close to your property as these could be boundary indicators.

6.  Look at air photos. There are several sources of air photos that may help you to determine features on the ground. Although air pictures do have disadvantages as they are generally two dimensional and if the plane has flown over during the summer, foliage and plant growth can obscure features on the ground. Similarly if the plane has flown at an angle, the pictures that are taken can miss key features. Air photos are however a good source of information and are well worth looking into. The photographs can reveal previous features that may not be visible from the ground. For example if a wall or building has been removed, although you may not see anything on the ground, the dark areas of the foundations will be visible in an air photo.

7.  Every day pictures and sales photos. The seller may have pictures that they took when they moved in and while they lived at the property. These photos are an invaluable resource to you if the seller is happyto give them to you.

A good way is to pay for the seller to get some of his or her negatives printed and sent to you. Another excellent source of pictures is the estate agent of the current seller and if you can find out the details of who the current owners bought the house from, the previous seller's estate agent, then they also may help. They will have a good number of pictures that they took in order to list the property and the key features are highly likely to be show in these pictures. The author, by obtaining the sales photos of his house, he was able to prove that the fence along one border did not extend all the way along the boundary as was claimed by the person next door. This prevented a dispute before it happened.

# Collecting and Receiving Data

## How to Verify Information

There are several ways to verify information that you have been given. If you are buying an old house, there may be useful information in the library or with the parish or local council. Check the library archives for information. If the house you wish to buy is a new development, check with the developer, as they will have records that will be useful to you. Any other questions can be posed to your solicitor or the sellers' estate agent to ask of the seller during the conveyance process. If possible, get the answers to all your questions verified during the conveyance, before you exchange contract. Do not forget any previous owners in your search for information. If they can be traced and contacted, they can be a goldmine of useful information. At the very least, you will be able to develop a history of the house you are proposing to buy, and at best, you will determine if anyone has ever had any issues or disputes while owning or renting the property so can take measures to avoid the same thing from happening again.

## Questions to Ask of Your Solicitor

Solicitors tend to undertake a standard set of activities when carrying out a conveyance. They check with the land registry for filed copy plans of your boundary and undertake a local authority search. In most cases, this is sufficient information to exchange a contract for purchase; however, most of these searches do not consider your neighbour's boundaries and their registered extents. This could lead to problems later, as many boundaries in the UK follow general boundary rules (explained below).

At the minimum, you should check your title deeds and compare them to your neighbours. To enable this, your Solicitor should be requested to do a boundary search on your neighbour's property as well as on your property. This is something most Solicitors fail to do during a conveyance and it is a major contributing factor to disputes later. The file copy plan at the land registry for both you and your neighbour's boundaries are the key sources of the information, regarding the properties registered extents as well as the latest ordnance survey maps (these will be inaccurate however). You will need to check all of these plans to see if your boundaries coincide with your neighbours. If they do not coincide, then you have an immediate issue that will need to be addressed by your Solicitor. If they do coincide, then the chances are that they will follow the general boundary rules and so this will also need to be clarified with your Solicitor.

Ask your Solicitor to reconfirm who maintains the boundary on each of your borders. Ask your Solicitor to verify if you are to maintain the boundary, then does your neighbour agree with this? A letter from your Solicitor to your neighbour may be necessary for this to be confirmed. If you have already asked your Solicitor, then this can serve as a formal confirmation of who maintains what on and around the property you are proposing to buy.

If there are any trees or bushes on or near the borders, ask who owns and maintains them and ask if there are any granted rights of access to your land or to your neighbour's land especially if these trees or bushes overhang on to your neighbours' property.

Ask about any past disagreements with the neighbours. Have they applied for planning permission in the past and has it been refused? Planning permission will generally show up on a local authority search; however it has been known for authorities not to record all information so it is always worth checking by visiting the local planning office directly. While asking about permissions, see if your neighbours' have any plans to develop their properties as this could be a source of problems in the future. The other benefit of looking at planning permissions is that if permissions have been granted for the property you are looking to purchase in the past, you may be able to use these permissions for your own works if they have not been completed.

Ask if there are any drains or drainage rights on your property or on, under or over your neighbours' land? Are there any rights on your land for drainage? If so what are they and how are they going to affect you?

Where does the main water feed come from? Does it traverse your land or your neighbours' property?

Where does the sewerage go? Is it passing through to the street, or does it go through a number of gardens before it hits the street? If it does, a blockage in the street could cause a problem to you as the water company or your neighbours are legally entitled to access should a blockage occur. If you have a sump, look at how the sump has been created as many older ones have a soak away attached to them. In many cases these soak aways run for several metres and they can run onto neighbouring properties. If these are historical, generally they do not present a problem. They can cause issues in some cases so you do need to know where they run so that a future dispute can be avoided.

Ask again who maintains the fences around the property? Are they jointly maintained or are they maintained solely by you or by your neighbour? Consider when they were last replaced or painted? Does this need to happen again?

Is there any land that has not been registered properly under your title? If so, can it be registered by using a First Registration Rights form (FR1) from the Land Registry? Can the previous owners of the property be traced?

Are there any public rights of way on or near your property? These can be a major nuisance to you as you can find people coming and going from your property as and when they please. If there is a public right of way on the property you will find litter, dog foul and people who will do what they want on your land. Importantly the law in the UK means that it is your responsibility to maintain the right of way and this will both be a cost and an annoyance to you.

Make sure everything is as it should be with your proposed new home. Check your understanding of the boundary with the neighbours' response. Compare this with the declaration of the seller. Look at old conveyance documents to see if there are any variations to the old plans and to the new ones.

Are there any restrictive covenants on the deeds of the property you wish to buy? Are there any restrictive covenants on your neighbouring properties? If so, an analysis of their implications needs to be made by your Solicitor.

Are there any statutory declarations from the previous owners that clarify the features on the property, do they describe the boundaries and the current or previous land use? If so, are these declarations clear and precise or are they ambiguous and open to misinterpretation or a different form of interpretation should a legal battle occur? Ask if it would be possible to receive a statutory declaration from the seller to clarify these ambiguities? Make sure however that you involve a surveyor in this process as you need to be as precise as you can regarding any features you find mentioned in any declaration.

What does the Land Registry state about the boundaries? If they say that the boundaries between your property and the neighbour are general boundaries, can this be recorded in writing? If they are general boundaries, then it is worth seeking a boundary declaration from the seller before you purchase.

## Insurance to Buy From Your Solicitor

Solicitors can also recommend insurance at the time of conveyance that will protect you should a boundary dispute occur. It is wise to purchase this insurance if you can, and you will need to make sure it covers civil action and the adjudication process. If it does not, then you may find yourselves in a position like one of the authors' clients where they took out insurance but were not covered for the adjudication process. When this clients' neighbour decided to go to Tribunal, this presented a major problem to them as the Tribunal Judge did not agree to refer the case to the County Court. Instead these people were left to pay their own legal fees as the insurer refused to cover them. This came to over seventy five thousand pounds in the end. You must read the clauses in your insurance very carefully and ask the following questions of the insurer if you are unsure of the extent of cover.

1.  Does it cover for a property dispute? A good policy will do so.

2.  Does it cover the costs of court action for trespass? If you have to prove trespass, this could be an issue. Make sure you do not have to prove this.

3.  Can you choose your own Solicitor? Most insurance companies employ their own Solicitors, and they do not

necessarily act in your best interests as they will try to save money for the insurer.

4.  Who determines whether you are covered? If it is the insurance company, this could be problematic as they could seek a second opinion. In the case of the authors' clients, their Solicitor said that the clients were covered; however, the insurance company's Barrister said they were not. Consequently the authors' clients had to fund their action themselves.

5.  Does the insurance cover civil action? Most building insurances cover only trespass. Civil actions for boundary disputes are generally not covered as a matter of course, so this clause must be written into any agreement. Be aware that you may have to pay a premium for this.

6.  Does the insurance cover the costs of the adjudication process? The adjudication process is a relatively new thing, and many insurance policies do not cover the costs of an adjudication case. The costs for adjudication are slightly lower than those of a court case; however, they are still costly and can run into tens of thousands of pounds.

7.  Does the insurer cover for all issues around your boundaries? If there are any issues that require legal attention around the boundary, then these could be covered in a general clause.

## After-the-Event Insurance

If you do get into a dispute with your neighbour, you can buy insurance to help pay for any eventual legal fees associated with the dispute should you need to pay them in the future. If litigation is pending, however, it is extremely unlikely that you will be able to get after-the-event insurance, as your legal case may not have a good chance of success, however well founded it is. You must always remember that the UK legal system is more of a lottery than a sound system of justice. Judges can decide the fate of others based on the character of the person in front of them or according to their mood rather than on the law and the insurance industry are well aware of this. If you can get insurance at all, it will likely be very expensive and will have some clauses weighted heavily in favour of the insurer. Even so, if you can get after the event insurance then do so as it could save you thousands later.

# Checks with the Land Registry

The Land Registry is a good source of information regarding any property you are thinking of buying or renting. The local office will have records of your land parcel associated with the property and should be able to give you some details about the property history. If you can, ask for copies of their records, these are worth keeping. These copies will, at the minimum, show you the registered extents and will also detail information about the past owners; they will show any past mortgages and any changes to the title that have been made in the past. When checking with the Land Registry, do not ever assume that they are experts at what they do. They are not, and because of their long-established history and the land registration system in the UK, they will always defer to a Solicitor or the law where difficult or awkward questions arise. By the same token do not ever assume that their records are accurate or that they are qualified in what they do or say. Again the authors' experience has shown that a number of the Land Registries employees are either incompetent, not qualified or a combination of both. Under no circumstances should you ever take the advice of the Land Registry without checking it with a Solicitor or a competent technical expert. If you do not check any advice the Land Registry gives you, then you can find yourself in a neighbour dispute due to poor advice. Never take anything they give you as fact until it is verified.

## Land Registry and Problems to be Aware of

The land registration system in the UK is not accurate for historical reasons. Mapping was undertaken by the Ordnance Survey, which created a system primarily as a way of mapping the country for defensive purposes, and this later developed into what it is today. The major issue with OS mapping is that it only looks at key features on the ground; OS surveyors have not normally been concerned with a high level of detail because inaccuracies in the scale on their maps would render such details useless. This means that many boundaries have either been inaccurately recorded by the Ordnance Survey or have been recorded too vaguely, as they were not key considerations for defence. Even though the purpose of these maps has now changed from that of defence, the same mapping process, scales and techniques have been retained. Key features are still not mapped and so this serves as a continuing source of disputes.

The Land Registry have inherited a system of recording land that causes a great deal of conflict, and, although steps have been made to try and improve the accuracy of land recording and of determining boundaries, the truth is that the majority of the land in the UK is not accurately registered to an exact position on the ground. As a result, boundary variation could be as much as several metres or as little as several centimetres on title plans.

A "registered boundary" is described in the Land Registration Act 2002 as the following:

*Section 60 Boundaries*

1.  *The boundary of a registered estate as shown for the purposes of the register is a general boundary, unless shown as determined under this section.*

2.  *A general boundary does not determine the exact line of the boundary*

These are the exact reasons as to why there are so many boundary disputes in the UK. The law does not enforce accuracy, so records are, as one would expect, inaccurate. The older Land Registration Act was even worse in its description of a general boundary. This means that anyone who wants to challenge you regarding the boundary lines on your property can do so, as the boundary line is a matter of interpretation and not a clear and precise fact.

Rather than modernise the boundary system in the UK it was decided by the government that the best course of action was to leave the General Boundary rule in place. This rule has created far too many problems for too many people and is the root cause of the high number of boundary and neighbour disputes in this country. It is time that the system changed. The government stated in 2003, however that it would be too costly to change the system and so they opted to do nothing and let you and I suffer as that only costs them are one or two votes at election time and they do not pay any money apart from the trivial amount they give as compensation if you can prove the Land Registry have made a mistake. The burden of proof however is on you and they do not provide any indemnity for "maladministration". This is the term they give to their mistakes so that they can abdicate from their moral responsibilities.

## Land Registration and Transfer Deeds

When land is first registered, a declaration as to the extents of the land to be registered is normally given with the conveyance or transfer, and this declaration is in the form of a deed or plan usually describing the boundaries of the land to be conveyed or transferred. This method of registering land can also cause inaccuracies and it is another root of many people's problems. When making these boundary declarations, the conveyor or seller is normally advised as to what wording to use in their declaration by a Solicitor, and unless the wording is absolutely specific and it details exactly what land is to be conveyed and the exact boundary positions to within ten centimetres, then it is not much use. The later interpretation of position is extremely difficult and this is any area that brings problems to many people. Their plans do not align with the words in their declaration and as a result the boundary plans and registered extents associated with their property are extremely inaccurate. Similar problems can arise when the words are very detailed and the associated drawn plan is inaccurate or if the drawn plan is detailed and the words on the declaration are inaccurate and do not describe key ground or boundary features in detail. Most declarations will also come with a map, and as these maps are not meant for accurate recording of boundaries, generally they will have a red line around the general area of the boundaries to denote the land within the owners' title. Court cases have shown that these maps are inaccurate and are only for defining the general area. Therefore if it comes to a court case, these maps are of little use to you.

## Problems with the Land Registry Title Plans

The land registry relies on ordnance survey maps, and on the land registration and transfer deeds of property owners to define their title plans within their records. This means that the land title plans held by them are not accurate unless they are specifically recorded as a defined boundary record. Typically an Ordnance Survey team undertaking a map survey will look at the key features on the ground and record them in their maps as they appear at that moment in time. Because their focus is on key features for map making purposes and not property boundaries, the boundary lines are not important to them and in many cases they have no idea where a boundary lays as they are not normally provided with this information at the time of mapping. It is therefore highly unlikely that they will record a boundary line. More importantly land features change over time, for example a 1966 Ordnance Survey map may show a key feature that in subsequent years has disappeared, for example a tree or a hedge line. This means that if your boundary title map was originally mapped to the feature shown in 1966, you have a real problem in trying to prove where the feature was originally as it no longer exists on the map. Moreover as maps are prone to scaling errors, it is extremely unlikely that you will ever be able to recreate the exact position of any removed feature on a map. This is why photographic evidence is really important and you should take photographs of your property frequently at different times of the year to record variation and changes on the ground.

Other problems around land registry copy plans are in areas such as roads and ditches. Sometimes there is an assumption that a property that fronts a road has its boundary at the centre of that road. Copy plans and OS maps will only show the road and not the boundary and unless you can show otherwise, it is difficult to prove that you own part of the road frontage. Most council's know this and take full advantage wherever they can when they build and expand the highway.

## General Boundary Rules

Because of all of the known inaccuracies in title deeds, the issues with land first registration documents and processes and Ordnance Survey mapping, the land registry decided that the best way to describe a boundary within a land registry title copy plan was as a general boundary. The general boundary rules effectively state that a boundary is somewhere in the vicinity of the marked plan held in their records. Any boundary line on a plan shows a general position for the boundary and due to difficulties around the accurate mapping and recording of information, the actual boundary position on the ground could be several metres away from the position recorded by the land registry in their title map. Taking one case in particular where the author advised a client regarding boundaries where there was a problem with one neighbour, there was a recorded line that translated to an area of roughly one point six metres in either direction of that line where their boundary could have been. One neighbour claimed the boundary line was one point six metres closer to the other neighbours' house. One neighbour thought differently to the other. As the features in this area had changed over time and had been inaccurately mapped, both neighbours were in a position where they had to get a boundary determination on this border. This cost both parties a lot of money as they had to pay a surveyor several thousand pounds to survey the land.

When one neighbour contacted the Land Registry, the Land Registry was not much use. Because of the current land recording system, they were unable to determine anything from their title plans apart from giving a general indication of where the border could be. Moreover not only was the Land Registry unable to determine where the boundary was, they had recorded both parcels of the land that was disputed as belonging to both neighbours as well. Because this information was in no way accurate and because both had title to the land in question, one neighbour took advantage of this and pursued the boundary dispute with the Land Registry Tribunals Service much to the expense of the other. When this case was finally settled, the Adjudicator did not award costs, but made a determination instead and his opinion did not match that of either surveyor. In the end neither party got what they wanted from the Adjudication hearing and it cost each neighbour around £45,000 to defend their positions.

## Boundary Declarations and Agreements

Because of the difficulties posed by the general boundary rules you can elect to have a boundary declaration or agreement drawn up between you and your neighbour. These agreements, if undertaken before a dispute arises can save you a lot of money and pain. If you have a dispute, a boundary declaration is normally the end result of the dispute as the boundary positions must be recorded to prevent further disputes and the court will normally order this when deciding a case should it go that far. It is always best to avoid court. If you have any of the following scenario's a boundary declaration and agreement is worth considering.

1.  Where you have inaccuracies in the map due to scale and these are reflected on the ground.

2.   The boundary that you want to go on record as determined goes across an open area where there are no distinct features that are referenced on a map. For example across a field.

3.   You want ensure that you do not have a boundary dispute with your neighbour.

4.   You have areas of common access with your neighbour and want to define the boundary between your access area and your neighbours. Driveways, roadways and pathways are areas of common access that can be determined accurately.

A boundary declaration is normally a sketch map of your boundary area with key features defined and the exact dimensions of the land noted. If you and your neighbour agree, a boundary declaration can be lodged with the land registry and it will be used as a part of the file copy plan in the future for your property. If you want to lodge a boundary agreement or a boundary declaration you will need to employ a chartered surveyor to draw the sketch map and to take the accurate dimensions that are needed. To start the process you can agree the sketch map with your neighbour and in order to prevent any dispute you could consider jointly instructing the surveyor. This way, as you and your neighbour are both paying the fee for the survey and determination there is a greater feeling of neutrality in the mapping process as the surveyor will work for you both. If there is any bad feeling between you and your neighbour it is best to work through a Solicitor who can instruct the surveyor on your behalf. The thing to bear in mind with any boundary declaration is that it has to be accurate so as to prevent any potential or further dispute. The declarations purpose is to describe the boundary accurately and it must do so to the extent that as the ground features and land owners change over time, the defined boundary is clearly established as it is accurately described, measured and mapped, and there should be no room for debate or any margin for dispute at any time in the future. The boundary line should also be able to be found later should you or your neighbour want to sell or alter your properties so must describe features that are unlikely to change over time.

## Determined Boundaries

The land registry and the government have long since recognised that there are problems with the current methods of registering boundaries and in particular they are aware that inaccuracies cause disputes. In order to try and deal with this problem as a part of the Land Registration Act 2002 they sought to make boundary registrations more accurate. To enable this they introduced the concept of the Determined Boundary. A Determined Boundary is the same as a boundary declaration however it is much more accurate and must be completed by a chartered surveyor. The aim is to get a land title plan to be within an accuracy of 10mm of the key features on the ground. This means that the surveyor commissioned to map and survey a piece of land is required to certify their surveys accuracy and the only way they can do this is by using time consuming, and therefore costly methods of measuring the fixed key features on the boundary. A determined boundary can be lodged with the land registry by a surveyor if the land is already registered or alternatively by your Solicitor when they lodge a FR1 form or from the first registration plan to be attached to your titledeeds. Because determined boundaries are drawn by experienced surveyors and they are to a high degree of accuracy, they leave little margin for debate, and so are one of the best ways to avoid a dispute with your neighbour as your boundaries will be accurately defined and their exact positions will be lodged with the Land Registry. Your title deeds will therefore be correct and not open to interpretation as there will be no incorrectly mapped or omitted features recorded in your deeds. If you have any reason to believe that there are inaccuracies in your title plan and can afford the surveyors fees, this is something worth considering.

# Maps

## Problems with Ordnance Survey Maps:

Although the United Kingdom is one of few countries that regularly maps features across the country, the sheer amount of land and features that need to be surveyed means that UK Ordnance Survey(OS) maps are only relatively accurate in their mapping. That is to say that OS maps are not accurate to the exact positions of features or objects on the ground and as such their scale, measurement and the influence of time and erosion all have interplay on the maps and have contributed to their inaccuracy. The most accurate maps are the national grid maps and they have published scales of accuracy with the best detail you can hope for at around 99% accuracy or within plus or minus 1 metre of the actual feature position on the ground recorded with a 1:1250 map. On a 1:2500 scale, the standard map size in the UK, this level of accuracy becomes a plus or minus 2.3 metres of the actual feature position on the ground. County maps are even less accurate and so can present further issues in relation to boundaries due to their relative inaccuracies. Depending on where you live in the UK, each of the above mentioned maps may have been mapped in your area; there is a strong likelihood that only one or two of the above maps will have been surveyed in your area so you will not have any reasonable accurate record of the mapping associated with your land.

The other problems with OS maps are that the OS teams do not map all features when they survey. They only consider the key features on the ground and as maps come in various scales and sizes, the features on each scaling may vary greatly. Importantly as far as boundary disputes are concerned, boundaries are not necessarily mapped by the OS and in most cases they are omitted from OS surveys unless they are themselves key features. This means that most OS maps will have limited value to your case should you get into a boundary dispute.

## Reading and Interpreting a Title or OS Map

Map reading and interpreting a title map are a complete skill set in their own right. If you are looking at multiple properties, particularly properties located in a rural context, the author would recommend that you buy a book on maps and map reading or alternatively visit the Ordnance Survey Website URL given in this guide and that you learn how to read, judge and interpret a map.

Many OS maps use the same symbols to represent different forms of the same structure. For example a wall, fence, stream, hedge and a ditch use the same line symbol. Other interpretation issues are based around the selection of only certain features due to space constraints on scale maps. For example on a boundary a hedge and a ditch side by side will only show a line for the key feature which will generally be the hedge and not the ditch. Small buildings if they are less than eight metres in size are normally not included in OS maps, so if you are looking for old out buildings to determine your boundary, you may not see any trace of a building on the OS map.

Another issue with OS maps is that of generalisation. This is where important features are not shown in their true positions due to them being located too close to each other. The Ordnance Survey has some rules that deal with this, however due to both space and a scale issue on a map, generalisation still occurs. An example of this is where two detached houses with a gap of less than one metre between them will be drawn on a map as being semi-detached on a 1:2500 map. The OS have a rule in that any parallel feature must be shown with a minimum distance from each other or they have to be merged. These distances represent 1 meter on a 1:1250 map or two metres on a 1:2500 map.

The best and safest way to interpret a map is to go out onto the ground and look at the physical features and compare them to the map. When you do this make sure that you align the map correctly north to south with a compass and then compare the map in alignment to each key feature. When doing this, make sure you take into account magnetic deviation. The figures for this will be shown at the top of the OS map and this then needs to be offset with your compass. This will give you the true position of north and south and the true alignment of ground features.

# Adverse Possession

Adverse possession is sometimes called squatters rights. The principle is that if someone occupies a piece of land and excludes the outside world from using that piece of land, the squatter can claim legal possession and title and so can be confirmed in law as the owner of that land. There must not be any kind of agreement with the true land owner before doing this, so for example the squatter would not be paying rent or leasing the land from you. As a land owner, the squatter will generally claim and do everything in their power to stop you from using your own land. In one case the author is aware of a real land owner put up a temporary protective fence to stop access to an adjoining property that needed repair and a neighbour claimed that the land on the other side of this protective fence was his; even though it was not. This neighbour made a claim for adverse possession on the basis that the land was exclusively his because of the fence being placed there. Even though the fence had an opening to gain access to the land and the property it was not a good move by the real owners. By placing the fence where they did this only strengthened their neighbours position regarding the land he was claiming and he won his case by lying, influencing others and by using this fence as evidence to support his claim.

There are rules associated with adverse possession, however if the squatter can prove they have had ownership of the land they are claiming for a period of twelve years or more if the land is unregistered or ten years if the land is registered (this changed in 2002 having being previously been ten years for unregistered land).

The problem with adverse possession is that the squatter will generally claim that the land in question belongs to them. If they have sought aggressive occupation of this land, they could have erected a fence, built a wall or in some way stopped you as the real owner accessing your property, they may have a case in law to take ownership from you. You have two choices to deal with this problem if it occurs, both of which choices are not palatable. Firstly you can consult with a Solicitor and commence legal action immediately. This will be expensive and will take a long time to see results. The second option available to you is that you could go and remove any barriers that the squatter has placed to bar your access to your property. The biggest problem with doing this is that your neighbour (if he or she is claiming adverse possession), or the squatter could call the police and claim you are committing criminal damage to his or her property, even though they are in the wrong. The experience of many people the authors have spoken to who have faced these problems is that the police want an easy life and so take the path of least resistance to deal with the problems. If the police are called to your dispute are as lazy as the police many of the authors clients have dealt with, then you are unlikely to receive any kind of support or sympathy from them, and this could mean you get a criminal record or a caution for affray or a breach of the peace for removing something from your own land. Simply put the police will not deal with civil matters such as trespass or squatters but they are happy to clear statistics, or clear a crime, particularly if you are an easy target or if they can get a quick win by accusing you of one. If you are contemplating removing any obstacles placed by your neighbour, do it in such a manner where there is likely to be minimal trouble to you, for example remove the obstacles when your neighbours are not in, or alternatively do it a night. Please note that under any circumstances the author does not advocate any criminal activity. If you are forced to remove a fence and erect a new one at the true boundary position, then when you do so, you must be respectful to any other property of your neighbour or the squatter and not create any unnecessary damage. The best course of action is to take legal proceedings immediately and not remove anything. If you do remove any obstacles, then this could add fuel to the fire and delay the resolution to any problems, if your finances are such that you have no alternatives, then you must consider your course very carefully and you should ask yourself whether you want a dispute. If not, then try and settle the matter as soon as you can with minimal cost and stress.

When you look at the purchase of your house you need to make sure that the land shown within the title plan of the property is as it should be and that no part of it has been occupied by your neighbour. If it has been occupied, then there could be a potential adverse possession claim to be made by the neighbour against you for that land. If they have been there for some time, it will be difficult to prove that they are not using the land for their own exclusive benefit and this means that if they wish to make an adverse possession claim against you, it will be difficult for you to defend against it. Be absolutely sure that if you do wish to defend any claim as these cases can be easily lost, and can cost you a lot of money in legal bills, that you have a clear and concrete case to defend against the action. Do not consider morality or principles in any legal dispute. There is no place for them as this will cost you money, heartache and time, particularly in an adverse possession claim. The law relies on good argument, past cases and fact. If your neighbour or the squatter has any of these elements in their favour, then they can win their case. When defending adverse possession, make sure you have all of the elements described on your side and always take the best legal advice you can afford. You must also consider the cost of the land that you are trying to retain. If the land is valuable, then consider the cost compared to the legal costs. If it is not valuable, do the same and ask yourself is it worth the cost of defence, and any awards should you lose your case. If it is not, then consider abandoning your case or negotiating a settlement.

## Ditches

These can be tricky areas to deal with in a dispute as a general assumption regarding ditches seems to prevail in the eyes of the law when a boundary problem that involves a ditch occurs. The assumption is that the real boundary owner dug the ditch to mark his or her land and that the soil piled up from the digging of the ditch was placed upon the edge of the land of the other owner, in the area where the boundary does not lie. Very often a hedge has been planted on top of this pile of soil as a barrier so hedges and ditches very often go together. The important note here is that the opposing side of the ditch is assumed to be the boundary by legal circles, that is to say the side without the hedge or the bank of soil is the location of the real boundary line. This is where the problem lies if you think it should be somewhere else.

In today's world of climate change ditches are becoming more contentious. Due to the need to dig drainage and irrigation ditches, there are increasing opportunities for conflict between neighbours based upon the above assumption. If your neighbour is an opportunist, then they could see a drainage ditch as a boundary line. Bearing in mind the relative inaccuracies of OS mapping and the law regarding adverse possession, this could lead to a dispute. Moreover as only key features tend to be mapped in OS maps, over time a hedge may appear on a map without the ditch being recorded or shown. This can add fuel to the fire with your dispute so when considering ditches, further references and proof may be needed by your legal team to determine the actual boundary position. Again photographs are a good defence and are useful pieces of evidence. If you can get aerial photographs, then these are a great defence.

## Fences

If your title deed says that a fence is yours, then you have a good probability that it is indeed your fence, and in most cases this denotes a boundary. If the fence is not shown in your title deeds, then you cannot and must not conclude that a fence is yours by default as this will lead to disputes with your neighbours. You must seek clarification if this becomes a problem to you. The only other areas where you may be able to determine ownership with a good degree of certainty is if your neighbour agrees that the fence is yours or if it is stated that the fence is maintained by you in the properties information pack or deeds.

A good number of years ago to deal with potential disputes, the T mark was introduced to signify fence or wall ownership on title deeds and associated drawings. The T mark is aligned to the fence or wall and if the T falls on your side of the map or drawing then this signifies that you are the owner and maintainer of that fence or wall.

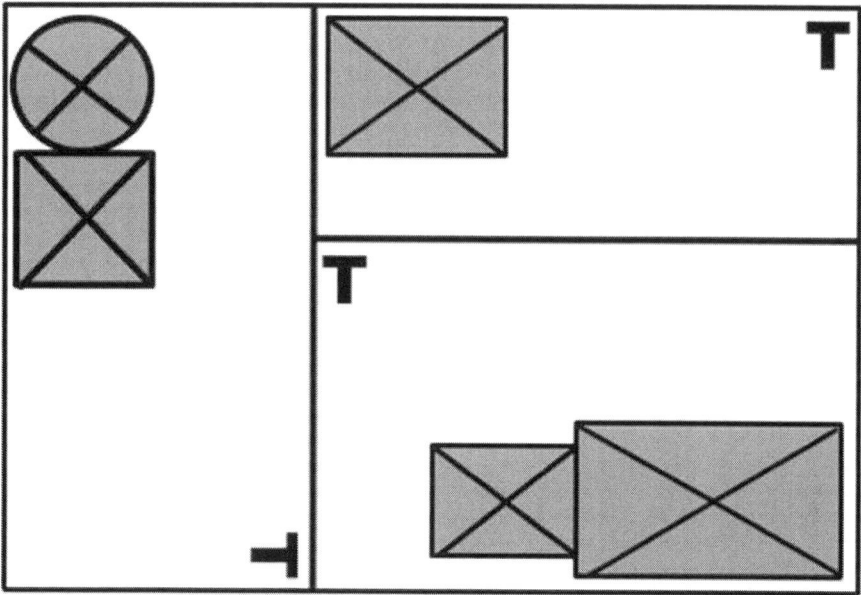

Some guides state that you can tell who owns a fence by looking at the rough side and the smooth side of the fence. These guides assert that the smooth side of the fence or wall is always facing away from the owner as it is public facing and the rough side will always be on the side of the owner as a result of this. Do not rely on this as a definitive answer to anything. It could be that the people who installed the fence wanted it that way or that they were just careless. Always verify your information with several sources as the author has seen conflicting information on many occasions. For example in one case both neighbours had details regarding fence ownership in their deeds and both details stated that they were the maintainers and owners of the boundary fence. This can happen if one owner gives up a boundary fence but does not update their title, while the other one, having taken ownership does. In cases like this, particularly where a new owner occupies the land, it can become very heated and difficult to prove who owns what and it generally leads to an expensive court case.

Another complication with fences comes around the ground where the fence is located, planning also plays a role and any restrictive covenant associated with yours or your neighbour property will also have an interplay. The true boundary may actually be further away from the fence line because of these complications and as a result the fence may not be a practical reference to the boundary location. An example of this situation could be reflected by the side of a road where fences cannot be right on the edge of the road or in the middle of the road due to traffic legislation and practicalities.

## Hedges

The problem with hedges is that they grow thicker and deeper over time. This means that when it comes to the establishment of the position of a boundary along a hedge line it is sometimes difficult to prove the exact line. As a result the generally accepted principle adopted by experts is that the root line of a hedge does not change over time and therefore these are a constant for the purposes of measurement and boundary determination. The problem with hedges however are that they rarely denote the boundary between properties as there must be a joint responsibility for its maintenance for it to be a boundary between properties.

## Walls

Walls generally have the same considerations as fences when it comes to boundary determinations. They have the added complication in that they are generally thicker than fences and as a result the actual boundary, if denoted by the wall could be the centre line, the cap, the face on your neighbours' side or the face on your side of the wall. Where there is any form of doubt, a surveyor needs to be consulted. As with everything, do not just rely on a map or conveyance or title deed to determine your boundary position.

## If Fences, Ditches, Hedges and Walls are Problems to You

If these are a source of a problem between a neighbour and you, then the first thing you need to do is engage with a surveyor who is an expert in these matters. They should be able to work to find the boundary line. If you want to do some checking yourself, either before engaging with a surveyor or if you cannot afford one, then check your neighbours title deeds and look to see if your borders coincide on each of your deeds or title plans. Search for any history associated with the properties. If you can find answers that show the true boundary position, then you may be able to agree the boundary by producing this evidence and by sharing it with your neighbour. If you can get agreement, then you can set up a neighbour agreement or can jointly apply for a determined boundary. This is generally less costly and friendlier than entering into a neighbour dispute.

## Restrictive Covenants

A restricted covenant on a property or a piece of land is defined as a provision in a title deed limiting the use of a property or land and it prohibits the land or property being used for certain activities or they have certain restrictions for use or further development.

A covenant is actually a contractual arrangement and is legally binding. A restrictive covenant also gives the rights to surrounding property owners, who also will have a similar covenant in their deeds, to enforce the terms of the restrictive covenant in a court of law. There are many reasons why there could be a restrictive covenant associated with the land or property; however in most cases it is either to preserve or enhance property values or the quality of life of an owner.

Property developers normally use restrictive covenants when they divide their property for residential or agricultural developments. An example of this is where a developer, after dividing his or her land into lots and streets, will impose certain limitations on the use of the lots in the development of any buildings or in its use. This restriction could see a limit on the appearance of any building extensions and conservatories or can be restrictive by specifying how far back from the road or fence an extension or outbuilding can be placed from another property, boundary or feature. Restrictive covenants can also specify what you cannot do in many cases, so for example some covenants might actually prevent you from building anything on your land, this can be anything from a building extension to a garden shed.

If you buy a property with a restrictive covenant you must adhere to the terms of the covenant, no matter how limiting these terms can be as the terms are intertwined with the property and are said to run with the land. If you break the covenant, the benefactor, usually a person living close by or on an adjacent property can ensure the restrictions are legally enforced in a court of law. If they go to court to enforce this, you will end up paying all costs and this can be tens of thousands of pounds. Think very carefully when considering any works on a property with any form of restrictive covenant. If you are unsure of the extent of any covenant restrictions, take legal advice before you do anything.

## Insurance Pre and Post Purchase

Before you purchase your property check what is and what is not covered as a part of your proposed household insurance policy. The major problem with household insurance is that it is there for when something goes wrong. Most people do not think about every event that could go wrong and so may not be covered for a boundary dispute even if you do have home insurance. You may think that you would be covered for a dispute as most household policies do have a clause for trespass. The problem with most insurance trespass clauses are that for trespass to be proved, you will need a determination of the position of your boundary and the trespasser must have passed onto your land to have trespassed. If your boundary line is unclear, you cannot prove the land is yours and so cannot prove trespass.

The author is aware that one of the biggest insurers in the UK states that the adjudication process (Tribunal Courts) and associated costs is not covered by their insurance policies. As the adjudication process is relatively new, after checking with many insurers the author has also found that many household insurance policies do not cover adjudication or land registry actions or even civil cases. This is a major failing by the insurers and the government as the government is pushing hard to remove boundary dispute cases from the court system as the number of disputes are increasing. It is therefore better to check what cover you have with an insurer before you buy. Any policy you are thinking of buying must cover legal expenses for any boundary dispute, including land registry costs, the adjudication process and the County Court process. If it does not, then you could find yourself with major legal costs in the event of any dispute.

## Costs of Boundary Searches and Pre and Post Purchase Insurance

The cost of a boundary search is around three to four hundred pounds and in the scheme of things is not too much. Specialist insurance at the time of purchase to cover a dispute costs is around six hundred to a thousand pounds on top of your purchase costs and this could be a valuable investment if you suspect that there could be any issue in the future with your neighbours or with your land title. Although you will never truly know whether there will be a problem, if you are purchasing an older property, a country property or one that has been extended, modified or altered in any way, then insurance is definitely worth the investment.

## Check List

What does the land registry file copy plan show regarding your boundary?

What does the land registry file copy plan show regarding your neighbours' boundary?

Does your neighbours' boundary align and coincide with yours?

Are you subject to general boundary rules?

If so, have you checked the latest Ordnance Survey maps? If there are key features, are they shown? Have you checked your own title deeds? For example are there any 'T' marks regarding boundary fences? Do they lie on your side of the boundary or your neighbours?

Have you sent a letter to your neighbour and confirmed who maintains the boundary? Can you come to an arrangement with your neighbour on maintenance of the features such as fences, hedges etc. on the boundaries?

Can you have a joint boundary search with your neighbour to determine where the boundary is?

# Chapter 3

## After Exchanging the Contract- When You Move In

The author is aware of several people who have moved into a new house who were so happy with their new home, they set about working to try and improve it. The new owners planted plants and trees on their borders and continued for several years happy in what they were doing. Then problems started and they soon found themselves fighting to prove that the land they had worked so hard to improve was actually theirs.

As stated, the best way to avoid a boundary problem is to prepare for one. There are a number of things that you can do to prevent a dispute and if you find yourself heading into one, with the preparation advice given to you below, you will be in a strong position to prevent the dispute growing into a bigger and more costly problem to you.

### Take photographs of Your Key Boundary Features

When the author moved in to one house he took a small number of photographs on special occasions such as Christmas or when it snowed and when his wife got a new car. He failed to take many detailed photographs of the house, garden, the boundaries and the neighbours' boundary fence at different times of the year. By not doing so if his neighbour had decided to expand onto his land, his neighbour could have changed all of the features in the area and there would have been no record of what the boundary actually looked like before any changes. The problem you face is that if you do not take pictures of your property you can lose the historical record and even the strongest physical features on the ground can be removed over time. Most importantly if you only have a limited number of photographs from the time when you moved in, your neighbour, if malicious or greedy, can claim that he had changed the features on the ground before he actually changed them and if you have no records, can claim they were there a long time before you moved in. This means that if there is no evidence to the contrary, your neighbour could claim adverse possession or squatters rights over land that belongs to you. When taking pictures make sure you are able to show from the time stamps on the camera, the dates and the time the photographs were taken. Make sure you take a lot of pictures of the key boundary features at regular intervals from different angles and in different parts of your garden at varying times of the year.

## What to Photograph

Take photographs of your boundary fence or wall, the fence posts or pillars and anything physical on or near your boundary. If there are trees on your side of the border, take a picture of them. The same goes with any plants, large rocks, holes, ditches and hedges. If you can take pictures of your neighbours' features then do this as well. Make sure you take the photographs from many different angles so that you cover each and every perspective.

Ensure that you take pictures at different times of the year. Be sure to photograph winter, summer, spring and autumn as the features in your garden will all look different at each time of the year and will expose something new or different as a result. The pictures need to show the key features from a distance and from a close up position. This means that you should take several pictures of each feature to get enough detail. If you can take a picture with a tape measure showing the size of the feature then this is perfect. Combine this with detailed pictures of the positions of each feature compared to each other. For example, the position of a tree relative to the location of you garden fence. Try and put a scale to the picture so that you can tell how far away the features are from each other. By doing this, you are able to show relatively accurately how far your boundary fence is to other items on your property. Although this is not totally infallible, the fact that you have a record is a valuable thing should you ever have a dispute or should you ever have to go to court. Moreover if you ever have any issues with the planning authorities, you will be able to show the time and date of when a feature was created or of how long it has been in position. The author had an experience where on day a local planning office came along and delivered a letter ordering the author to demolish a shed or apply for a certificate of lawful development for the shed. At the time of issuing the notice, the planning officer said it was unlikely that permission would be granted to keep the shed so be prepared to demolish it. When the author produced photographic evidence to show the shed had been in its location for over fourteen years, the council backed down as they could do nothing about it. If the author did not have those pictures, the council could have enforced their order to have the shed demolished.

## Take Some Measurements

When you have taken your photographs, take some measurements and record the distances between key features. For example record the distance from the hedge line to the fence line or the distance between your garage and the fence between you and your neighbour. Take the measurements at different times of the year and re-visit your measurements every few years or so. This is because plants, trees and hedges change position over time due to root and foliage growth. Similarly if you or your neighbours are trimming trees or hedges on the border you will see the shape of key features change over time. If any features have been removed, try and record their old position. For example in a case where a neighbour removed a number of trees from a border with another neighbour, the real land owner was able to dig down and show the stumps, and the first neighbour had difficulty in proving that they were not key features delineating the actual boundary between properties because of this. If you have pictures that have been taken on your boundary and in your garden, then record the dimensions of the features and the details on the back of your photos or better still, place them in a photo book with records of times, dates, areas and dimensions relative to each place within your garden and with a reference to the photos taken of those places.

## Draw a Sketch Map with Dimensions if Possible

Draw a sketch of the key features in and around your property on a piece of paper and place it somewhere safe, if you have created an album, place it in there with all of your other records. Try and be as accurate as possible in your sketch and incorporate the measurements that you collected. Record as much detail as you can in your sketch, key features to record includes hedges, trees, fences, bushes, walls and ditches. If there are tree stumps, remnants of old walls, fences, paths etc. make sure you record these as well as any other feature that could be meaningful to you later.

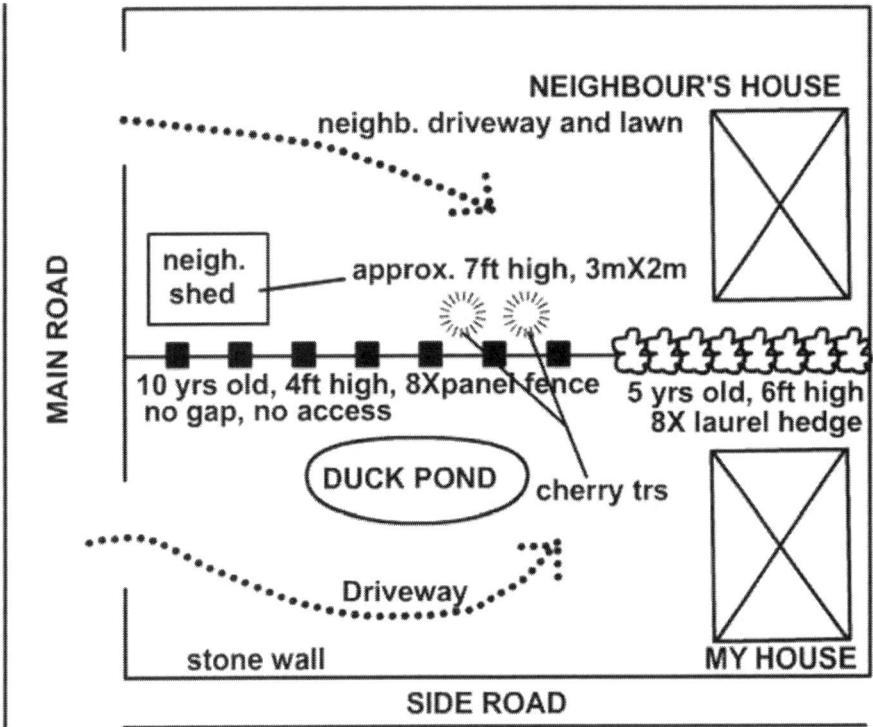

## Record as Much Information as You Can

From the first time you go to your new house to the time when you leave to go to a new home you should make and keep notes and keep records of all correspondence or key discussions pertaining to your home and property. Make sure you keep all of the letters sent to you from neighbours and received from your Solicitors during the time of the conveyance. Keep any conveyance information you may have from other sources such as the estate agent and the original owners from whom you purchased your home.

You must ensure you keep copies of all correspondence between you and your neighbours. This includes thank you letters, birthday cards and Christmas cards as well as any other notes between you. If a dispute ever does develop you will need this information as it will prove invaluable. In one case the author observed at a trial, a neighbour tried to say that his immediate neighbours were hostile to him from the day he moved in to his home and claimed they were never friendly to him or his family. This person looked a complete idiot in court when the supposedly hostile neighbours produced several thank you letters, birthday cards, barbeque thank you notes and Christmas cards that were sent to him by the supposedly hostile neighbours when they did not have a dispute. His point that these neighbours were hostile to him was shown as false in court and this in turn destroyed much of the credibility he had with the Judge. In the end, when it came to the benefit of doubt, the Judge awarded in favour of this persons neighbours because of his outright lies.

Be sure to keep a record of any meaningful incidents or developments in and around your home. These could include any decoration or renovation works carried out by you or your neighbour, record any significant gardening activities, and document any changes to their property and any social events such as parties, arguments and large family gatherings. The author is not suggesting that you should spy on your neighbours but each of the events described above can have great significance in case of a dispute. Again as an illustration in one case observed in court by the author one neighbour remodelled part of his garden when he did not have any dispute with a particular neighbour and was about to get rid of a small willow tree. His neighbours asked him for the tree and he gave it to them. When a case came to court several years later this neighbour claimed that the tree was on the disputed land that he was making a claim for. When he was shown pictures of his remodelling and a specific photo showing where the tree was originally planted, it discredited his claim as these pictures were time stamped and dated two years later than he was actually claiming in court. This had a massive effect on the Judge at the trial as this neighbour was shown not to be telling the truth. Needless to say this person lost his claim and suffered a very large legal bill as a result.

It is also worthwhile carrying a small camera whenever you are in your garden. Not only can you photograph any wildlife that is there, you can take pictures of what is going on at different times of the year and you can record significant events as and when you come across them.

## Planting a Tree

This may seem obvious, however but many people do not consider the consequences of planting a tree. Most people do not realise the rate at which a tree grows and so the planning of the tree's placement is not undertaken in the first instance. It is generally only years later when the tree has grown substantially that people see problems that their planting has created. Trees planted in the wrong place can cause several issues that can lead to a neighbour dispute. These include the trees' growth, and its subsequent diameter and height after several years as well as the roots and the shadow caused by the tree. The shadow that the tree creates, and the subsequent leaf drop in autumn can be a major thorn in a neighbours' side, and these factors alone have lead to a high number of court cases involving trees. By law your neighbour has the right to cut the branches and roots of any plants that come onto his or her land. By doing so he or she can damage your trees so that they do not grow properly or alternatively they fall onto your land thus causing you further problems.

When planning to plant a tree, make sure you know the height and width that the tree can grow to. You must also look at its annual growth pattern. Consider how the tree can be pruned when it is planted on your land or close to your boundary. Think about shade and shadow at the trees maximum height and consider the sun at different times of the day. If you are planting close to your border make sure you make room for tree and trunk growth so that the tree does not encroach over the boundary to create a problem at any time in the future. A typical rule of thumb is to plant the tree before its full spread. For example if your tree has a full spread of one metre, plant it no closer than one point five metres to your boundary, thus giving room for growth, pruning and border discrepancy. By giving the tree room, you will also preclude any tree growth going over your boundary and onto your neighbours' property. Some surveyors or organisations say plant the tree one meter away from your boundary so that the trees maximum spread can denote the boundary. Sadly plants do not adhere to their growing instructions and so could extend beyond the boundary if planted too close. Alternatively they could grow in a manner where they will be vigorous in one direction and slow growing in another. If the fast growing side of the tree is facing your neighbour, then this could present a problem in the future. The authors' advice is to steer clear of any potential for dispute and make sure you plan your garden and any trees or shrubs that you plant should be deliberate and carefully considered. Play it safe and you will save a lot of money, time and grief in both the short and long run.

Many people look to fast growing hedge varieties on their boundaries as they create an instant barrier. Varieties like Leylandii hedging can certainly grow quickly and present a near instant border or barrier. As these plants mature however they can become problematic as they are difficult to prune and as they are vociferous growers, they can become very tall and can create a lot of shadow after a small number of years. If you are looking for fast cover plants, look at laurels as an alternative as they grow thick and can be topped easily.

# Fences, Walls & Gates

Fences and walls can be the cause a number of issues to a property owner. In some cases it may be difficult if not impossible to identify who is responsible for the upkeep of a fence. This is because it may not have been identified on a conveyance or on a title deed. There is any number of reasons for this to have happened and it is something that you should be able to pick up on at the time of conveyance. Firstly the fence or wall could have been put in place to prevent livestock such as sheep or cattle wandering if the fence or wall is in the countryside. If the fence or wall is in a town property it could have been put in place to prevent dogs from wandering where they are not wanted or could have been placed to ensure they stay within a defined area for security reasons. For these purposes, a fence or wall may not actually be the boundary of a property but they could turn into one if the fence or wall remains in position over a long period of time.

Other reasons for not taking fences or walls immediately as a boundary are any issues such as any restrictions enforced by planning regulations. An example of this could be a fence or wall placed by the side of the road, where the planning authorities restrict the wall or fences proximity to the road. Other considerations could include terrain and features on the ground that limit fence or wall placement. An example of this could be large rocks or trees on the edge of the fence or wall that could not be removed at the time of its placement. In the authors' case, an example with his previous neighbour is where he erected a fence in front of a row of large trees that he did not want to remove. The fronts of the trees were the boundary and not the fence.

Make sure that you know who is responsible for maintaining the fence or wall on your property as you cannot take anything at face value. If you are unsure as to who is responsible for what, make as many enquiries as you can before approaching your neighbour with any issue or questions and when you do so, get an agreement in writing as to who is responsible for what if you come to a settlement.

If you are able to identify who is responsible for the fence or wall and if it is on a boundary, the front face of the wall or fence is normally the actual boundary line. If you have reaches an agreement, then generally this will serve as the boundary line in the future. This is why it is extremely important to document everything that you can.

# Chapter 4

## Dealing with Neighbours

### People are People, Ego's, Feelings and Aspirations

The statement people are people may seem crass or obvious to some, but the fact remains however that everyone has their wants, needs and expectations. Everyone has an ego and everyone has ideas and dreams. The same goes for you as for your neighbours wants and expectations too. If you are lucky you will be seen by your neighbour's as a person who works and lives within their set of values and beliefs. If you are unlucky and you do not match their ideas or beliefs, then you have the seeds for disagreement as your foundations for life will not be the same as your neighbour's. Not all people are bad or egotistical, however to illustrate the depth of feeling amongst most people, just visit one of the many conversations on any public blog site or on face book and you will see people who get upset with so many things, and it is difficult to understand why. Some of the issues that seem to upset people appear to be petty and insignificant to others but highly meaningful and emotional to some. The problems with beliefs are that they are very personal and are the result of many factors and influences; there are a whole plethora of ideas, thoughts and misunderstandings that can come as a result of an actual or perceived challenge to those beliefs.

If you look at people's behaviour, when you get into their home they get more protective and defensive when in this environment. When you consider that people spend most of their lives at their home, they get very emotive as both happy and sad events happen there. People associate things with both good times and bad times alike and the home is the hub of all of this. For example when the author got married, he planted a tree to celebrate the wedding. The tree was a lovely ornamental willow and if someone was to cut that tree, either by accident or on purpose, the author would find it upsetting and would likely become angry. Although this is a simple example, the act of planting of a tree could have a great emotional significance to someone. If you look at this as a single event in isolation, most people have thousands of emotions that are either attached or associated with their house and family, their home and the objects in and around it.

When dealing with a neighbour you must consider your approach to them from day one. You must remember that their home is a very personal thing and that if you upset their ideals or views, or if you become outspoken on what can be seen by many as a trivial matter, your neighbours can become a nightmare to deal with as they could easily be offended. Everything you say or do when you interact with other people, be it in a friendly or an unfriendly manner will be recorded in some way or the other. They will either mentally record their view or impression of you and the conversations, where the aim of your neighbour is to build an overall impression of you, or they will record things physically via correspondence, notes or cards. Even the simplest gesture such as the sending of a Christmas or birthday card is important and its effect must not be underestimated.

Nobody ever wants a dispute with another person or wants to be unfriendly towards them, life however is different and even with care, and the best of relationships can turn sour and cause you future problems. If your relationship with your neighbour leads to a dispute, then the history between you will matter greatly. If legal issues follow as a result of the dispute, the past relationship between you both will be considered by the legal authorities. For example, if you go to court or adjudication over a boundary dispute, or if you are before the court for any other issue for that matter, then any previous correspondence between you and your neighbours may be used against you. Similarly if your neighbour raises a complaint about you with any authority such as the council or the police, you will have a record of the relationship between you, and this can work in your favour, particularly if they claim that you have been unfriendly or aggressive towards them from day one and you have proof to show you have not. The other point to think about here is that people have different beliefs and values so if an issue appears perfectly reasonable to you, it may not be perfectly reasonable to them. These types of problems and misunderstandings are prime ground for the beginning of a dispute so beware and invest in a good friendly relationship with your neighbours. Even though it may be difficult for you, always try and see things from your neighbours side or point of view as well. You may not always be perfect or right so always consider this aspect as well.

# Living Peacefully With Your Neighbours

Although most people do not have any issues of problems with their neighbours, most people do have their ups and downs for many different reasons, and there are times when relationships can be strained. There are a number of areas that can cause the relationships to be strained at different times with different people and different neighbours. If your neighbour is a reasonable person and you maintain an informed relationship with them, then things need not get out of hand during any ups and downs you may have. Given below are specific problem areas that can cause issues between you and your neighbours and also detailed are ways of dealing with these problem areas to ensure that you stay on good terms with your neighbours.

## Communications

As mentioned previously the way that you communicate with your neighbour really matters and as a golden rule, you should always deal with anyone in the way that they expect to be dealt with themselves. For most people that is in a friendly, polite and respectful manner. When you see your neighbour, always acknowledge their presence and spend a little time to exchange some form of pleasantries, even if you are in a hurry. If you are polite, friendly and give them the time of day, most people will get along with you and if you have to ask anything of your neighbour that is reasonable, then they will normally try and help as not only will they see you as being reasonable, it is unlikely that they will feel threatened by you.

There are however always exceptions to the rules of what is normal and what is not. The author has come across people who are just downright nasty to everyone they meet. These people are aggressive, hard to talk to and hard to deal with, even on the simplest matters. In these cases it will be very difficult to maintain good communications between you so limit your interactions to the bare minimum. With people like this it is always best to be polite, to listen before speaking and when you do speak or ask something of them, be neutral, non-aggressive and polite even if it may be very difficult to do so and even if they are aggressive in their tone. If you respond in an aggressive manner initially, it may pour fuel on to a fire and may create a dispute where one may not exist. The thing to watch out for however is bullies. If your neighbour is a bully then you may need to take advice on how best to deal with them, as bullies pick on who they perceive to be weak people. If they see you as a weak person then they are likely to create problems where they do not exist, just to feel powerful and just as an ego trip. If you cannot take advice or cannot afford it, please see below.

## Dealing with Bullies

Most people are reasonable, descent and honest in their approach to everything in life. However there are some people who are not and these people are generally seeking to get anything and everything they can for themselves. By doing so, these people will not hesitate to bully, cajole or use violence to get what they want and they do not care about you, nor do they see you as a victim, you are just prey and as such they see a challenge in making your life a misery. If they can make you unhappy, these people feel stronger for it. If you are ever in the unfortunate situation to be living next door to a person like this, then they will try to force their views on you if you upset or disagree with them in any way. These people are bullies and like most bullies they are cowards. They like to feel powerful by stepping on others who they see or perceive to be weaker than them. The best way to deal with a bully is to give them a taste of their own medicine. If they think you are an easy target they will pick on you and will make your life difficult. If you are not weak and you give them a hard time in response to anything they throw at you, then the chances are that they will leave you alone. Do not be deceived by thinking that bullies can be reasoned with, they cannot as they are not reasonable people. If they were, they would not attempt to bully you so make sure that you stand up for yourself at every opportunity and do not be frightened of them. Bullies are difficult to deal with as they tend to try to get the upper hand at any opportunity. You will need to keep them in their place but when doing so remember that the likelihood is that you will not ever be friends and any counter actions taken by you may see an escalation in any dispute that you have, even if the bully does back down, they will always remember it and look for a moment to try and get the upper hand again. Conversely if your neighbour knows that he or she will get a dose of their own medicine but only stronger if they try to bully you, this may be enough to deter them and will make them leave you alone

# Problems, Remedies and Their Prevention

## Be Careful What You Say and What You Write. Estoppel!

Because Solicitors and Barristers are very often misunderstood they have invented a language of their own that corresponds to the amount of money they bill for. If they can use a long or Latin word such as estoppel they can add a few hundred pounds to your bill as whatever it is they are suggesting sounds good and official. Besides which they have to pay for their classical education somehow and high rates of billing for hot air is a prime example of this.

Estoppel is the word Solicitors or Barristers use where a circumstance or an event sets an expectation that can be relied upon from a legal perspective. Put simply, if you say something that disagrees with a given position of another party, later this could be used against you in a court of law, even if it was not meant or even if it was only spoken. A prime example is if you say yes to your neighbour for a border position and agree a fence at a certain point in the garden. You cannot claim later that the neighbour is trespassing with this fence if it is on your land after authorising them to do something as they have your permission and the law states that you cannot unreasonably withdraw your position without good reason The concept is that of using reasonable behaviour for your actions as a defence. Another real world example is if you owe money to a bank and the bank agrees to write off the money you owe, they cannot come back to you and claim you still owe a debt of money to them.

Estoppel is a very important concept to you because if you make any form of agreement with your neighbour and then you change your mind, this can be used as a defence against you by your neighbour using estoppel as the excuse. The key is to be careful with what you say and what you agree with your neighbour, be it either verbally or in writing. Again it is worthwhile taking the appropriate advice before committing to any agreement even if the agreement appears reasonable, as it could disadvantage you later if you do not consider the consequences in their entirety or if you do not take the correct advice. Typical problems that develop around estoppel come from allowing access or use of your land or in you agreeing to cut a tree or hedge on the boundary of your property.

## Bonfires-What If You Need to Burn?

The first thing to consider with a bonfire is that you do not need to burn anything at all. Some councils collect garden waste and any additional rubbish, so look to see whether yours does and let them collect it rather than burning it. If your local council does not collect waste then think about chipping your wood to use as covering on your garden beds or paths or think about taking any excess rubbish to the tip. There are also many different ways to use of your grass clippings or the leaves from your trees. Grass clippings and leaves can be used as mulch around plants and can save you water during the summer or they can be composted to be used in your garden in the coming seasons. Try and be friendly to your neighbour and the environment by not burning anything unless you really have to. That way it is unlikely that you will encounter issues with your neighbours and we will all have a cleaner environment

If you are going to have a bonfire because you cannot mulch, chip or take your waste to the tip, let your neighbours know in advance that you will be burning rubbish or wood. Try and hold your fire away from any sensitive parts of your neighbours' property as stray embers can cause a fire. For example do not hold a fire close to your neighbours' house or garage where they may be working or storing flammable materials such as oil or petrol for their mower or car. Similarly if it is a fine day, make sure that your neighbour has not hung their washing outside to dry or opened their windows for ventilation. If it is also a fine day, make sure that any grass near your fire is not so dry that it will catch light and carry the fire to another part of your garden or your neighbours.

When you have lit your fire be sure that it is tended at all times and ensure that it burns evenly by raking your wood and rubbish into the centre of the fire where it is usually the hottest. Make sure that it is dry when you burn your fire as wet wood or leaves tend to create a lot of smoke. This is a major problem as smoke drifts and under the Environmental Protection Act 1990 Section 79; a smoke nuisance is a prosecutable offense by the police and the council if there is too much of it or if it drifts across a road and obscures visibility on the highway.

When you burn your garden or household waste, burn it as quickly as you can and leave no embers smouldering afterwards. If you do have a large amount of rubbish or garden waste to burn, consider having several small fires at different times over the day or over a number of days.

## If Smoke or Fires are a Problem to You

If your neighbour burns wood or rubbish regularly then this may be deemed by the authorities or your legal adviser to be a nuisance and you may be able to get an injunction to stop them from burning. The problem however is this. Firstly this process is costly and unless you can prove that your neighbour has been burning wood or rubbish frequently and by doing so, has been interfering with your enjoyment of your property or of life, it is unlikely you will win your case. If your neighbour is causing a nuisance and he or she is endangering you by burning close to a fire hazard such as your garage, or gas supply or any supply cylinders then you stand a better chance of getting an injunction against them. To further any case in the courts you will need photographic evidence, a diary of when your neighbour was burning, how often and a note of how you felt at the time of burning. You can get the council involved and they will likely ask you to keep a diary and take photos. They will also talk to your neighbour and will warn him or her of the consequences of their actions if they continue. If you are lucky, they will stop burning. If you are unlucky they will continue and you may have to send Solicitors letters to warn them of the consequences of their actions or re-engage with the council. The last resort to any problem is to go to the court and take legal action and so you must try and avoid it at all costs Your chances of success are not high for the reasons stated above as you must be able to show how your neighbours fires have affected your life and you must prove that your neighbours have been careless or unreasonable in their actions.

## Fireworks - If You Are Having a Fireworks Party

Everyone likes to see colourful fireworks on a special occasion. They are pretty, vibrant and in some cases very loud and great fun. They are also dangerous and explosive and so can create damage if they are not set off in a controlled manner. When planning to use fireworks in a celebration make sure you are safe in your handling of the fireworks and make sure that they are as non-intrusive to your neighbours as is possible. The author has had some bitter experiences with fireworks where one of his neighbours launched fireworks from her garden and because she was reckless, these fireworks hit the authors' house, smashing a window as it exploded just inches away from the house. There was a violent explosion as the firework hit and flying glass went around the room. Luckily the author was in the room next door, otherwise he could have been very badly injured by this flying glass. The other considerations for fireworks are that they are flammable and as such they can set fire to things. Again the author had another bad experience with fireworks with the same person as above where a firework from a neighbouring property came down that still hot and it set fire to a wood pile that had been stored for use over the winter months. Although the fire was quickly put out, it could have been very damaging if it was closer to the authors house or garage. When planning on using fireworks it is always best to notify all of your neighbours that you are having a fireworks party. Make sure that you have taken all safety precautions before starting your firework display and this includes having water available should there be a fire. It is important to check your home insurance to ensure that you are covered for any accidental damage to either your own property or that of your neighboursbefore having a fireworks party at home. On the day of your party make sure that all hazards are dealt with that could create problems for you in the near vicinity of your launch area and that they are removed or are clear of hazards. This includes your neighbours gardens if your fireworks will be going anywhere near them. Make sure that your firework launch area is cited so that the fireworks go up in the air as straight as possible. If you do not consider your launch area, the fireworks could go off at an awkward angle and you could easily watch them exploding and either creating a nuisance for your neighbour or even worse damaging their property or your own.

## If your Neighbour is Having a Firework Party

This has to be one of the most irritating things a neighbour can do if you are not expecting it. Sadly unless your neighbours have their party at unsociable hours there is little you can do about it. The author once had a neighbour whose teenage daughter loved firing fireworks on special occasions, and because this neighbour was inconsiderate and irresponsible, she launched her fireworks directly at the authors' house. She especially enjoyed launching rockets so that they exploded as close to the author's windows as they could. The noise was sometimes deafening, the experience was not pleasant and the police did nothing when it happened as the neighbours claimed that the fireworks were carried close to the house by the wind. Unless your neighbour has regular fireworks parties that damage your enjoyment of your property, there is nothing you can do apart from give them a taste of their own medicine. Sadly however this will likely lead to an escalation of problems and issues with your neighbour. If however they are having regular parties that are unlicensed at night, then you can get the council to take action as there are now restrictions on the times of day that fireworks can be launched.

## Barbeques &Parties

There is nothing like a barbeque on a good summer's day, or a garden party to celebrate something special in your life. Sometimes a spontaneous party or barbeque is a good tonic for your morale and is a nice excuse to get together with friends and family. In any of these cases parties or barbeques are good for you, but can be a real pain for your neighbour especially if they are private people or if they enjoy their peace and quiet.

If you are planning a party or barbeque and are on good relations with your neighbour, then why not invite them to attend? If you do not want your neighbours at your party or barbeque, then the courteous thing to do is to tell them in advance of your party if you can. Give them an idea of when it is going to be held and how long it will last. When you finish your party, make sure you leave nothing that can blow onto their garden and create a mess and if you can, either talk to your neighbour after your party or send them a quick note the day after to apologise for the noise and thank them for their patience.

If you are playing music at your party or barbeque, make sure that the music is as low as is practical so as not to disturb other people unnecessarily. If holding a barbeque on a windy day, consider the drift of smoke and the smell of cooking onto any adjoining properties. Try and reduce the smoke from the barbeque by using a cover to your barbeque and by ensuring your coals are very hot before placing the food on the grill to cook Always remember that you are responsible for your guests behaviour so make sure that they are not too noisy and that they do not park anywhere that could be a problem or nuisance to your neighbour. If you are having a late night party, make sure that your guests understand the need not to disturb your neighbours and that they are quiet when they leave to go home after the party.

## If Your Neighbour is Having a Barbeque or Party

If your neighbours' party is a one off then there is little you can do about it but put up with the noise and the nuisance it may create. If your neighbours hold parties or barbeques on a regular basis and if they disturb you, it may be possible to involve the council and follow the options given in the noise section in order to try and reduce or prevent their intrusion. Outside of this, there is not much you can do apart from talking to them or in the most extreme of cases, sending them a Solicitors letter. In the end though, court action will be costly and you are unlikely to get too far so you may just have to live with it.

## Gardening and Repairs / DIY

For most occasions regarding gardening and DIY around your home you do not need to contact your neighbours' to let them know what you are doing as generally it will not concern them. This is particularly the case if any noise or disturbance is made during the day and if it is temporary. If however you are doing things that may involve your neighbours' in any way, it is always best to let them know what you are doing in advance so that they are aware of it and can plan alternatives.

The things that may concern them are things like the pruning of trees and bushes on your borders if your neighbours' own the overhanging trees or bushes. Other considerations are things like painting your boundary fence or the undertaking of any DIY to any areas that are considered to be joint areas. If you are doing anything at all to your neighbours' property you must seek their permission to do it. For example if you paint or repair the boundary fence without your neighbours permission and if the fence is owned by your neighbour, it is considered criminal damage to do so.

If your neighbours' trees are overhanging on your side of the boundary then you do not need to consult with them to cut them although it is polite to do so. If you cut your neighbours trees or shrubs because they are overhanging, you must give them back the cuttings and any fruit that was on them. A further point to note is that you cannot trespass onto your neighbours land to prune or cut the trees or bushes without legal permission. If your neighbour is unreasonable and does not take action when you request them to do so regarding any overhanging bushes or trees, you must send several letters requesting permission to carry out the proposed works to your neighbour before you take any form of action. For example you must send letters that ask permission and request what you would like your neighbour to do and why. If your neighbour refuses to do as you ask, and you must never ask anything that is unreasonable, then the next step is to ask them for permission to access their land to carry out the task or for a third party to carry out the task. You must be exact and precise as to what you are asking of your neighbour and in describing what you are proposing to do. As an example if you are using a third party, you must state what the requirement is to your neighbour, you must tell them who is going to carry out the requirement, their approach, times and dates, when the activities are proposed and any further details such as how access will be gained to fulfil the task they have been given. It is always advisable to give any insurance details that either you or the third party hold to cover any proposed activities. If your neighbour still refuses permission for you or a third party to carry out the proposed works, then you can apply to the court for access to your neighbours' land under the neighbouring land act 1992.This act allows you to apply to the court to obtain permission to carry out a specific essential maintenance task or tasks on your neighbours' property if it is causing you any issues. Essential maintenance activities include the trimming and pruning of trees, the repair and maintenance of things like sewer or water pipes, drainage and cess pits that are also connected to your property. When applying to the court you must be specific in your requirement and request to the court and will need to provide a good reason as to why you need access to your neighbours' land and you must detail who is going to do the work. Your last letter detailing your requirements to your neighbour should have most of the details you would need to apply for a court order to allow you access to your neighbours' land. The court cannot prevent you undertaking essential maintenance activities, however if your neighbour objects, they can impose restrictions on the way you carry out the proposed work or can place a restriction on when or on what works you can carry out if any elements are deemed to be non-essential. Before going to the court however, try and ensure that you have exhausted all options with your neighbour and that if you do go to court, you can demonstrate that you have made reasonable requests of your neighbour that have either been ignored or not agreed to by them.

---

*Dear Neighbour,*

*As you are aware, there is with regret, an existing dispute between me and you about the laurel hedge next to my kitchen. In order to end the dispute and to be neighbourly I offer to accept that I shall trim my hedge to the level of 6 ft in height. However, as the hedge is at present 24ft tall, I request that you should cover half of my costs for the initial work. When the hedge is cut to 6ft I shall continue to maintain it to that level by me free of charge.*

*I really hope that we could find a mutually acceptable solution to our dispute therefore I look forward to hearing from you. Please note that my offer is valid for 28 days after that it will automatically expire.*

*Yours faithfully,*

---

When carrying out the essential activities that have either been agreed by your neighbour or as they have been directed by a court order, make sure that you do not stray in any way from the agreed tasks or approaches that you have agreed to. If you do stray, although you have permission to be on your neighbours land, you could still be committing trespass if you stay too long after completing the task or if you wander into a different area of your neighbours' garden without their express permission. Once all tasks have completed, leave quickly and make sure you tidy up and make good any damage. Under no circumstances should you ever do any additional works without express permission otherwise this could construe criminal damage.

## If Your Neighbour is Carrying Out DIY or Maintenance

The same rights that apply to you also apply to your neighbour, so consider this if they are doing DIY or are gardening. The best way to avoid any form of trouble in the garden is to maintain your garden so that it is at least tidy, trim your trees and hedges and make sure nothing overhangs your neighbours' garden or so that nothing can blow into their garden that could be a nuisance or that could cause damage. Leaves can do this so if you can, ensure that you collect them before they are blown by the wind onto neighbouring properties. With regard other DIY activities, take a common sense approach to your work and do not create issues if anything is not a real problem to you. Try and avoid any conflict if you can and so do not do anything that your neighbours' could be concerned or worried about without good reason.

## Extensions &Building Works

The biggest investment in life for most people is an investment in their home. At some stage in the ownership of their home, most home owners will want to remodel, change, extend or build something extra to make their home just a bit more special to them. This may be something like building a new kitchen or a new extension or could include just plain redecorating. Whatever it is that you are planning to do to your home, consider its impact to your neighbour, particularly if your works are external. For example if you are remodelling the house or garden, will it change the view from your neighbours' house? Will it obscure light or create a problem later for your neighbour such as increasing maintenance for them on their own property? If you are not changing the physical features of your property that impact your neighbour consider the nature of the works themselves. If you are getting a new kitchen for example, will your contractors need a skip to take your old kitchen and rubbish away? If this is the case, where is it going to go? Will there be a large number of contractors on any given day working in or around your home? If this is so where and how are they going to park? Will these contractors make a noise while working? When are they going to be working? Will they be early or late and if so on what days will they be working? If you are going to carry out the work yourself, you will still need to consider these points as your work will most likely need to be planned in the same manner as that of a professional particularly if you are getting deliveries or a skip. Whether you are carrying out the work yourself or whether you are employing a third party it is always best to send a letter to your wider neighbours' explaining to them that you are having some work done on your home and for how long. Apologise to them in advance for any inconvenience that it may cause them and give them all the necessary information to make them feel comfortable about what is that you are proposing. If you are going to undertake the work yourself, ensure that you try and stick to the times and days and details as you have given in the letter to your neighbours. If you are employing third parties to do the work, then try and build the agreement or contract with them around the letter that you sent to your neighbour. If you or your contractors cannot stick to the details of your letter, then let your neighbours know of any deviations if they could cause them concern and when the work is all over, make sure that you send a thank you note to your neighbour's to thank them for their patience and understanding. With your immediate neighbours it is best to talk to them frequently and to send a letter in a friendly and polite manner just to remind them of the dates that you are starting your building works. After the event, a small thank you present would also be a good idea.

---

*Dear Neighbour,*

*As you are aware after our initial agreement to trim the laurel hedge to 6ft in height I have now contacted Trimmytree & Sons Ltd and received a price quote which we both agreed to pay jointly.*

*Last Friday the contractor carried out the work and trimmed the hedge to 6ft in height and disposed of all excess wood from the site.*

*I would like to thank you for your patience while the work was carried out. It was a rather noisy three days. Please also let me tell you that I am very pleased that we were able to resolve the dispute peacefully and I very much appreciated your co-operation.*

*Yours faithfully,*

---

## Fences & Boundaries

Fences and boundaries are one of the biggest causes of disputes between neighbours' in the UK. Sadly the land recording system historically defined by the government does not define exactly where most boundaries lie as they are measured by the general boundary rule.*(Please see previous chapters with more detailed References)*.When painting or repairing fences be sure that they belong to you and not your neighbour as you could be committing criminal damage if you have not got their permission to paint or repair. Check your title deeds before you start work as it could lead to problems otherwise.

## Pets

Pets can be a major cause of grief between neighbours as animals can be responsible for many things and in many cases you cannot control them. For example dogs can bark and create noise at different times of the day, and this could create friction and tension with your neighbour. Cats can also be a problem as they are totally uncontrollable. They tend to wander around the neighbourhood doing whatever pleases them and as they are very territorial, they mark their territory to show where they have been. This can be a problem to neighbours who tend their gardens and grow plants or vegetables. Cats can also be quite aggressive if they want to be and the author once had a cat that would sit on one neighbours' roof and would patiently wait for this person to let their dog out into the garden. As soon as the dog came out of the neighbours' house, the cat would jump from the roof onto the dog and would dig its claws into the dogs back, causing the dog to react by barking and by running in all directions. The dog would also react by chasing the cat and the cat, being practical would always take the shortest and quickest escape route which in this case was always via the neighbours' rubbish bins. The dog, being slower to react would always collide with these bins and resultantly there would always be a mess where the rubbish from the bins would always end up on the floor afterwards. At first this was highly amusing to watch but after a few occurrences the neighbour got fed up and the author received a letter requesting that he control his cat. Another issue with the cat was that one day the cat attacked a dustbin man and afterwards this person refused to come anywhere near the authors house or anywhere near the adjoining properties in case he got attacked again. Incidentally this dustbin man was around six foot tall and was very thick set, the cat was very small but fast and aggressive and this man was petrified of the cat. This also became an irritation to the neighbours as again they first thought it was amusing that a little cat had beaten up a very large man. After the rubbish was not collected for a while due to this mans' fear, the amusement quickly wore off and the author received letters from his neighbours' requesting him to control his cat.

## Noise

Noise is one of the most common problems that you can face as a home owner, particularly if you are in a neighbourhood comprised of a lot of people, or if you live in attached or semi-detached housing. If you are lucky enough to have no neighbours close to you, or considerate neighbours who do not make noises at awkward times of the day or the night then you are one of the extremely lucky few. Noises are a real issue to many people and one statistic said that one in three people had complaints about their neighbours and noise was one of the top reasons for their complaints.

The problem with noise is that it is not normally a continuous occurrence, that is to say noise does not normally happen all the time and so you need to keep a diary and log of when it happens and when noise becomes a problem to you. Even if you do keep a log or diary, the loudness of the actual noise is difficult to measure as what may be loud or irritating to you may not be a problem to others or alternatively if you manage to record the noise, the actual noise level would be difficult to prove as being high without specialist equipment. A real world demonstration of this is if you are unlucky enough to be on a train near a person who has their music on so loud in their headphones that it can be heard halfway down the carriage. It would deafen most people at that volume; however it does not appear to be a problem to the person listening. This leaves you with several issues if your problem is at home. If you ask your neighbour to keep down the noise levels and they fail to do so you only have a few alternative methods of dealing with this noise nuisance. Firstly you can approach the local council and ask them to get involved to measure and monitor the noise. Under the Environmental Protection Act 1990 the local authority are obliged to take all reasonable steps within their powers to investigate noise nuisance and if they can prove a nuisance, they can bring proceedings against the offender. The authors' experience of this course of action that it is effective for a short period of time as the neighbour, after receiving a warning will generally stop until they think you have forgotten about it and will soon start again when the council are not around or when they appear to have lost interest. For the council to do anything meaningful they must be able to prove a nuisance and if your neighbour is a slippery person, the chances are that the council will be able to do very little to help you.

This now only leaves you with one further alternative. The next option is to try and get legal proceedings started against your neighbour. This will cost you a huge amount of money and in most cases it will not get you too far. Even if you get an injunction against your neighbour because you have proven noise as a problem, and in most cases it is difficult to do so, for an injunction to be effective it has to be enforced. Generally speaking the police are not interested in noise enforcement or any other kind of neighbour dispute as they feel that it is not really a crime and so the net effect of this is that you may win your case in court, your neighbour will have received an order to stop making a noise but will continue to do so as no one is going to stop them. It is a complete waste of money and time. The legal system needs to change in this regard and the police need to be made accountable for dealing with these types of issues if the court has ordered an injunction.

## Burglar Alarms

One of the most common and most irritating things in today's modern world is a burglar alarm that constantly rings. The law requires that alarms reset themselves after twenty minutes. If the alarm becomes a regular problem you can report it as a noise nuisance to the local council. If the alarm is deemed a nuisance and if it has been ringing for more than twenty minutes or on and off constantly for over an hour, the law allows for a council worker to enter the building with the alarm having first shown that it is a genuine noise nuisance and having first obtained a warrant for entry. If the council worker cannot get free access to the building, the warrant allows them to enter the building by force. If they do so, not only can they damage your property, they can charge you for the time of the council worker who has entered your property and silenced the alarm and most likely damaged your property as a result.

The local council also has the powers to declare an area an alarm notification area. In essence this requires everyone in the area to give the contact details of a key holder to a property within the area. If the alarm is triggered and is deemed to be a nuisance, then the local council can contact the key holder to have them silence the alarm. The council and the government take this matter very seriously and they have written the requirement for key holders to silence these alarms into legislation. This means that if you live in an alarm notification area and do not give the contact details of someone who can silence an alarm or alternatively if the person who is contacted by the council does not turn off the alarm when requested to do so, then it is a criminal offence that can carry a fine and in extreme cases a prison sentence. If you think that you live in an alarm notification area, then contact the council and they will advise you of what you need to do to comply with the law in your area.

## New Cars or Items (Keeping up With the Jones's)

It is not uncommon for your neighbours to take an unwelcome interest in your successes and failures or your major purchases. An example of this is where the author bought a car and within a week of buying this car, a neighbour had bought a bigger and more expensive car and had begun parking it in full view of everyone to show it off. This particular neighbour was a complete idiot and everything the author did had to be bettered by this neighbour in some shape or form. Another example from the same neighbour was where the author laid a patio outside of his kitchen and placed a table and chairs there for outside eating during the summer. Again within days of completion, the neighbour did the same, only his patio was bigger with a much larger table set and he added lights, trees and a very large pergola. If you are inventive you could have some fun with people who are obsessed by buying bigger and better things than you. For example you can hire a sports car for several weeks and watch your neighbour react. Ultimately it does become irritating and sadly there is nothing that you can do about it as there is no law to prevent it.

## Weeds

You are responsible for everything on your property and in many cases, anything connected to your property. If this influence affects a surrounding property then you could be held accountable for any damage that this may cause to that property. Typically this influence extends to plants, animals, and odours etc. An area that people tend not to think about however is weeds. Although in many cases weeds are not normally an issue to property owners, a number of people take ownership of properties with weed problems, sometimes they do this without realising that there is a problem. Properties with weed problems are not just limited to the countryside but they can be in the cities and towns as well. Up until the early eighties, plants like Japanese Knotweed were seen to be good ornamental and acceptable plants to be planted in the garden. The plant is highly decorative and grows quickly so was used in a variety of ways, from edging ponds, to feature plantings in plant border beds in both small and large gardens. The plant grows so quickly that it is now considered a pest and as a result the government drew up legislation to prevent its use in the future. It is now an offence to encourage the plants growth, to plant it or to trade it in any way. For knotweed this includes cutting it as this also encourages its growth. There are also other weeds that are also invasive and that are considered a nuisance and you need to be aware of these as well. Should they spread to neighbouring properties then you could be forced to pay for their removal and for any damage they cause. In the case of Japanese Knotweed, not only does it have to be removed by specialist companies that are licensed for its removal and disposal, you will be inspected by the government if a problem is found and if you have not complied with legislation, you could be prosecuted. If an invasive weed such as Knot Weed has strayed onto your neighbour's properties, then you could find yourself with a massive bill for its removal, a heavy fine and damages that will need to be paid to your neighbours. If you suspect that you have a weed problem consult an expert immediately. If your weed problem is proven right, then they can recommend the best treatment to kill the weeds or to prevent their spread. Be aware however that this is not likely to be cheap so prepare yourself for a large level of expenditure starting at several thousand pounds upwards.

# Trees & Shrubs

# Your Responsibilities

Like weeds you are responsible for the trees and shrubs on or protruding from your property. You can also be responsible for any trees or shrubs that have grown as a result of seeds that came from your property. This means that trees are an area where you can inadvertently find yourself with problems. The areas where most people get into dispute around trees and shrubs are above the ground as they are most visible here. Trees and shrubs can grow and take away a lot of light so they must be trimmed and maintained regularly. Their leaves and fruit can also cause a problem to you and your neighbours, particularly in circumstances such as if there is a pond nearby, as fish can be poisoned by falling leaves or fruit. Bear this in mind if you have a neighbour with an ornamental pond. Similarly leaves and fruit can stain items so if you have trees overhanging a patio or driveway, this can also cause problems to your neighbours. Make sure that you keep your trees trimmed and regularly pruned and if they do bear fruit, make sure you pick it before it starts to drop onto your neighbours property.

If the trees or shrubs are on or near the border you must also consider what is going on below ground as well. During dry spells, tree and shrub roots grow vigorously to try and find water. If there are dry periods with intermittent and infrequent rain showers, roots can grow and rise to the surface of the ground or they can grow and move towards damp spots in your garden to extract water from the soil. If a tree or shrub is growing close to a house, a path or a driveway, any rising roots can damage virtually any surface including tarmac, cement and flags. Although this does not happen overnight, it may be difficult to stop the growth without causing damage and so could again leave you with a bill. If you have not seen the problem and you have plants close to your neighbours, then you could easily get into a dispute regarding the repair of any surfaces or foundations that have been damaged as well as getting into a dispute about the removal of any offending trees or shrubs and their root systems. If you have to remove the entire root system because of growth over a long period of time, this can be very costly to do as you may have to remove a complete driveway or path.

## If Your Neighbour Has Trees or Shrubs That Are Causing Damage

If your neighbours trees and shrubs are causing damage to your property you must consider what this damage actually is. For example if you come home one autumn day and you find your pond full of leaves and your fish die due to them rotting, then the requirement on your neighbour will be for them to trim back the tree, bush or trees and bushes that caused the problem in your pond. Generally if you have suffered actual damage you may be able to claim for the damage on your own household insurance or on your neighbours' household insurance. If your neighbour is able to deal with the issue, ask them to do this as soon as possible or better still send them a letter stating the exact nature of the issue as concisely and as clearly as you can. If your neighbour fails to act when requested, or if they do not react in a reasonable timeframe, get your Solicitor to send a letter to them.

Where there has been damaged caused due to your neighbours negligence, it is also best to get the opinion of an expert who can record the damage and make a reasoned assessment, they can also detail the exact cause of any damage and can note any specific information around the damage. Once you have this in your possession, you will be in a better position to take any action necessary for nuisance against your neighbour if you have to. If you do take action leading to a court case, you must be able to show that you had informed your neighbour of the issue in a clear and concise manner, at the earliest opportunity to you and you must prove that they have not done anything about it despite your reasonable requests to resolve the matter.

# Wildlife

## Your Wildlife

This is currently an interesting area of law in the United Kingdom that is awaiting a test case to determine who is responsible in law should any wildlife that lives on your property cause damage to a neighbours' property. The law is not currently clear as to the totality of responsibility so this leaves a gap for interpretation by legal professionals. Where animals are declared to be vermin, animals such as rabbits, squirrels and foxes and where these animals actually live on your property, then you may be held accountable for any damage that they create if you have not taken all reasonable measures to have these animals removed, contained or eradicated. Rabbits are a particular problem, as again if you have not taken reasonable measures to prevent them from moving and entering your neighbours' property by measures such as by putting up a rabbit proof fence, then a Judge may feel that you have not prevented their travel and have done nothing to prevent any increase in population, as a result you could be held liable for any damage these animals and their offspring causes to your neighbours' property. As with anything that is not clear cut and where there is a potential for dispute, then it is best to consult an expert who can advise you on the best course of action to either prevent or contain the problem.. By doing this, should the matter ever come to court, you will be able to show that you have taken measures to prevent the problem and as a consequence, any punitive action by a Judge will be reduced accordingly as you have proof that you tried to do the right thing.

## Your Neighbours Wildlife

If your neighbour has wildlife living on their property that is causing damage to you or your property then they are obliged by law to take reasonable measures to prevent these animals from entering or passing through your property. Before you take any action against your neighbour, you must be one hundred percent sure that the animals coming on to your land are indeed from your neighbour property and that they actually live on his or her land. Wild life travels, and although they may appear to come from your neighbours property, they may only pass through your neighbours' property and they may actually live elsewhere. In this case it would be difficult to show the court that your neighbour has not taken adequate preventative measures with these animals as they may be as much a problem for him or her as they are for you. Again if you have any doubts, consult a wildlife expert who should be able to assist in pointing out where the wildlife may actually live.

## Fumes and Smells

If your neighbour constantly causes a nuisance by dumping strong smelling things like manure close to your property you may be able to call the council and get them to act against them. Again as with noise, smells are very difficult to record and can be treated subjectively by your neighbour and by the council. For example the author had one neighbour who used to regularly place manure on their garden during the spring. Sadly to do this they would bring in several tons of manure and would pile it up for use over a long period of time and because he knew it annoyed the author, this neighbour would place the manure as close to the authors' kitchen on the other side of the border hedge as he could. After doing this several times the author called the council who, although not entirely unsympathetic, did nothing about it as they deemed that the smell was natural and the neighbour had the right to spread manure on his garden. The author was unable to open his kitchen windows at certain times of the year because of the unpleasant smell. If you are going to involve a Solicitor or the council in a matter concerning bad smells, take photos of the items causing the bad smell or if you cannot do this, make sure you keep a diary of when the smells started and how long they lasted as well as their effect on you and your family. Getting an injunction to stop the smell or fumes may be costly and extremely difficult as smells are hard to prove a nuisance. You may just have to live with it until either law changes or until you have enough evidence to persuade the authorities that the smell is a nuisance.

## Trespass

Trespass is a civil offence and not a criminal one. Therefore if someone trespasses onto your land you have to deal with it yourself. The police will not get involved as it is not a criminal matter unless the trespasser has caused actual damage to your property. If you are in the unfortunate position to have people trespassing onto your land or if you have a neighbour who undertakes the act of trespass by occupying or using some part of your land without your permission you cannot forcibly prevent them from doing so. If the people undertaking the trespass have a legitimate right to be there, you cannot claim trespass against them. In order for you to prove trespass you must show that they occupied your land in some way without your permission. The key here is that you must own the land that is being trespassed upon and you must be able to prove that the trespass actually happened. Moreover if you are to take any kind of court action against the trespasser you must also show that they have created some kind of damage to your property and that you as an individual have suffered otherwise you may go through great deal of expense with Solicitors and get nothing from it, as the courts may just order the person or persons trespassing to stop entering your land without permission and make no cost or damage award in your favour. This would mean that you would have to cover all of your own court costs in order to get an unsatisfactory outcome.

If someone does trespass onto your land without your permission, you will need to record evidence of the trespass and the damage their act of trespass has created. If the trespass is as a result of a boundary dispute it will be extremely difficult to prove that trespass has been committed as the land in question is under dispute. If you are one hundred percent clear that the land or property trespassed upon is yours, then you will be able to take civil action against the trespasser although the costs of doing so may be expensive and your return in the form of a remedy or a fine for damages is not likely to be very high even if there has been a lot of damage. In most cases you are only likely to cover your costs if you take any form of action against a trespasser as most cases of trespass only result in minimal damage. There are however alternatives to employing a

Solicitor directly, as there are now many companies that specialise in raising injunctions via the Internet. Although an injunction is a serious thing, a letter from one of these companies threatening action is sometimes enough to modify the behaviour of the person trespassing and to stop them from venturing onto your land without your permission.

# Chapter 5

## When You Have a Dispute

### If You Find Problems

If you find there are issues with your neighbour and you have tried everything in your power to avoid a dispute, the first things you need to do is stop and assess the exact nature of the problem that exists between you. The thing that you must not do until you have taken advice is to write to your neighbour detailing your complaint or the problem between you. If you do this without taking advice you can weaken your case as you are acknowledging the fact that there is an issue with your neighbour, and if he or she is legally represented, his or her legal team will use your letters against you if he dispute gets worse. The other point to take into account here is that if you write the first letter detailing a dispute, your neighbour may be able to claim that you started the dispute by using the letter as evidence against you. This is an especially important point to note if your neighbour is claiming adverse possession, squatter's rights or is claiming that you gave him or her right of way or an easement allowing the use of part of your property. An example of this is if you have a land dispute with your neighbour and he or she has actually moved onto the land in dispute, or if your neighbour puts up a fence on your land. Another example is if you ask him or her to leave your land or to cease activities on it, then this is actually acknowledging he or she is in occupation of the land in question, or he is using it and you definitely do not want to state this in a letter without taking expert advice as this could be the heart of your neighbours legal argument for taking possession and it will be picked up by any smart Solicitor or Barrister. Sometimes it is better to threaten legal proceedings against a person and to obtain an injunction via a Solicitor than to do it yourself. If you do go down this path however you have to have good grounds and a strong case against your neighbour. Only a legal expert can tell you this and if you have written to your neighbour acknowledging a problem, then this could count against you should you have to fight it out in court.

When your neighbour problem first occurs, write down a description of the exact nature of the problem on a piece of paper. Do not get tied up in the meaningless and the trivial or in emotions. Get straight to the heart of the matter that is bothering you and look good and hard at what the problem is and what is actually causing the dispute between you. The issue may be down to a boundary dispute or the fact that you have had an argument with your neighbour or you may have been insulted or assaulted and this can cloud the issue between you. If you do not deal with the issue correctly and without emotion, then there will be continued bad feeling between you and your neighbour and further opportunities for arguments and trouble will still be present. Importantly if you do not address the issue directly and quickly, you could find that your neighbour makes a case for litigation against you and it will be you that ends up paying for the problem they caused. You must always bear in mind that the law is not fair and impartial and in any form of dispute there is always ultimately a loser and a winner. Although both parties end up paying a high price, either in money, stress or time, right and wrong do not matter in the eyes of the law, Try and make sure that you come out of any dispute with as little damage to you and your family as possible. The only way to do this is to look good and hard at the problem and the causes of it. Do not get emotional and always try and put yourself in your neighbours' shoes. Ask yourself what is it that your neighbour actually wants?

# How to Deal With the Issues and the Other Side

## Correspondence

Your first indicationthat there is a problem between you and your neighbour could be in the form of a letter you receive out of the blue or some other form of attempt by your neighbour to force you to agree a position and deal with them without taking expert advice by putting you under some form of pressure. Time is a weapon in this case and usually they will put a time limit on a proposal or on the time you need to take to respond to their letter or attempt to force a position on you. To communicate with them in any great length is a mistake and do not be fooled by time pressure. In trying to be reasonable and by not taking the correct advice before corresponding you can compromise some or even most of your case if it deteriorates further and goes to court. Your first step to take before entering into any kind of letter exchange with your neighbour or his or her representative should be to assess the problem at hand. Do not start a dialogue with the other side until you have an assessment and a second opinion. Even if you believe in being reasonable and you feel that you have to respond out of correctness or politeness, this will not work. You must think that you are dealing with the unreasonable when you are in dispute and when it comes to trial all of your correspondence will be taken into consideration by the other side and by the Judge. The fact that the correspondence sought an end to the dispute could be seen as immaterial, because by making counter offers or recognising the other sides' position you can weaken your case. This is especially so if they make an offer that you refuse and they ultimately win their case. They could claim that you were unreasonable and that the dispute could have been avoided if you had accepted their offer. This has a major bearing on costs as they will claim that you started the dispute and caused the legal expense as a result

The problem with not starting a dialogue with your neighbour, or in not acknowledging the other side however is that this can also go against you in court. If you receive any correspondence from your neighbour or their legal representative, just send a letter back to them acknowledging receipt along the lines of the following.

---

*Dear Mr / Mrs*

*Thank you for your letter dated 12<sup>th</sup> May 2008.I am currently taking advice and will respond to you at a later date.*

*Yours faithfully,*

---

Do not allow yourself be bullied into responding by the other side. As an example the author assisted in the resolution of a dispute that had come to trial, where the authors' client had a neighbour who had employed a typical smart ass Solicitor to represent him. This Solicitor was like most of the bad Solicitors who give the law a bad name as this person was not interested in the law; this individual was just about making money and was only concerned with winning his case, no matter how they did it. From day one this Solicitor used every trick in the book to try and extract information from the authors' client, to get them to commit to a compromised legal position or to get them angry so that they would react and then the Solicitor could take advantage of this. Do not ever react to a proposition without considering it and without taking advice. By reacting, particularly if you feel strongly about the proposal, you are giving the other side ammunition to further their case. This is exactly what the other side wants and before taking the authors' advice his client fell for this Solicitors aggressive letters and his threatening tone. By reacting you are taking a position and by taking a position the other side can prepare a defence against your position or can develop a case that can destroy yours. The most important point to remember in a legal dispute is that the person who issues an action first has the upper hand in the dispute as the defending party will need to respond to whatever case has been outlined by the other party. By being forced to respond, you are usually on the back foot as Solicitors and Barristers prepare and try cases for a living, they know the best approaches to case preparation and so can mask or hide the real issues that need to be addressed or dealt with in any correspondence. If they are forceful, they can get you to reveal a lot and subsequently they will use it against you. Even if their tone is not threatening or aggressive you must not react without taking advice as the same thing will apply.

After many letters and a lot of frustration the authors' client decided they would not correspond with the other side at all. They were plain fed up of their threats, the attitude of the neighbours Solicitor and the way the neighbours' legal team behaved. When it came to the court trial as the aggression and correspondence led to a court case, the other side had sent letters demanding actions and issued many fait a' complete. As these were clearly aggressive letters stating that if you do not do this, we will do that, the author assessed what it was they were really proposing and considered their actions were just about acceptable so long as they complied with the courts directions when it came to the preparation of legal papers. The neighbours' legal team did not comply with court directions and tried to introduce new information into the trial without the approval of the Judge and without the approval of the authors' clients. They claimed that as the authors' client had not acknowledged every one of their letters, and as a result they claimed the authors' clients were being unreasonable by not doing so. During their correspondence, in a single paragraph missed by the authors' client, the other side had asked if they agreed with the trial bundles list. In this list they had inserted documents that had not been seen or known about by the authors' clients. The fact that the neighbours legal team were being unreasonable by doing this did not matter to the Judge as he stated that by not writing a letter objecting to the papers, the authors' clients were tacitly agreeing to the list from the outset. The author recommended that his clients went to a Solicitor or a Barrister to help with their case. They refused at first and when they were finally pushed, and when they did engage with a Solicitor, the opposition were placed into an untenable position and their case did not succeed in court as the Solicitor ripped them apart by using their aggressive correspondence against them. The key points here are that correspondence is a very powerful weapon in the hands of people who know what they are doing and who know how to use it. Conversely if you are in a bad position, it can be used as a powerful weapon against you.

# Actions to Take

## Letters or Threats

If you receive letters or threats from your neighbour or their legal team, consider the content of their letters or the threats very carefully. Respond back that you have received their letter or that you have been threatened and that you are considering the contents of their letters or the form of their threat and that you will get back to them after taking the appropriate legal advice. If your neighbours are chancing their luck, this may stop them if you state that you are taking legal advice and they see that you are taking the matter very seriously. It may not stop them however and so you must be prepared for this.

## Legal Advice –Solicitors

You must try and take some form of legal advice as soon as you can. If you can employ a Solicitor then this is the best bet. They can respond to the letter or threat and deal with the issue either by countering or threatening a counter action or an injunction. This might stop your neighbour. Always take the best advice that you can afford and when looking for a Solicitor, make sure they are specialists in the area that you need them to work. Taking the example regarding the court case and the aggressive correspondence, the authors' client eventually employed a specialist in land law and the neighbour who had started the case was using a Solicitor who had a general practice and so was not specialised in land law. The result was that the specialist destroyed the generalist and the case was won by the authors' clients

## Local Council

Other areas to approach for support are the local borough council who may have an anti-social behaviour unit. Depending on the issue, they could be of major assistance to you. Council resources are usually limited however and so they may either be slow to react to you requests or they will want a good degree of evidence from you describing in great detail what the problem is, how long it has been a problem and what you have done to try and resolve it before they take action. The local borough council can advise you even if they cannot take action themselves and they have many different leaflets and forms that are good guides to assist you in dealing with the majority of problems you may have. Because most councils have encountered these issues before they can particularly useful in advising you on evidence gathering so that you can be prepared should the matter make its way to the courts..

## Police

You can go to the police if there are threats made against you or your property. The police however are generally reluctant to get involved as most neighbour disputes are seen to be civil not criminal matters. Moreover even where it could be deemed to be a criminal matter, a recent survey has shown that the police do not view neighbour disputes or anti-social behaviour as major criminal issues and so rarely deal with them in a matter that is satisfactory to the wider public. As a result of this the usual response from the police is to recommend that you talk to a Solicitor as they believe at they are best placed to deal with any matter with neighbours. If the police can however be bothered to deal with the matter that is causing you concern as they deem it worthy of their attention, the fact that they are involved and that they go and speak to your neighbour is sometimes enough to stop your neighbour undertaking certain actions and threats against you. For example in a case known to the author a neighbour made allegations against another neighbour with regard to the use of a firearm. The author suggested to the accused neighbour that this be reported to the police as the misuse of firearms are serious matters and it was further suggested that a demand for an investigation be made by the police. As soon as this happened, the police spoke to the neighbour making the claim and reminded him that it was an offence to harass people and make false allegations. They also asked why the matter had not been reported to them instantly if it was so serious and why a letter had gone to a neighbour making an allegation without their involvement. Naturally the accuser had no excuse as the events did not happen. The allegations then ceased and this neighbour did not cause any further issues after that.

## Mediators

If you are genuinely in a dispute with a neighbour there are strong chances that it could escalate into a major problem and as a result, it will be costly to you in many respects. In order to try and avoid these high costs and to resolve matters quickly it is best to try and mediate with the other side before any action is taken further especially if there is an attempt to take the matter to court.

After assessing the problem it is best to employ an expert in the problem area. If it is a boundary dispute, use a good chartered surveyor. If it is another form of dispute use another form of expert, for example if it is trees, use a qualified tree surgeon. If your dispute is due to noise, use the council or a noise expert. If you go to a Solicitor they will generally recommend an expert. If the Solicitor cannot, the author has appended some details of the Royal Institute of Chartered Surveyors who can recommend some good surveyors in the appendix at the back of this document as well as giving links to other forms of expert. Generally a Solicitor is used for legal advice and an expert such as a surveyor is used for gathering, interpreting and presenting the factual and technical information around your land, or technical problem and can give a lot of detail as to the nature of a problem and can propose a technical solution or gather technical evidence to support your case.

## Chartered Surveyors

Chartered surveyors have a wealth of knowledge about land, land surveys and boundary issues. By employing a chartered surveyor as soon as you can you will be able to determine the validity of any claim that your neighbour may have very quickly in any land matter.

When you instruct your surveyor you will need to provide him or her with as much information as you can about your property, the dispute and your neighbours land. The first information to give them will be your land registry filed copy plan and your property reference number. If you can give them your neighbours' property reference number then that will speed up the survey process. These two pieces of information will allow a good surveyor to gather a mass of information and they can quickly address any issues when armed with both copy plans.

In the UK surveyors are regulated by the Royal Institute of Chartered Surveyors and as Chartered Surveyors, they are recognised professionals who have to undertake a recognised training course to meet the institutes standards. They are therefore suitably qualified and certified by the institute as professionals. For the purposes of boundaries and mapping if they are recognised expert witnesses and have completed this course, they can be used as experts for the determination of land and as expert witnesses they can prepare papers that are admissible as evidence in court and can give oral evidence in court hearings. The surveyors listing in the Chartered Institutes web site will give you details of their exact qualifications and whether they are expert witnesses or not.

Good surveyors usually have many years of experience of neighbour disputes as it is probably their biggest source of income. They will have good sources of information pertaining to boundaries, mapping, features and disputes that you will not have access to. They are an excellent source of additional information and should you get into a dispute about boundaries, after first employing a Solicitor, you must employ a surveyor. Many Solicitors will know the intricate details of the law of the land and even though surveyors are supposed to be independent, Solicitors will normally instruct the surveyor on your behalf as you have to consider the case if it goes to court. If you are the initiator of a boundary dispute case or the respondent in one, this has an advantage in so far as the surveyor and the Solicitor will be able to prepare a case for winning based upon their instructions. Even though surveyors are not supposed to cooperate with a legal team, as their cooperation will turn a case from a technical argument to a legal one, many surveyors do cooperate and this makes a case difficult to defend if you do not employ your own surveyor. If you can afford the combined Solicitor surveyor team, then this is good news for you. If you cannot afford it and you have to represent yourself and your neighbour can, then this is very bad news for you.

## Move or Stay Put: Disclosure of a Neighbour Problem

When a neighbour dispute starts your best hope is that it will go away as quickly as possible. If it does not go away you will see your quality of life slowly deteriorate, and you will be strongly affected by the dispute in many ways you had ever imagined. Whatever happens however you cannot ignore the problem and you have to take some form of action so as to prevent it going into a downward spiral of ever more problems and increasing costs. If you are like most of the UK population you will likely be in a position where you may be able to afford some legal advice, but may not be able to pay for a full court case or because of your own personal circumstances, may not be happy to pursue any action in court because of the antagonism your neighbour may give you and the effect it may have on your family. This leaves a major problem. You either have to live with your neighbour or you have to move home. Both of these are major considerations as the first issue means that you may have to experience continual problems with your neighbour and the second issue may mean that the home that you have lived in, have raised your family in and set your dreams upon may be lost and you may have to look for a new home. If you want to move quickly, this could mean that you have to sell for a low price for a fast sale. This will further compound and aggravate any sense of injustice you may have especially if the neighbour dispute is no down to you.

The Law in the UK now requires that when you sell your home you must disclose all relevant information to any prospective buyer in a Sellers Property Information Form (SPIF).There is a section within this form that asks questions regarding your neighbours and specifically asks you if you have had any disputes or disagreements. If you fail to complete this form correctly, or if you omit information from the form, or if you give misleading information you may find yourself liable to be sued by the new buyer if you sell your home and your new buyer has issues with your neighbour. The new buyer must be able to prove that there was a history before he bought your home if a court case happens as a result of a dispute after they moved into your previous home and if you have had issues with your neighbour in the past, there is likely to be a record of this somewhere. This is a major problem to many people. Another important element to understand with regard to neighbour disputes is that legally you must declare them to any buyer and any agent selling your property and by doing so; it will have an effect on the sales price of your property. After all who wants to live next door to a bully, or a problem neighbour? If you firmly believe that you will not be able to get along with your neighbour in future, before an issue escalates into a full blown dispute, take serious consideration to moving as quickly as you can. Although it may be traumatic to you in the short term, it may be better in the long run and it will save you money in legal fees and in the devaluation of your home as well as many years of pain and hassle with your neighbour

# Instructing a Solicitor to Deal with Nuisance

If you instruct a Solicitor to deal with a nuisance, then you will need to show or demonstrate the following items as a minimum for them to take any form of action against your neighbour.

You must show that the nuisance your neighbour is causing is a permanent occurrence or that it happens to you or your family frequently.

You must be able to show that your neighbours' actions were deliberate and not accidental.

You must be able to demonstrate whether there has been actual damage to your property or whether there is a case that your enjoyment of life has been affected by your neighbours' actions or behaviour towards you or your family or your property.

You must be able to show consideration in your neighbours defence. Is the nuisance a key part of his or her livelihood? For example is your neighbour a farmer and therefore has a genuine reason for waking you at 4am in the morning by revving his or her tractor?

You must be able to show evidence as to the nuisance your neighbour has or is causing and must be able to demonstrate the frequency, severity and the affects the nuisance has had on you or your family.

Solicitors will use the above as a basic baseline for any decisions they make and should be able to advise you on the best course of action to take when they are armed with this information. Even if you have the above information and have provided it to a Solicitor, there is still no guarantee of success in either stopping the dispute or in preventing it from going any further or into court. A Solicitor can advise you on how to reduce the problem and if your defence is a good one, can help in a legal remedy. You must always remember that a Solicitor is a legal expert and so will always take that stance. Sometimes common sense and rationality are not brought into the mix so always consider the advice they give in the legal context and not in a pragmatic one. Before acting upon any advice, always take the time to evaluate it and always ask of the consequences' of taking the advice that is given to you.

## Insurance: What is Covered and What is Not!

Most people believe that their home insurance covers almost every kind of problem a home owner could have or could ever face. Sadly this is not the case with most types of home insurance and the insurance companies know this but do not tell you. Sadly the insurers are commercial entities and they try to resist against every type of claim that they can as it costs them money. An example of this is where a policy holder made an insurance claim which was with the UK's biggest insurer. The house holder believed that the policy they had gave them insurance against trespass. The specific terms of their insurance even stated that they were covered for this very thing.

The policy holder requested that her insurers cover her under trespass and fund her to take action against the wrong doer in the County Court. The insurer sent her request to their Solicitors who determined that there was a case that the insurance company could cover if she could prove trespass had occurred. The insurers Solicitors then sent the case on to a Barrister who determined that there was a boundary dispute, therefore the determination of the boundary to the property was not possible as the policy holder claimed it was at point A. The neighbour determined it was at point B because each neighbour disagreed on the boundary point, the insurer stated that it would not be possible to fund a trespass case without a specific determination of the boundary. The insurer said that they would not fund a boundary determination as they stated it would be a precedent if they were to fund the case and flatly refused to take it any further. After the policy holder got the answer back from her insurer she requested her files back from the Solicitor appointed by the insurer to determine the case. Within the correspondence between the insurer and Solicitor the author foundthat the Solicitor was trying to limit the insurer's costs and liabilities. Both the insurers Solicitor and the insurer were clearly not acting in the policy holder's best interests as they were approaching the case from a money saving perspective. Insurance companies are commercial organisations with a responsibility to their shareholders. As a result, any payment that they may make affects their bottom line profitability and in turn it affects their shareholders profits. Resultantly there are very few insurance companies that will fund a trespass or boundary dispute. Where they do, there must be a better than 50/50 chance of winning the case and before they take a case forward, they will send it to their own people for an assessment. You can choose who the document goes to, however again as the insurance company has a vested interest in the outcome, the Solicitor or Barrister that you choose has to be agreed and recognised by the insurance company. Before you purchase your insurance make sure that it covers all adjudication, trespass and civil action and that you are able to choose your own legal team.

This lack of insurance cover is going to be an increasing issue for many people in the future as the UK government are committed to moving from the courts service to Adjudication Tribunals where it is cheaper for the government and simpler to resolve matters as there is a single Judge sitting with each case. As seen with the situation above, this drive by the government to lower costs has seriously compromised the chances of getting justice in the UK. The government will not give any form of legal aid for civil action and so if both the government and the insurers will not cover a dispute, the only sources of funding left are the people who have the dispute. This puts tremendous financial pressure on the people who get into disputes with their neighbours, particularly if they are the victims of an unwarranted and aggressive case.

# Costs

## Chartered Surveyor Costs

Surveyor's costs vary depending on what it is that you are asking of them and depending on the skill and reputation of the surveyor. If you require a survey, then this can cost from five hundred to one thousand seven hundred and fifty pounds depending on the complexity of what you are asking the surveyor to do or to prepare. If surveyors have to search records, travel to the land registry, order archive information or find aerial photographs, then they will incur additional expenses that will be added to your bill. The costs of each of these items can vary from tens of pounds to hundreds of pounds. When employing a surveyor, allocate budget costs of around two thousand to two thousand five hundred pounds if your dispute goes to court or Adjudication. If you are instructing jointly with your neighbour, make sure that you get a good quote up front to cover all works and budget around a thousand pounds for the costs.

## Solicitors and Barristers Costs

As soon as a dispute emerges between you and your neighbour there could be a need to contact a Solicitor for advice. The first requirement is for the Solicitor to assess the situation between you and your neighbour and to either start a correspondence with the other party or to make an assessment from a case perspective with a view to court action. Solicitor's charges vary depending on the skills of the Solicitor and level of the individual representing you. These charges start at around one hundred and sixty pounds per hour for a junior / trainee Solicitor to five to six hundred pounds per hour for a partner. Most Solicitors book their time in billing blocks of six minutes. If they charge one hundred and ninety pounds per hour, then this equates to nineteen pounds for every six minutes of their time. Be aware, that the bills soon increase as you ask them questions and their opinions. Very soon you could be into a potentially massive bill if you employ your own Solicitor to fight your cause as they charge for everything they can generally. Again Solicitors are commercial people and so exist to make money. Everything they touch has a value and even if they just answer the telephone to take your call, they will generally charge the call back to you. If your case goes to court and you lose your fight with your neighbour you will have to pay for your opponent's Solicitor as well. Make sure you consider this when budgeting for your costs.

For a Solicitor to undertake an initial investigation to determine if you have a case, you are looking at costs of between five hundred pounds for advice and letters and at around three thousand five hundred pounds for a mid-range case assessment with a relatively experienced Solicitor within a good practice. For a really good Solicitor you will have to pay more and wait in line for your review. Once a Solicitor has determined that there is a case to be fought, they will want to send the case and its associated files for an assessment with a Barrister and this will involve further costs as the Solicitor will charge to prepare the brief and papers to give to the Barrister and the Barrister will charge for their time and written opinion based upon this brief.

A Barrister is generally instructed by a Solicitor and although there is a direct access scheme in the UK where you can contact a Barrister directly, the authors experience has shown that this does not work very well with most Barristers. This is because the Solicitors undertake a lot of activities that Barristers just do not want to deal with or alternatively are not licensed to deal with. These activities include writing letters to the other parties and preparing court papers. If you go to a Barrister under the direct access scheme, then the costs associated with the engagement of a Barrister are similar to those of a Solicitor and are looking to pay in the region of around three to five hundred pounds per hour and you will have to pay the Barristers directly for each piece of work. They will invoice for each element and generally ask for their fees in advance as they are not allowed to hold any money on account. If you go through a Solicitor to access a Barrister, you pay an additional overhead to the Solicitorfor instructing the Barrister and you can typically see an additional bill of around one thousand pounds from your Solicitor for instructing a Barrister. Barrister fees for a case assessment come in at around two thousand to three thousand pounds depending on the time and complexity of the review or of the case.

## Land Registry Process Costs

You may end up paying title plan order fees if you want to see the title plan of your neighbours' property. Also there may be some printing cost if you wish Land Registry to provide you with the copies of your files or the files of your neighbour. Again if you wish the Land Registry to conduct a land survey or boundary survey this may cost you anything upwards from seven hundred pounds for them to conduct the survey. If the land registry have made mistakes in their records, you may be able to get them to cover the costs of your searches and surveys. They will have to agree to this and you generally have to apply to them in writing for them to do this. You must also bear in mind that the land registry will do everything in their power to save money and will not necessarily agree to your requests even if they have made some mistakes. Where they have made mistakes, they will generally try to limit their financial exposure and will actively seek to reduce their costs wherever they can.

## Adjudication and Court Process Costs

The adjudication process is just about as costly as a court case to the people using the service and as such can be very expensive. The costs of a hearing, trial and the associated preparation are exactly the same as for a court as they are prepared by Solicitors and Barristers in the same way. The adjudication process is relatively new in the UK and as such there are many opportunities for Solicitors to make mistakes and a lot of room for them to manoeuvre as the Tribunal processes are not clearly defined or mature. Because the processes are currently ill defined and due to the limited exposure Solicitors and Barristers have had to the Tribunal service, it can lead to a lot of expense for you as there is very often a need for the Solicitor or Barrister to seek clarification from the Tribunal Service. If the court, Solicitor or Barrister have made mistakes, you end up paying for them. There is no court cost associated with the Adjudication process; so you do not yet have to pay a fee for filing or lodging documents with the tribunal, however you still have to pay for your own legal defenceor advice and normally this is a very hefty fee.

Even if you decide to defend yourself in the adjudication, your minimum bill could be in the region of ten to twelve thousand pounds as you will need to prepare papers, get some form of legal opinion and to lodge your papers and defence. This figure mentioned is only the cost for preparing the case for a hearing. If you lose the case your costs may be doubled or tripled if your neighbour has used his or her own legal team to prepare their case as you may have to pay for them as well. If you go to appeal, then this can cost you even more money. The court is supposed to take into account a persons' ability to pay costs but in most cases does not. Invariably the Judge sitting has a simplistic view in so far as that as you are in a dispute and if you defend yourself against your neighbour, you are making a choice and so must be prepared to pay the costs and consequences of your actions to the greater or lesser extent depending on how much they feel you to be at fault. Most Judges however have never been in a neighbour dispute and have never had to defend themselves from unwarranted aggression. Therefore their view is highly simplistic and until most Judges take the opportunity to visit the real world, they will still perpetuate this opinion and justice will not be served.

# Dealing with Incidents

## Assault

Assaults are the worst kind of incident that can happen to you in any dispute and the perpetrators of the assault may try and justify the many reasons for them commit an assault against you. The authors believe that these people are the lowest forms of life on the planet and no matter how they feel, they should not commit assault under any circumstances. The sad fact however is that assaults between neighbours are very common and as a result, you have to know how to deal with them should they happen to you if you are having any form of dispute with your neighbour.

At the time of an assault all of your emotions will be on overdrive, you will be very angry, shocked, upset and your world will have been turned upside down. In many cases there is no rational reason for the assault to have taken place. During and after an assault it is hard not to be emotional. The first thing to do before you do anything else assuming you do not need immediate medical treatment is to stop and think. Even if you are not the aggressor, re-evaluate everything that has happened to you. Write down all of the events, including all of the ones running up to the assault and examine them carefully.

If you are assaulted, call the police as soon as possible. Tell them what happened to you and tell them the time and place where the assault happened. Record the names and numbers of the police who attend the scene. Ask them for the crime reference. If there are any marks on you, or cuts or bruises photograph them before they go away. To take things forward the police will need evidence that you have actually been assaulted and if you have no cuts, bruises or red marks, they will automatically dismiss the assault. Make an appointment to see a doctor or go to casualty to have the marks recorded if you can. Do not fail to do this as it will prove a trail of evidence if you need it. This information is critical if you need to get an injunction against your neighbour for any future misdemeanour so it must be recorded.

The law regarding self-defence is interesting and worth knowing. In one case the author discussed with the police at a seminar, the discussion focussed on an assault where one neighbour who knew the law precisely stated that she acted in self-defence in an assault case against her neighbour and that due to her being assaulted first she was in fear of her life so thereby was defending herself by hitting and kicking her neighbour first. She lied about this to the interviewing police officers and the police knew this but it was a perfect legal defence and so they were powerless to intervene or do anything about it. You can attack someone first if you feel that they are going to attack you and that you are in fear of them assaulting you or you are in fear of your life. If you just claim self-defence, and if there are no witnesses the police will be unlikely to take any further action as they will have your word against your neighbours only and as there are no witnesses, it will not go anywhere. The author's suggestion is that you learn self-defence when you have a neighbour dispute and should you ever be in the unfortunate position where your neighbour attempts to attack you, consider the law and the defence given above as well as your self-defence training. If you are arrested as a result of defending yourself, the policeman who discussed this case with the author suggested that you do whatever the police ask of you and that you do not talk to them until you have spoken to a Solicitor. They recommend politely telling them that you wish to speak to a Solicitor before speaking to them. Legally you have a right to speak to a Solicitor and the police cannot question you until you have done so. When speaking to the Solicitor remind them that you are not the aggressor and that you were acting in self-defence and were in fear of your life or of being hurt. The Solicitor can then advise you from there and it is highly unlikely the police will pursue the matter.

## General incidents

If you are not assaulted by your neighbour, it is highly probable that your neighbour will try and do everything they can to disrupt, discredit or generally annoy you during the dispute. Where any incident between you and your neighbour takes place, make sure you photograph or record what is going on. If you have a Dictaphone, use it to record any conversation between you and your neighbour, be sure to capture the details of any threat or incident you encounter with your neighbour. As an example of this, in the case of one neighbour dispute made known to the author, a neighbour used his gardener to threaten and intimidate his immediate neighbours'.The author advised the people that were being intimidated to photograph the gardener and make a recording made of what he said and when he said it. This neighbours' girlfriend also made threats to the immediate neighbours and the author advised that they should also photograph her. Although most normal people would not dream of threatening or intimidating another person, it is sad to say that you must prepare for the worst and always carry a camera with you in your garden. If you do you can take pictures of any incidents, should it come to a court case you can show the evidence to the court and prove your point. If you do not take pictures or record the events, the other side will try and discredit you when you raise these incidents and you will be at the disadvantage as you will have no evidence to prove or disprove the claim. If you are in a very hostile dispute, always try and ensure that you do not do or say anything without witnesses. Sadly sometimes accusations will be made against you by your neighbours that are not true and if you do not have witnesses to the events, they will be difficult to prove as unfounded in a court.

# Chapter 6

## When it All Goes Wrong and the Dispute Heads for Court!

If you have tried to be reasonable and deal with your neighbour sensibly to try and stop or resolve a dispute and it has failed, then there are only a few options open for you to take to solve your problems permanently. Even though you may be angry, upset and may fantasise about taking a more direct action with your neighbour that could involve dark alleys and heavy blunt implements, this is not practical and you have to stop and think before the dispute gets any further out of control. In terms of the options available to you, you must have a clear head and if it does go wrong you must consider how to minimise any damage, disruption or costs involved or associated with your dispute. If you take the wrong course of action with your neighbour or if you dig your heels in to prove a point, and do not see reason then a dispute could cost you a fortune if it escalates to the court or to adjudication. You must also consider this. Even if you are right and your case is unfair and your neighbour is the aggressor in the dispute, when it comes to a battle there are no rules and people will be unreasonable and stubborn just to prove a point. If your neighbour is an unscrupulous individual or if he or she has more money than you have, he or she will always have the upper hand in any dispute. If they can afford good Solicitors or Barristers, they can and will get away with things that are clearly wrong and unjust. Sadly the law in the UK is a joke and most of the Judges that decide the interpretation of the law are incompetent, useless, powerless or opinionated. Of the Judges that the author has observed in courts and at tribunals, only two were reasonable people who had any kind of understanding of the issues that people face when forced into an aggressive defence by an unscrupulous neighbour. If you are not forced into a legal defence and decide that you wish to take action against your neighbour because a problem needs resolving, you will also be disadvantaged. You must also consider that the time and energy you spend on the formulation or on the defence of a legal issue or on a neighbour dispute will never be recovered. Even if you win your case, you will not recover the time or the energy that has been wasted. There is no compensation for sleepless nights, for the arguments and tears between you and your partner or your children. Nothing will ever be worth the pain and anguish that you will go through. The worst part of any dispute is that no one will understand you or your position and no one will want to talk to you about it as they will not know how to deal with you or how to talk about your issues. Throughout the whole legal process you will be on your own and will get no support from anyone apart from your immediate family. Even if you can afford a Solicitor to defend you their costs are prohibitive and you will end up paying a lot of money for a result that in most cases is less than satisfactory. If the dispute does go to a trial, you will either be a winner or a looser and it is highly unlikely that you will get an apology from anyone. The problem with justice in the UK is that most people cannot afford the fees to pay for a Solicitor or a Barrister as there is no legal aid available and so they end up borrowing money to pay for their defence or to win their case to resolve their problem. During the dispute all of your dreams and ambitions will go on hold and you will be subsumed into the dispute as you will be unable to talk or think about anything else.

## Immediate Actions to Take

You must try and detach yourself from the disputeas it starts to escalate into a full blown legal conflict. If an escalation does occur, you must be rational and need to record the details as it will be vital information should you need to go to mediation, court or to tribunal. Get a piece of paper and write down exactly what you feel the issue to be between you and your neighbour. Ask the following questions to help you clarify your situation.

1.  What is the dispute?
    Is it a boundary dispute, nuisance, or is it something else? if so what type of dispute is it?

2.  What is your neighbour claiming in the dispute?
    Is your neighbour being reasonable in their claim, or is their claim wild and outrageous? Is their claim genuine or is it a lie?

3.   How did the dispute start between you?
Did you start it? Did they start it? Exactly how did it start? Try to remember the conversations and events that lead to the dispute? Did you say something to upset them, or did they say something to upset you?

4.   When did the dispute start?
Is this dispute a bolt out of the blue or has it been something that has been bubbling away in the background? Have the seeds for dispute been there all along without you recognising it?

5.   Ask yourself did I do anything wrong?
There are very few innocent victims in a dispute, even though you may think you are; the chances are that you have added to the dispute in some way, shape or form. Something you may have said, something you may have disagreed with. You may have taken some form of action to annoy your neighbour and add to the dispute. Even if you are not the cause of the dispute, your neighbour will see things differently. Ask yourself the cold hard question, did I do something wrong? Try and place yourself into your neighbours' shoes and ask the same questions again of yourself as if you were your neighbour. Then ask what your neighbour has done.

6.   Ask am I being objective in my understanding and dealings with the dispute?
In many cases disputes escalate due to people's unreasonable beliefs or ideals. Everyone has a set of principles and sacred cows, so when the right buttons are pressed, they will dig their heels in and will not move from these principles or ideals. Is this right? Are your values different to your neighbour? Are they based upon belief rather than fact? If so, then try and rationalise how your neighbour thinks. Put yourself into their position and then question your own principles.

7.   Ask yourself; Is the dispute really important to me?
Although you may think so at a given moment in time, a dispute may be the result of something that is not really important to you. When disputes escalate into legal cases

and you end up spending a fortune and a massive amount of time, where you end up without sleep, end up arguing and spending your time deep in dispute with nothing else to talk about, ask the question again and again. Is this dispute really important to me? If it is not important to you seek to end it as soon as you can, with minimal damage to you and with minimal costs. The thing to bear in mind is that even the seemingly important issues can become unimportant when you take the time to look at the wider picture. The wider picture is simple to understand "Ask yourself do you want to lose everything you own over the dispute?" "Do you want to be in debt for years to come over the dispute?" If the answer is no to either of these questions then remember that there will never be a winner in a neighbour dispute case. There will be a looser with a massive bill to pay and another looser that has just recovered seventy five to eighty percent of their legal costs and none of their time spent dealing with the matter.

8.   Ask can I settle this dispute now? If the answer is yes, do not wait for the opportunity. Act immediately and engage with someone who can assist, be they a mediator, Solicitor or a Barrister.

## Opposing Solicitors / Solicitors Representing Your Neighbour

If things do go wrong between you and your neighbour, then you can be sure that you will receive a letter from a Solicitor at some stage representing the other sides' case. When you receive this letter from a Solicitor, he or she will normally be making an accusation of some kind against you or will be mentioning some form of behaviour that they want you to stop. The will also likely want some kind of remedy, be it a financial remedy or a promise to do or stop something.

When you receive a letter from the oppositions' Solicitor, they will want you to answer them immediately and will try and put you under time pressure to get a response as soon as they can. Solicitors are employed to win a case and some Solicitors are more than willing to use their own forms of intimidation, veiled threats. Solicitors are employed to win and false accusationsto win their case for their client. Some Solicitors are not interested in what is wrong or what is right with a case or claim, they are interested in winning. The problem with the approach of these Solicitors is that they will deliberately make you angry, they will try and bully you by making statements about things you have not done or will try and threaten you by stating that they will prevent you from winning or from undertaking any of your rights. Although the author acknowledges there are good Solicitors out there that are not bullies and have real moral values, the author has come across a number of bad Solicitors as well. Until you face them, you will not know their agenda so be aware at all times.

### They Are in the Same Club!

Your Solicitor is regulated by the same organisation as your opposing Solicitor, the person or firm that is representing your client. The chances are that your Solicitor will know your opposing Solicitor to the greater or lesser extent particularly if they practice in the same town or geographical area. Not surprisingly, the world of law is a very small place and as a result, the majority of Solicitors tend not to take on things that will either disagree with their career or their ambitions. Although they may be willing to take a case, they will not do anything that they feel will jeopardise their position now and in the future with their betters or peers. The net effect of this is that although your opposition may be unscrupulous and aggressive bullies, your Solicitor is unlikely to do too much about this apart from send a polite letter asking them to be reasonable. As the paying party to a Solicitor this can be incredibly frustrating to you as the tone of the letter they send, instead of dealing with the matter directly, is likely to ignore or water down the issue causing you concern. On the other hand, if Solicitors' are dealing with the opposition and the opposition is unrepresented, then most Solicitors will not hesitate to send nasty letters worded in such a way so that they annoy you, but you cannot do anything about them. The last thing in the world you want is to get angry and respond in such a way as to jeopardise your case. Barristers are exactly the same as Solicitors; however they will do the above in court and not via any written correspondence.

# Pre-Action Protocols

Lord Woolf wrote a series of recommendations for the reform of the English legal system. He rightly recognised that there were fundamental issues with the legal system and that the law was weighted in favour of those with money and influence. He made a series of recommendations for the reform of the system. Some of these recommendations were adopted by the government and as a result the way some Judges think has been changed by this new legislation. The biggest change to court thinking is that legal action should be the last course of action to take and that before you undertake any form of litigation, you should have exhausted all other options for the resolution of the dispute. If you have not done so, whereas in the past the situation was that the losing party in litigation paid all the costs, today's thinking is that if you win and have not undertaken the correct pre-action protocol or undertaken any form of mediation or any Alternative Dispute Resolution then the chances are that you will not recover all or most of your costs when costs are awarded. If you find yourself in any dispute with a neighbour, seek mediation first before you undertake any kind of litigation. If you find that you are forced down the path of litigation then you must ensure that you follow all pre-action protocols as otherwise it would be detrimental to you when it comes to the court as they now require that you exhaust all options before litigating. First and foremost you must show that you have tried to settle the dispute before the litigation. There must be an audit trail to show that you have made a series of reasonable offers to try and resolve the dispute. You must also demonstrate that you have sought to avoid any increased costs and that you have clearly warned your neighbour of the consequences of their actions and the costs of litigation as well as the potential outcomes. When you have exhausted all options, only then should you consider litigation. The other important point to bear in mind is that your Solicitor must also behave in a way that demonstrates to the court that he or she was seeking to avoid any extra costs and that they also gave the opportunity to the other party to settle the dispute before and during any litigation. Before any court action or before any papers are served, you must ensure that your Solicitor sends a letter before action and that they advise your neighbour to seek legal advice. It is worth noting that as your Solicitor acts for you, if they misbehave or are seen to be aggressive before or during the litigation it will be you that is penalised and not them. Although there are codes of conduct for Solicitors, these are open to interpretation in places and so although a Solicitor may have upset a Judge by his or her actions, the authority that regulates Solicitors may see their behaviour as inside their guidelines and you will have no comeback. Instead you will have a large bill.

## Without Prejudice Letters

A without Prejudice Letter is normally a letter that you receive during the course of a negotiation, or is some form of offer, or is an outline to an agreement. The letter normally consists of a reservation made on a statement or an offer that it is not an admission of anything, or cannot otherwise be used against the person or parties who wrote the letter in any future dealings with you, or in any litigation against you with any determinative legal effect. You really need to be careful with these letters as you may get an offer or an agreement on one of these letters that may have serious consequences and if you do not fully understand the implications or the meaning in the letter, it could be detrimental to you to agree anything without taking the correct legal or technical advice. Typically a neighbor who has a problem and has employed a Solicitor will try and deal with the issue or matter by some form of negotiation first before they take the matter to the court. If they want to reserve their case for any future court action or adjudication, they will write a without prejudice to first try and solve the case without need for any form of litigation. Always be very careful how you deal with the letter, as although the letter may be without prejudice, the offer may have a bearing on any future proceedings or litigation taken against you. Most courts now will impose penalties on party's who do not behave in a reasonable manner. This includes the refusal of any offer of negotiation or mediation made by any party. These penalties can include the award of costs and if the court determines you have not been reasonable, then you will end up paying the costs of the other party in their action against you. This can be tens to hundreds of thousand pounds if the case ends up being long and protracted and if it goes to appeal. Without prejudice letters are openers to discussions and so you must view them as such. You do not have to accept them, but you do have to be aware of the consequences of not accepting them.

## Open Letters

An open letter is a letter that is admissible in court and so is not seen to be without prejudice. The content of the letter can be seen by the court and can be used as evidence both for and against you in a litigation case. Open letters can be a double edged sword if you choose to use them as their contents can either help or hinder your case. Their content must be thought out very carefully before sending them, however they do have a tactical use and that is with regard to forcing of an agreement if the matter is reasonable one, or forcing the matter regarding costs. If you make any kind of offer in an open letter, then it can be included in the trial bundles at the time of preparing the case or can be included with the courts permission during the trial and so the letter can be made visible to the court. If you have made a reasonable offer in your open letter and your opponent has dismissed the offer, then he or she may be held liable for costs up to the point the offer was made if the Judge takes the open letter into account. The court may conclude that the other party has been unreasonable in not accepting the offer and so may incur all the costs the court case or alternatively may have to pay all or some of your costs. Open letters can be very powerful in influencing the outcome on costs or on a settlement so their use is worth considering if you need to force an issue.

## Letters Before Action

A letter before action is generally a letter sent by either you or your Solicitor to the opposing party telling them of your grievance or the issue you have with them or with some form of action they have taken that is prejudicial to your rights. The letter will generally tell the opposing party how you want them to remedy your grievance and it will generally tell them of the consequences of not remedying the grievance. Letters before action are important to the pre-court process as they are seen to be one of the major steps to take before you litigate. When outlining your letter before action make sure you are clear in what you want from the other party and ensure that you set a time limit on the letter for them to respond so that if the opposing party fails to undertake the desired action by a given date, then they will be clear of the consequences and the next steps you will take against them. Again like all documents, if you are unreasonable or unclear in your requirements or if you are aggressive or threatening in your tone to the opposing party you will see this come back and haunt you should it go to trial as the Judge will read this document to see that you have followed the appropriate court processes. If you have not followed process then you will take a hit when it comes to determining costs and outcomes. Do not skip on a letter before action as it could cost you thousands of pounds whether you win or lose your case.

# Personal Issues

The hardest part of any dispute is the effect the dispute has on those close to you and on yourself over time. Even the most resilient and strongest people cannot fail to be affected by a neighbour dispute. As the dispute progresses through time you will find yourself dealing with false accusations and hurtful issues. You will be subject to an immense amount of stress and will likely be spending a lot of time arguing with your loved ones over matters concerning the dispute. The author has observed that neighbours generally use every trick in their arsenal to try and discredit the people they are in dispute with and they generally try to divide their neighbours' families and in order to try and win their case. This is very divisive and so you must make sure that you and your family are prepared and that you stick together through the good times as well as the bad times.

## It is a Hard Path

The feelings that you go through when you have a dispute with anyone are extreme and are generally worse when the disputes are very close to you. The more the neighbour dispute progresses, the harder it generally gets for you to deal with. In the UK there are relatively few people that would understand the pressure and the anguish that you go through when you have a neighbour dispute and even worse there is nobody out there to help or who will listen or advise you in any way apart from either superficially as with the charities or with the councils or in depth at a high cost as with a Solicitor or Barrister. The majority of this advice is about your case and its handling and there are relatively few people or organisations that advise you on the personal aspects of any form of neighbour dispute. As you progress through a neighbour dispute you may see a number of small victories in your favour and defeats against you. Depending on your own character and personal psychology these will affect you in a number of different ways. You may find yourself feeling happy and elated one minute and then sad and weepy or angry the next. You may feel that the issue between you and your neighbour will never end and that you will lose everything you have. On the other hand the reverse may be true and you may feel that you will win and get more from your neighbour. However you feel at a given moment in time you can guarantee that over time the dispute will wear you down. You will end up losing sleep and you will worry about it at some stage. You will also see that the dispute affects your social life with your friends and family as well as your finances. At each and every point in the dispute you must ask yourself again and again, is the argument worth it? Ask yourself if the dispute can be ended in a different way with a better outcome for you and your family? If you can see some ray of light, when you are feeling at low ebb, remember this and see what you can do to start down the path of getting a resolution with your neighbour. Disputes are not fast or sometimes they are not easy things to resolve and they can take many years to finally put to bed. The author, at the time of writing this book was supporting a friend that was coming to the end of a dispute that took seven years to get to a conclusion, having gone from letters, to the court process, to appeal to finally reaching a settlement. That is seven years of hard work, tears and stress that has been endured by the authors' friend and their family. This persons' case is the principle reason this book was written as although the author has seen and been involved as an advisor in a number of cases, this case was extreme and the outcome was not good for all parties involved. The clear injustice of the case was an epiphany and there were many lessons that were observed by the author.

## It Will Test Your Relationship to Breaking Point, Sadly in Some Cases, Beyond

Because there is not much help available to people who have a dispute with their neighbour and because of the very nature of the issues you generally have in a neighbour dispute, most people will avoid you when you mention the fact that you are in a dispute. Over time your friends will either start to avoid the subject if you are lucky, or if you are unlucky your friends will avoid you all together and will slowly but surely disappear from your life. Extended family members will also try not to talk to you about your issues with your neighbour as they will not know how to deal with them or how to deal with you. This means that the only people you have available to talk to you about the dispute are those that are very close to you. The emotional roller coaster ride that a dispute brings to you and your loved ones is difficult to deal with and if you only have your immediate family to take the brunt of the emotions you will feel when you are in your dispute, then your relationship with your family will get very strained at times and if you are not careful, could collapse altogether. They say that one in three people have a neighbour dispute of some description. They also say that there are a high number of divorces in the UK and although there may not be a direct connection, there may not be an entire disconnect between the two. The strain on your relationship can become immense and only the strong survive. If you want to maintain your marriage, or your relationship with your children and your friends, then you must learn to deal with the stress and strains and must seek to moderate the problems that come with the emotions of a dispute. The best way is to try and take your mind off the dispute whenever and however you can, both as an individual and as a family. Make sure that you do get out and away from your problems at each and every opportunity, even if it is for a few minutes or hours. You must also learn to appreciate your family and your friends for what they are and you must never take them for granted. Show your appreciation to them whenever you can and invest in your relationship at all times.

## Time and Trivia

The biggest loss that you face with any neighbour dispute is the loss the of time that you or your family will end up spending to resolve the dispute. Although most people would agree that the loss of money in a dispute is bad enough, time is more precious than money as it can never be reclaimed or earned again. If you waste an hour, a day or a year then you will never be able to recover that time. Neighbour disputes are a massive waste of time and the trivia you contend with, the correspondence that you will have to write, and the dealings you will have with the legal community and the aftermath are all a tragic waste of your precious time and those of your loved ones. The problem you have however is that unless you can resolve your dispute quickly, you are doomed to spend a lot of time dealing with it. If you are able to do so, make sure that you do not allow the dispute to take over your life completely. You must always try and ensure that you spend your time on meaningful matters and do not waste it on trivia. When an opportunity comes before you to get away from your dispute or for you to recharge your batteries, do not waste the opportunity.

Seize the moment and make the best of it. Try and make sure that you do not end up looking back and saying you wasted your time as the dispute will be bad enough.

## Obsession

As the dispute progresses it takes over your thoughts, whether you are asleep or awake it will slowly but surely take over your life. You will find yourself constantly looking for ways to win your case, to prove yourself right in the dispute with your neighbour and will seek to have absolution, sometimes without considering the cost or the consequences'.The problem with this obsession is that it takes over your life and any time that ever you had that was productive for you soon get swallowed up in dealing with your neighbour dispute issues. Whether you employ a Solicitor or decide to go it alone and fight it out yourself, you will have to deal with correspondence from the other party, you will have letters to write, research to do in order to win your case and you will have people to speak to. It can soon become a full time obsession to win and you can easily sacrifice all of the things that matter. The difficulty you may face is in letting the matter go or in letting someone else deal with the problem. In all cases you have to ensure a balance and that it does not take over your life completely. You must ensure that you are able to deal with only the matters that need to be dealt with and that you leave the rest to the point that they must be completed by you or handed over to someone else. Do what you must do and do no more. Spend your time wisely and do not obsess.

## You Are the Loser

In any civil dispute or form of litigation there are no winners. There are only losers as even if you do get the court to agree you were right in the dispute between you and your neighbour, and that Judge has determined that you have won your case, the chances are that you will have spent many months or years going through hell to get to the result that you have got to. The probabilities are that even though you may have won your case, or even if you have lost your arguments' at the trial, you will still have the same neighbour living next door to you for some time to come. You will still have to try and live together as neighbours in the best manner that you can without future antagonism. This can be extremely difficult to deal with as there will likely be clear reminders of the dispute between you and these will affect you each and every time you come across them. If you are lucky enough to be able to afford to move away from your former neighbour and foe and buy a new home, then this is definitely worth considering. If you cannot afford to do this as your finances will not allow, then you must try and either make peace with your neighbour or alternatively look at ways of moving on with your life to forget things. The most difficult part of the whole affair is likely to be that whatever the outcome to your case, whether you have won or whether you have lost, you will always have some kind of bad feeling or memories of the dispute and it will take many years of hard work to get over them. The very nature of neighbour disputes is that they are very personal and as such there are events and aspects of the dispute that will stick in your memory for a very long time afterwards. If you can, try and find ways of escaping. Get a hobby, go out more and above all try and live a better life. Look upon the good points that you have learned from the dispute and use the knowledge you have acquired to its best effect.

## Personal Issues Check List

Ask yourself if the dispute is worth it?

Do you have any alternatives that will allow you to deal with the issues with your neighbour; can you mediate through a friend, a third party, a formal mediator? Can you negotiate through a Solicitor or Barrister? If you can, do not wait for the dispute to deteriorate any further. Act as soon as you can.

Use your time wisely and do not spend hours of sleepless nights thinking about the dispute. Try and deal with the dispute or elements of it as quickly or efficiently as you can so you can move on with your life.

You must look to the good things in life and must remember to focus on what is important, not what is unimportant or trivial. Think long and hard about what these are and then act upon them.

Remember you will never be a winner in a neighbour dispute case as there will always be bad memories and issues at the back of your mind even if the court has decided that your case was valid. You must learn to move on and must put the dispute behind you if you can.

Get a hobby or a form of recreation that you can do yourself and with your family. Make the best use of any time you have available to you and ensure that you get the most out of it. Time is precious so make the best use of it.

# Chapter 7

## Possible Solutions to Disputes

### Neighbour Agreements

The costs of the legal process are very high and for most people the process involves the expenditure of far too much money for the achievement of a very small and in most cases, unsatisfactory outcome. If you can avoid litigation in the first place then this is the best course of action available to you, even if you are not the aggressor. If you can seek to get an agreement with your neighbour as to how to deal with any issues between you, particularly around any area that you or they feel strongly about, then this is probably the cheapest and most effective way of dealing with any issues.

A neighbours' agreement is an agreed course of action between two neighbours, and they form the foundation of dealing with any areas that you may dispute or disagree about A neighbours agreement is a document that is normally drawn up by a Solicitor and signed by both parties in the presence of a witness. Once signed, this document then becomes a legally binding agreement between both parties for them to adhere to the details that have been set out and agreed within the document. The cost of these documents is not too great compared to the total cost of a litigation case and they are well worth considering if you believe that both you and your neighbour can live within the agreed terms of the agreement and that you can reach an agreement without too many problems between you.

When signing a neighbours' agreement you must bear in mind that the neighbours' agreement, once signed is enforceable in law. If you do not want to have this enforced by the courts or if you know you cannot observe the requirements of, or the actions set out in the agreement, then ask yourself the following question, what will not signing or adhering to the agreement lead to? The answer to that is probably that you will see a further deterioration of relations between you and your neighbour and if you are not careful, this will lead to litigation. Neighbours agreements generally come out of joint discussions or mediation between both involved parties and if the process has been done correctly, you will have been guided through the process of creating the agreement and it should not be too unpalatable to you or your neighbour.

## Approaching your Neighbour

If you are able to approach your neighbour and discuss matters that are concerning you with them, then it is always wise to do so before the dispute between you gets out of hand. When approaching your neighbour you must consider several things. First and foremost, will a discussion between you be fruitful and secondly, will it resolve the problem or will it add to the issues between you? If it is beneficial, try and involve a party who you can trust and who can assist you in the discussion process. Consider meeting your neighbour with a friend or alternatively with another neighbour as they will be able to assist and witness the discussions between you.

When approaching your neighbour try and be objective. When making your approach to your neighbour, make sure that they know the discussions between you will be without prejudice. By making your discussion without prejudice, if the discussion goes nowhere or if it breaks down, then what you have said or agreed cannot be used against you or them in court and so they are more neutral. When undertaking correspondence or discussions with your neighbour do not be personal or rude and do not be aggressive in your tone or manner. Try to be neutral in both tone and approach. When discussing issues with your neighbour, listen before you make any comment. Sometimes problems can be solved by a good discussion and by getting issues and perceptions off your chest. When answering a comment or a criticism, try and see what is behind the comment or criticism. Do not react out of hand as both you and your neighbour will have strong feelings on matters. When you are confronted with an issue, consider the many different ways that you can think of to resolve the issue. Do not just think of an ordinary solution; look for unusual and practical ways to resolve the problem as well. When looking at a potential solution also consider the areas that you could compromise or modify in order to meet the agreement or to resolve the issues between you. You must be prepared to modify your behaviour as well as it is likely that something that you are doing is also adding to the problems and differences between you and your neighbour. When you agree each point or issue, pause, reflect and document what you have just agreed or what you have just said. Not only will this form a record of your discussions and agreement, it will also act as an aid memoir for the future agreement and discussions.

# Mediation or Alternative Dispute Resolution

The authors' introduction to the mediation process was via a Barrister who thought that his clients would benefit from this approach to the resolution of a dispute but the client was unsure of the process and of the Barrister making the suggestion and he engaged the author for his advice. The authors view and that of the courts is that mediation or alternative dispute resolution definitely has merits and they are a good way to reduce both your costs and your exposure to any potential litigation by your neighbour. If at all possible you should enter into mediation between you and your neighbour as soon as possible before any disagreement you have turns into a full blow legal battle between you and your neighbour. Mediation and alternative dispute resolution if undertaken correctly, will allow you and your neighbour to get a better understanding of the reasons for dispute between you and your feelings between you and your neighbour and by exploring and dealing with these each in turn, it will lead to a resolution between you that is in many ways better than the resolution you would get from the courts or the legal process. Mediation or alternative dispute resolution are the only places that may see you get an apology for any injustice or issues that have been given to you by your neighbour. The courts or Tribunal just make a decision and you have to abide by it. They will never instruct for an apology to be given so they always leave an element of bad feeling whatever the outcome.

The courts are now very keen on mediation as an alternative to trial and this has happened only recent post the Woolf reforms. The courts view is that mediation should be sought wherever possible as the court should be the final resort and not the first and if you refuse to agree to mediate and make attempts to do so then they take a very dim view. The refusal to mediate can have a direct bearing when it comes to deciding costs or the case outcome. If the court believes that you could have avoided the trial process in the first instance and that have entered into litigation unnecessarily, it could go heavily against you and you could end up paying higher costs as a result or with a result that is not entirely in your favour.

The concept of mediation is that you and your neighbour employ an independent mediator who works with both parties to bring you together to discuss the problem or problems between you. Their job is to assist in resolving the differences between you and your neighbour and to help both parties come to an agreement that will end the dispute. The process of engagement with an independent mediator is that the mediation is generally proposed by one party and agreed to by the other. The costs of the mediator are normally shared between both parties equally so that they are paid on a neutral basis, i.e. the mediator cannot be seen to have bias as both sides are paying their bill. When a mediator is proposed, the other party will generally review the mediators' qualifications and any past case history. After approving the mediator or approving an alternative, the mediation process will begin. The normal start of the process is to agree a location for mediation and to agree any parties that need to be involved. These parties may include a Solicitor, a Barrister or both as the aim of the mediation is to get a legally binding resolution between both parties. As the agreement concerns legal matters, it is best to employ an advisor wherever possible. The mediator is unable to assist in giving any advice to the mediating parties as they act as an independent third party to try and encourage a settlement so cannot take a side nor advise on a course of action if it involves breaking neutrality. Mediation is relatively new to the UK legal system and of the mediators the author has spoken to; he agrees with their methods but does not agree with their approach to mediation for the reasons given below.

# When Not to Mediate

There are certain circumstances where it is not possible or wise to mediate. These circumstances include the following.

1.  Where there has been a serious crime that has been committed

2.  Where there are other more appropriate actions to take. These actions may include the notification of another party for them to take action. For example a land lord or land owner if you have problems with a tenant or with a part of your rented property.

3.  Mediation or negotiation is not appropriate in circumstances where it has been attempted before and where it has failed.

Unless you have a good reason to believe that it is worth trying again, there is very little point in attempting to do something that has failed previously.

4.    It is not appropriate in a compensation claim or a claim that involves a large sum of money. There are specific rules of law that deal with these areas and so it is best to take the advice of a solicitor in these circumstances.

5.    Where there is a court case or civil or criminal prosecution of the person you are proposing to mediate with. Under these circumstances it may not be appropriate due to the case that is being prosecuted against them. If you have a problem and are unsure of how to take this forward, contact a solicitor and they should be able to advise you of the best course of action under these circumstances.

## The Benefit of Formal Mediation or Negotiation

Mediation offers an opportunity to you to resolve the dispute in a way that you will not get in court or in the adjudication process. The mediation process allows you to confront the other side with the issues, problems and concerns that you really have and these may or may not include legal matters. Because mediation also includes non-legal elements it means that hopefully you can cut to the heart of the dispute and deal with the matters that are most pressing and important to you. Because boundary or neighbour disputes are not always about the land or the boundary, or the legal issue this gives you an opportunity to get something meaningful to you so you can resolve the dispute once and for all. For example in the previously described dispute where the Barrister recommended mediation, the neighbours' girlfriend assaulted one of the people who engaged the author for his advice. The party who was assaulted was looking to mediate and they wanted an apology and the recognition that their neighbours' were wrong to commit assault. It was pointed out to the mediating party that an Adjudicator at an adjudication trial or a Judge in court would only focus on the land dispute, and would not want to know anything about the disagreements and events between each party unless they affected the outcome regarding costs, or legal issues directly relating to the matter at hand. The court or Adjudicator will not enter into discussions with anything that has happened apart from the law relating to the land or the technicalities of the dispute and whether or not a party had sought mediation prior to the trial or hearing. The neighbour who committed the assault did not want to proceed with the mediation process and simply went to the court instead and as a result the mediating party did not get the apology she wanted and felt slighted as a result. Mediation if successful would have given both parties involved in this particular dispute an opportunity to redress the imbalance between them and may have dealt with the bitterness that they still have towards their neighbour and anyone associated with them. To be beneficial, mediation has to be something both sides subscribe to and the compromises met need to be palatable to both parties. Mediation cannot be one sided if they are to be successful.

The principle benefits of mediation is that it is relatively cheap to undertake when you compare the costs of a mediator to the payment of legal fees for a court or adjudication case. Even if you are paying for your legal advisor and the mediator on the day of mediation, it is still very cost effective. For example, a day's time of an advisor to assist in mediation would likely cost around two thousand pounds and the cost of the mediator will cost about five hundred to one thousand pounds depending on who the mediator was and on his or her experience. The cost of the mediator is generally split between both parties involved in the mediation, so a day's mediation can cost each side between two thousand to two thousand five hundred pounds for the best mediator and legal representative. Although this seems like a lot of money to most people, the costs of losing a court or adjudication case can equate to forty to eighty thousand pounds depending on the complexity and animosity of the case. For all of the reasons mentioned above, from the costs, to getting a resolution on a matter important to you, mediation is worth pursuing at the earliest opportunity and it is something that you should try and use to get a resolution to your problems without going to court. The mental, physical and legal costs of a court case or adjudication are not worth it.

## The Disadvantages of Mediation

The skills of the mediator are very important to the outcome of the mediation and there are many useless mediators in the UK who appear to have the necessary certification and are fully paid up members of the appropriate bodies and the organisations. It is therefore extremely important to find a mediator with a good solid track record of resolving difficult and complex cases. Remember the mediator will not represent you or the other party in the mediation so their skills towards impartiality and in getting to the heart of complex and sometimes personal issues are extremely important.

The clear advantages of mediation are that the process enables you to discuss and deal with the matters that the courts cannot deal with as it they are outside of the legal process or alternatively because they are not a consideration for the courts. The disadvantage of mediation is that you may need to compromise on areas or matters that could be detrimental to your interests unless you are advised correctly at the time of mediation. Events during the mediation process can happen quite quickly and a good mediator will seek to resolve and close down all issues as soon as possible. With the speed of mediation, the benefit of good advice is very necessary to you as you may not see the legal advantages or disadvantages of what is being proposed due to your feelings towards the other party and so it is always best to have representation with you during any mediation.

The other main disadvantage with mediation is that it may not solve all of your legal or personal issues or problems and this is where the author had a fundamental misalignment with a team that a Barrister approached to deal with his client's mediation. The authors view is that unless you are prepared both mentally and practically, mediation may not achieve what you wish or alternative you may end compromising in areas that are important to you. This can only lead to longer term resentment and bad feelings. The team approached in this particular mediation were a team of Barristers and with their approach to legal matters, they struggled to bear in mind that sometimes it is the little things that matter in a dispute and it is the resolution of these matters that will ultimately see the end of any problems or issues between you and your neighbour. The approach of the team that the author worked with was generally that of a matron or of a governess in the fact that they wanted you to swallow the pill no matter how bitter it was and reach a settlement, as in their view it does you good and is the ultimate aim of mediation. The mediation team did not necessarily take into account the personal issues that mediation can bring to individuals and so discounted the personal feelings of the authors' client. Although some sentiment and emotion can be ignored, many disputes have deep a rooted clement to them and sometimes these are emotional or personal issues. In this particular case, all the authors' client wanted was an apology and recognition that they could enjoy their life without their neighbours' intrusion every time they went into their garden. The mediation team thought the issue was a boundary issue. They wanted to focus on getting the boundary problem resolved whereas if the authors' client had received an apology, he was willing to concede the boundary line. They did not suggest the abolition of the line until the author mentioned it to his client. After doing so, both parties agreed to refrain from their behaviour and a solution was reached that was satisfactory to both sides. By focusing on the boundary, the Barristers felt that they were protecting their clients' interests. By not discussing their clients' actual wants and needs, they were leaving the roots of the dispute in place and it could have grown again at any time.

## Think About What You Want From Mediation

Although you should not go into mediation with any pre conceived ideas about the mediation it is worthwhile preparing a strategy before you start. Think about what you really want from the mediation and from your neighbour. There will be several things that may come to mind during this thought process. These may be things such as retaining your land or part of it if it is a land dispute. If you have had a bitter dispute with your neighbour about something else then you must consider the reasons for the dispute and what you may be prepared to concede, and then there may be other issues or considerations that may be important to you. Focus on what really matters to you and what is the real root cause of the dispute and not on the trivial issues or minor problems that distract you in a dispute. If you are in a situation where you need to mediate then the chances are that you are in a serious dispute with your neighbour and if it fails then you will end up in court. Along with your considerations regarding the dispute, you must remember that you need to save on the costs that will be associated with the court process. When you go through the mediation, the opposition will have key areas that they want to deal with and while considering your own strategy and approach, you must also consider theirs. Think about what you are prepared to compromise during the mediation and what you are not prepared to concede. Look at what you must compromise to end the dispute and look at the potential outcome of this compromise. Ask yourself it will finally resolve the matters between you and your neighbour. Write all of these points down on paper so you have a guide to refer to during the mediation process. Mediations can move very fast so a quick reference guide and any associated notes will be very helpful to remind you of key points and matters that may get lost as the mediation progresses.

When looking at the mediation process, consider this as the key point. If you cannot reach agreement between you and your neighbour, ask yourself what are the consequences of not solving these issues between you both? Ask yourself if you are prepared to face these consequences? In summary ask the following of yourself to start your thought process.

1.    What is your aim or goal? What do you want to take away from the mediation?

2.    What really matters to you? Is what matters to you a fact or is the issue between you and your neighbour down to principles? Is the dispute about something of material value or is it something less tangible that you want, possibly something like an apology?

3.    What does your neighbour want from you and from the mediation?

4.    What is your neighbour prepared to compromise? What do you think they may compromise?

5.    What are you prepared to compromise to your neighbour?

6.    What is the potential outcome to the mediation?

7.    Is the outcome likely to be what you want? Is it only going to partially meet your needs? Is it not going to meet your needs? Consider all outcomes and scenarios.

8.    What happens if you cannot reach agreement with your neighbour? If the answer to this question is not palatable to you as your only recourse could be to live with the problem or take it to court. If this outcome could cause you emotional or financial damage, then go back to step one and start this process again and ask yourself the really painful and truthful questions you need to in order to reach an agreement between you and your neighbour and focus on what really is important and not on the trivial and meaningless.

When you enter the mediation the mediator will ask you what you are trying to achieve from the mediation, they will be neutral in their approach to both parties but will guide the discussions forward depending on the answers they receive and on the strength of feeling between each party. During the mediation, you may or may not be close together to your neighbour and his or her legal team, possibly you will be in the same room at some stage, so you may have to face your neighbour at some point. For the largest part of the mediation however the opposition as well as you will have a legal advisor who will represent you during discussions and will advise you on any legal matter that may arise out of the mediation, they are likely to require a quiet room for discussion and they can act as middlemen in the most bitter disputes, isolating you from your neighbour and any bitterness between you. When you are in this situation make sure that your legal representative works in your best interests during these discussions, and you must ensure that they fully understand your strategy to the mediation and that they know your needs and understand your desired outcomes. Set boundaries with them before the mediation. You will have to be open and flexible and you cannot refuse something that is either practical or reasonable. You must think of alternatives and compromise and you must discuss this with your legal team or if representing yourself, with the mediator. Do not think of the ordinary things in this case, think of the extra ordinary things as well.

## Appointing a Mediator

If you appoint a formal mediator check their background and their qualifications, ask them how many similar cases they have dealt with? Ask them the outcomes to these cases? If you can, talk to the mediators past clients if at all possible in order to get references about the mediator and if you can, ask about their approach. Try and determine if the mediator is doing this part time, for example they may principally be a Barrister or Solicitor but may take mediation cases as well. Ask if it their main line of work even if they are a Solicitor or Barrister. They may be growing this particular element of their business and so could have had a number of successes. Ask if they are certified and if so what are their qualifications? Ask them their likely strategy to reduce costs and speed up the resolution process.

# Negotiation

The difference between mediation and negotiation is that a negotiation is normally undertaken by your legal team. It is undertaken either by your Barrister or by your Solicitor and they do not normally involve a middle man or mediator and therefore are not independent in their representations to the other side. In this case your Solicitor or Barrister are acting under your instruction and so will not be viewed by the opposition in the same way as a mediator. The benefits of this approach to resolving a neighbour dispute are that your negotiator can liaise directly with the opposing sides' team and can jointly agree a course of action to settle the dispute. Negotiation can sometimes be more beneficial in neighbour disputes as a number of points can be discussed, explored and agreed without the time pressure of mediation. A negotiation tends to be more to the point and more direct in outcome as the Solicitor or Barrister is likely to have discussed all of the negotiation points with you before approaching the other side. Negotiations tend to take place in situations where mediation is not possible or where a quick outcome to resolve a problem is needed. Negotiations generally happen in order to prevent something from going forward to the court or from progressing to a final outcome in court such as an appeal hearing.

When starting a negotiation with your neighbour make sure that your legal team are appraised of exactly what you want from the negotiation. Tell them how much you are prepared to compromise and what you are prepared to compromised. Then tell them how much or what you are not prepared to compromise and tell them what you are not prepared to concede. If your negotiator is a good one, they will explore any underlying issues that concern you and your dispute and will seek to find an answer to them before they approach the opposition to initiate the negotiation.

When a negotiation starts there is generally some discussion and documentation exchanged between both parties to set up a framework agreement for the negotiation. Once this framework or agreement has been set up, each party will then review their position and the points raised by each side at the start of the negotiation. Your legal team should advise you of what are good points and what are bad points and they will generally seek to protect your interests from a legal perspective. Sometimes this protection of your interests will see a compromise of your requirements from the mediation or a change of course that may challenge your ideal. This compromise is generally in your interest so bear this in mind when discussing it with your legal team as they are employed to ensure you get a good outcome. Negotiations can be slow to start as the initial discussions involve the laying of rules, boundaries and principles. Negotiations can gain momentum all of a sudden and the negotiation can conclude very quickly if it is felt that all ground has been covered and an agreement reached. Be mindful of this fact as you can find yourself with a commitment to do something within a very short period of time. If this commitment involves some kind of expenditure or the signing of a legal document quickly, make sure you have the money or the resources to make a payment or to adhere to the agreement within the given timescales.

Once a negotiation concludes each party will sign the agreement that has been reached and the document that has been produced will generally be lodged with the court for them to agree or endorse as well. This is a formality that most Solicitors or Barristers require and it is in your interest to get a legally binding solution to your problems once signed and agreed. If this agreement involves payment to the other party, the payment will generally be set up within a Tomlin agreement. (Described later in the book)

# Chapter 8

## Preparing for the Court

### Representing Yourself

If you cannot afford to pay for legal representation you are in a very difficult position and you have very few choices ahead of you. Legal aid is not available for many different types of civil cases, you cannot get legal aid if you earn above a certain amount or have assets above a certain value or if the case is an adjudication case rather than a court case. The government is wholly unsympathetic to peoples financial situation and do not take victims into account when interpreting strict financial policy. This means that if you are in an unfortunate position where you cannot afford to pay for a Solicitor yet are forced into defending yourself because your neighbour has more money than you, your only choices are to borrow money to pay for a Solicitor and recognise that if you lose, you will lose a lot of money and potentially your home, or alternatively you could defend yourself in the hope that you will win. In any event you have a severe problem and it will cost you money.

### Considerations Before you Defend Yourself

The biggest issue facing you when considering whether or not to defend your self is that irrespective of whether or not you can afford it, you will need some legal advice at some stage. If you neighbour has employed a Solicitor or Barrister knowing your financial situation, then they will have paid to win. Solicitors and Barristers are not primarily concerned with the law when they take on a case; they are concerned with winning the case for their client. Whether the case they are pursuing is legitimate or not, they will argue and work to win their case as it is their job to do so. They work for their employers as it is them that pay the bills and not the law. This presents a particular problem to you. Even if you are one hundred percent correct in your plight and the case being presented to the court is unjust and unfair, the opposition has employed a legal team to destroy any argument or case you have, however right it may be. Their job is to win full stop. Bear in mind there are some Solicitors or Barristers who will not lie, cheat or deliberately influence you or the Judge to destroy your credibility and hence your case, however there are others who are unscrupulous and will do whatever it takes to win for their client. It is a lottery as to who you get opposing you and even if your opposing Solicitor or Barrister is a good one, they are still employed to win.

When you think about defending yourself, you must consider that unless your neighbour is defending his or her self, you will be facing a legal team that will have many more years of knowledge and experience that you do not have. They will also be able to call upon vast resources that you do not have access to and more importantly, they will not hesitate to destroy your case in order to win, no matter how strong and well founded your case may be. If you are right it does not matter to a Solicitor or barrister. In court it is not about right or wrong, it is about a legal argument and not morality. Most Solicitors and barristers will try and seek settlement outside of court wherever possible, however be assured that when they do seek settlement, it will generally be in favour of their client and not you.

The legal system is also of no use to you when defending yourself as the law is indifferent to your plight and although the law should allow equality as you will be a litigant in person you are generally viewed as the lowest form of life in the legal system. Most Judges are opinionated and status orientated, therefore if you do not meet their expectations or ideals, you are at a disadvantage immediately. Even where the Judges are not opinionated, there is very little they can do to help you. This means that if you do not present the right legal argument, the Judges cannot advise you of what to present. Moreover the courts or the adjudication service do not assist with legal advice and are slow to react if you have questions or are unsure. Even worse their websites and guidance documents are of limited value. In cases where they recognise that you need legal assistance, yet cannot afford it, they will refer you to the citizen's advice bureau, which although generally helpful, can only assist so far. Generally citizen's advice staff are not lawyers and so in most cases can only give general advice. If you do defend yourself you are likely to be completely on your own and if you have any kind of money, savings or value in your home you will not be able to get any free legal aid or support. Your best hope is to work towards an early settlement that does not cost you the earth. The path to follow is that of mediation or negotiation as with both of these courses you do have an element of control on your outcomes.

If you do decide to represent yourself, in order to win or defend your case you must focus on legal and not the moral argument as they are not the same thing. Even if you think you are right and that your neighbour is being vindictive, this is not relevant. The law is predicated upon case law and upon a better argument in relation to this given case law. When preparing a case, the opposition will look at your skeleton argument, or if they are the aggressor, will look to precedence, and they will call upon case law to show how weak your case is in the eyes of the court. In one case the author observed in court where an owner had title ownership to land that was disputed by his neighbour and where he could prove that it was his he was still disadvantaged. This was because of his neighbours' social standing and because he could call upon other more prominent people to back him and his argument, and along with the presentation of a good legal argument by his Solicitor, this person's neighbour took a wholly vindictive case to the County Court. The result of the trail was that the real land owner did not win his case as he did not have the level of support that his neighbour had and because he was not represented by a Solicitor, his legal argument was seen to be weak. Simply put the "better standing" neighbour showed a better legal argument and had his "friends" to back him in court. The opposing side, as a litigant in person was completely disadvantaged due to this persons word and the word of this persons friends and due to the superficial strength of the case presented by his legal team, the Judges' biased and dubious behaviour also contributed as he was not prepared to listen to the litigant in person when he was not precise in his legal presentation or case law. The number of people who were prepared to say the opposition was a "good person" all worked in the aggressors favour. He destroyed the case with the word of his friends and legal argument even though the material evidence showed a different story to that being presented by the aggressors' legal team. The fact that the real owner could prove the land was his was immaterial to the case and to the Judge as the real land owner lost and their neighbour took adverse possession of his land. Legal argument, character and good presentation in court win cases. Everything else is incidental and it adds to the lottery.

You must think very carefully before going down the path of representing yourself. If you cannot afford legal representation, then see an early settlement as soon as you can, before legal costs accrue and before the case becomes too advanced. Because litigants in person have no support in court or in their case, and the legal community know this, you are at a disadvantage throughout the whole legal process. Unless you firmly believe that you have a strong case, whether you are right or wrong, the odds are stacked against you winning. If you can, consider mediation or alternative dispute resolution to solve your issues before you resort to court action or adjudication. If you do decide to defend yourself consider the following areas that may be able to assist you.

## Experts

Your words alone will not be enough to persuade the court that you are right and that the case you are presenting is a valid one in the eyes of the law. To formulate your case, you will need to call upon an expert within the area that is problematic or that is central to the case. If it is a boundary dispute, call a surveyor. If it is a dispute over a hedge, trees or plants then call a tree surgeon or a horticultural specialist. Look in the appendix at the back of this book for more help. These experts will be able to help and advise you of your problem and can be called upon to represent your argument in court. Bear in mind however that unless they are legally qualified, they cannot officially give you legal advice. When employing an expert, consider that they should have experience of disputes and disagreements that have been settled prior to court and should also be able to present evidence in court and so should be able to assist in the formulation of your case prior to and during the case hearing.

## Preparing Your Case: Statement of Case or Particulars of Claim

Whether you are defending yourself in court or whether you are preparing to take action against your neighbour you will need to prepare a statement of case if it is going to tribunal or a particular of claim if it is going to court. In essence these are the documents that you will present to the court or Tribunal to outline your claim in legal terms and the claim details what you believe the issues to be, it gives an outline understanding of the matters affecting or influencing the case from a legal perspective and it makes a suggestion as to a remedy to settle the case. A statement of case or particulars of claim must include the following at a minimum.

1.   The names of the claimants and the defendant or defendants.

2.   A brief outline of what the issue or issues are

3.   A history in summary, set out in chronological order

4.   The legal argument in outline to support the case

5.   A prayer or a claim, in essence this is what you want to see as the outcome to the trial or case.

6.   A statement of truth where you sign the document stating that your claim is correct and true to your knowledge and belief.

A statement of case or a particular of claim are extremely important documents as they are the cornerstone of any legal case that you wish to present to the court or tribunal. They must be factual, concise and must detail exactly what you want and why. Once a particular of claim is submitted to the County Court or a statement of case is submitted to the Adjudicator (The Tribunal Court Judge), then the court or Adjudicator will serve a copy on your opponent and will request a response from them.

Make sure that you meet the deadlines of the courts "Directions", as these are the requirements that are issued by the Judge for you and the other side to follow in your case and they are requirements you should comply with. The issuing of directions is the only way the Judge will correspond with you and the other party on matters relating to your case; therefore you should pay particular attention when you receive a direction as it is generally a call for you to provide or comply with something. You should carefully consider what the Judge wants you to do and in what time scale you should satisfy the requirements of his or her direction. If you fail to respond to directions you may be severely penalised and you may even lose your case if you have no reasonable excuse for not complying with them.

If you have legitimate reason to request an extension for a deadline, if you disagree with a direction or if you have a request for the Judge to take in to account while he or she considers your case you should submit a formal letter to the Judge or in some cases, you must submit a formal application where you should fill in a specific court form and send it to the Judge's office for Judge to consider that particular issue.

When the Judge considers the case or request the result of the request or ruling becomes a "Decision". You are entitled to receive a written decision about the case as well as a breakdown of the reason for the reaching of the decision. After the decision has been given the "Court Order" is made. This is the final Judgement where the Judge orders the parties to take certain actions, for instance, one party may be ordered to pay the other party's costs or you may be ordered to remove something, or not do something such as not trespass. The order is legally binding and if the decision and order are upheld, if you contravene the order it can be a criminal matter in certain cases. If you do not understand a decision or an order take immediate advice as it will have an effect on you.

## Responding to a Statement of Case or Particular of Claim

If you receive a statement of case or a particular of claim from the court or Adjudicator you have only a limited amount of time to respond to the claim or case. This time period is usually fourteen days and you will need to respond to the court or Adjudicator and state whether you wish to defend the case or whether you wish to settle the case. If you wish to settle, then you must tell the court that you wish to do so and they will arrange for this to happen. If you wish to defend yourself in the court or adjudication case, you will need to use the court documents sent with the claim or statement of case to tell this to the court or Adjudicator and you will need to outline why you are defending yourself or if you are not defending yourself, you will need to tell the court or Adjudicator who will be defending you. You must also state your reasons for your request and your case should be given in outline and what you believe the outcome of the case should be. You will be required to sign the documents you send to the Adjudicator or court with a statement of truth, this is essentially where you are signing and stating that you believe your defence or desired outcome to be true and correct.

## Skeleton Argument

Once you have either received a response from the opposing party, or if you are making a claim yourself, after you have issued a particular of claim or statement of case, you will need to prepare your skeleton argument to outline to the court what your argument is in brief legal terms. Each element of your legal claim must be included in your skeleton argument and it must make any relevant reference to legal documents or any supporting evidence that you wish to use in your case. Once you have issued your skeleton argument to the other side, if making a claim you will need to wait for your opposition to give their skeleton argument to you. If you are in opposition and your neighbour is making a claim against you, you will need to respond to their skeleton argument with your own argument once you have received their skeleton argument. Once both parties have exchanged skeleton arguments, the court or Adjudicator will normally then set a date for a court hearing to be heard and for the case to be tried. A link to the court template for a skeleton argument is shown in the appendix at the end of the book.

## Amending Your Skeleton Argument

You can amend your skeleton argument at any time and can reissue it via the court to your opposition before the trial. To do so you will generally have to pay a fee to the court for them to stamp and issue the skeleton to your opposition if your case is being heard in the County Court. If your case is being tried via the Tribunals' process, you will generally not be required to pay a fee to have your argument issued. It is extremely important to remember that you can amend your argument at any time if you are representing yourself as it allows you to change your approach if necessary. The issue of a document does not mean that it is final. If you find new information or evidence and want to use it then add it to your skeleton argument, an amendment is a powerful tool to do use so bear it in mind.

## Disclosure of Documents

Once skeleton arguments have been exchanged, the court or Adjudicator will normally order the disclosure of all documents relating to the case. The request for disclosure will normally be a direction telling you that you must release all documentation that you have in your possession regarding the case and that you will be using to rely upon to support you case in court. You will be ordered to release any document that supports your case and any that you have in your possession that may not support your case. The County Court has different rules regarding document disclosure to that of the Adjudicator and the County Court can impose strict penalties if documents are not disclosed due to them being detrimental or if they are not presented to you in a timely manner. If you believe that a document should be disclosed to you by your opposition, you can request the court to order your opposition to disclose it via rule 25.1 of the civil procedure rules 1998.Once you make this request to the court, along with your reason as to why the document should be disclosed, then the court will assess its relevance and if they think the document should be disclosed, they will issue an order or directions for it to be released. The Adjudicator has different rules regarding evidence to that of the court. The Adjudicator can only request disclosure under rules 14 and 47 of the practice and procedure rules for the disclosure and inspection of documents. They cannot however force disclosure under rule 25.1 of the civil procedure rules and so if your opposition does not disclose a document they cannot be forced to do so. This leaves a problem and it is another major failing of the adjudication service.

For you to defend your case you must be aware of all documents and of the issues that may affect your case, whether this effect is beneficial or not. If you know about a document that could be of benefit, the Adjudicator cannot force its disclosure from your opponent. The court can force disclosure however so if you are considering a case and you know that your opposition is being underhand and you suspect that they are withholding evidence, take your case to the County Court rather than to the Adjudicator as they have the power to force your opponent to reveal the information that is vital to your case. The Adjudicator however can do nothing in this regard apart from waste time, money and tax payer's resources with this and many other matters.

## Witnesses

When preparing your case for the County Court or Adjudicator it will very often get down to your word against your opponents word in court. If your opponent can show more evidence to support their case, be it in a written format or an oral format, then they have a better chance of winning their argument and this will have positive outcome at the trial. Wherever possible you should consider the use of witnesses to support your case and argument and if possible get them to present evidenceto the court.

## Expert Witnesses

Expert witnesses are generally people employed by you to give evidence to the court to support your case and technical argument in County, High Court or Adjudication. Generally although they are employed by you, expert witnesses are obliged by CPR 35.10 to maintain integrity in all court matters. Many expert witnesses do try and maintain their independence and objectivity however in one case the author observed, there was clear collusion between the Land Registry and an expert witness and between a legal team and his expert witness. It is still questionable whether this collusion was detrimental, however the fact that it occurred raises strong questions over the matter of integrity in court matters. You need to be assured when you employ an expert that they have good credentials and that they are recognised by the court as expert witnesses. It is therefore essential that you check their qualifications and background with a registered body and if you can, search their history online and ask them for details of cases where they have appeared as expert witnesses. An expert witness can be a surveyor, a tree surgeon or any other expert with professional credentials. When a decent expert is employed they will give evidence based upon a founded argument to the court and if they have information that supports your case they will present it personally to the court. If however the information they have does not support your argument, you must consider their information and its use carefully and should try and seek settlement before the case goes to court. Expert witnesses can be vital to your case and so their use and employment will be critical if you are a litigant in person. They are sometimes the only people that you can rely upon to support your argument so treat them well and use their knowledge to your best advantage. They are absolutely crucial to your case and to your argument so make sure you employ them before your make any technical representation to the court or opposition and ensure you include their ideas and opinions and documentary evidence in your skeleton argument.

## General or Other Witnesses

A case can be made in court or it can be broken by the evidence provided before going to court. If you or your opposition can present a credible witness to support what is being said, then you or they have a chance at winning as the witness will add weight to whatever is being presented. When considering your case, try and see what witnesses you can call upon. They could be friends, other neighbours and previous owners of your house. Do not think of the ordinary, think of the extra ordinary. For example in one case known to the author, a gardener gave evidence at a trial and because he could remember great details of the land in dispute, particularly around what plants were growing and when they were planted, he destroyed another person claim because of this. Whoever your witness, they need to be credible and need to support your case and argument. Before calling upon them you must be sure of your facts and they should be sure of theirs. If you have a legal team, get them to ask questions and to prepare your witness for the hearing. If you are representing yourself, then you must do the same preparation. When your witness or witnesses are in court they are going to be cross examined and so they will be open to a whole series of questions and in some cases allegations. Your opposition will try to discredit them and the information they present as it is crucial to the outcome of their case. Your witness will need to know that the opposition will likely ask awkward and penetrating questions to discredit their information and therefore they need to be prepared. If your witnesses are not prepared, then your case and argument can fail very quickly as barristers are like a dog with a bone when they get hold of something that supports their argument or case. If your witnesses are able to support you and your case and are not concerned with the questions or tactics of the opposition, then they are good people to use to support your case and argument. The opposition will try and discredit your witness, however this is not a question of challenging the integrity of your witness in many cases; it is about a question of the completeness of memory or understanding of your witness. For example in a boundary dispute if you call upon a previous house owner, they may have a recollection of the boundary that is different to the boundary as it stands at the time of your dispute. Features change over time and memory also alters over time. Therefore it is sometimes easy to show that there have been changes and that your witness has a recollection or has given a statement that does not entirely bear resemblance to the situation as it stands at the time of your case. If your opponent can pick up and pursue this, then they will do so. Invariably they will also try to use it against you.

## Witness Statements

In order to support your case in County Court or at a Tribunal hearing, if you have any witnesses that have evidence that is in support of your case, it is always best to record what they have to say in a document and once this information is recorded, you can present this document to the court in the form of a witness statement. A witness statement can be an invaluable tool as it is a documentary record of what the witness has to say about the matters of your case or has recalled about something in support of your case. When the information is presented to the court, a good, well written witness statement should support your case and should force your opponent to think and re-evaluate their argument. If they cannot defend their case because the witness has presented compelling evidence in their witness statement, then it may force your opposition into early negotiation or settlement. Be aware of the power of this as it is a good tool to use before a case gets to court. If however your opponent does not choose to negotiate, then a witness statement adds weight to your case and as such must be rebuffed by your opponent. This means that they may have difficulty in preparing a case to challenge the information if you present it correctly. This can be a very difficult thing for them to do as any well prepared witness statement adds to your opponents anguish and can weaken their case. If you can call upon more than one witness and they can support each other's information, then your case becomes even more compelling and so you will have a better chance of winning at the trial and in beating your opponent.

## Other Forms of Witness or of Evidence

## CCTV

There are many different sources of information that can be used as evidence or that can witness what you are saying. In terms of witnessing events or actions, Closed Circuit Television or CCTV can be used to support what you have to say or what you have seen. If you do have any form of dispute with your neighbour deploy CCTV cameras as soon as possible and make sure you record everything, if you can use CCTV with a microphone as well, then this is even better. Keep an archive of all recordings and make sure that the information held in your archive is kept safe and secure. Do not delete anything, even if you think that there is no information of value on the recording. The reason for this is that even insignificant events may have a bearing on your case and on many occasions, you will not know what is or is not relevant until your neighbour has presented their skeleton argument to you. Similarly by keeping a record of events over time, when your case does finally come to trial, you should be able to see a chronology of events and any changes within the area monitored by the CCTV and you will be able to build these into your case. A prime example of this happened in a case where a neighbour made false claims that an owner had altered the boundary of her property. By showing CCTV evidence and additional photo's the owner who was accused of moving their boundary was able to prove that it was the accuser who changed the boundary features over time and not the accused owner. The accusers' case was subsequently dismissed and they had to pay all costs. The key to the usefulness of the evidence in this instance was the chosen placement and positioning of the camera on the land where the problems were occurring. When considering the use of CCTV to build up a picture of events, make sure you place the camera or even better a number of cameras in positions that are likely to capture the information you need and that cover as much of the area as possible. Think about covert and overt placement. Are the cameras a deterrent to your neighbour creating problems for you or are they placed to capture evidence. If they are a deterrent make them highly visible to your neighbour and place a sign near them to tell your neighbour that they are being recorded. If the cameras are there to capture evidence, they need to be more discrete. Therefore make them small and obscure them so that they cannot be seen easily.

## Photographs

Photographs are a fantastic source of information as to the history and the changes associated with your property or your neighbour dispute over time. If you have a dispute try and source or take as many photographs as you can that have a bearing on your case. If you have a problem related directly to your property, the photographs could be sourced from your town or county archives, also consider aerial photographs from special companies. Some photographs may not be available from the air so look to photographs from previous owners or from the time you moved in. Whatever the source of the photographs, they can bear witness to events that have happened over time, moreover photographs are hard to dispute. When looking at photographs you must bear in mind that they were taken under certain conditions or that they were taken from a certain angle or from a certain place. This may mean that the information they convey may not be just as you want it, however if the information conveyed in the picture supports your case, then there is no reason why you cannot use it as evidence in support of your argument. Resources that may assist you in looking for different sources of photographs are given at the back of this book or alternatively look at the chapters about buying your house for further ideas on information and areas to research to help you find pictures or drawings to support you case.

## Documents

Documents are a good source of evidence to support your case. Documents include any official papers held in government offices such as the land registry or the council. These documents can be OS Maps, Title Deeds, Statutory Declarations, Land Survey Reports, formal correspondence etc. Other document to consider in your case includes anything from the previous house owners'; they may be copies of correspondence between you and your neighbour or between you and your Solicitor at the time of the properties conveyance. The chapter about buying your house and researching the area where you are proposing to live gives good information sources to show where you can find any additional documents that may support your case. Title deeds for your property and your neighbours' property are also invaluable and they should be some of the first documents you obtain, particularly if your dispute is land or boundary related. The Land Registry has these and they are also available from many companies online. They can be searched in any search engine with the key words title deeds.

## Land Registry

The Land Registry are supposed to be experts in their field, this being the field of recording and listing boundaries and conveyances. They are also the legislative repository of information regarding boundaries and conveyance in the UK. Although the Land Registry do maintain records of the above described events and titles, they are far from expert at dealing with the information they hold and the interpretation of it. Moreover the laws that govern and regulates the Land Registry are such that the Land Registry are not able to record information conclusively or to a degree of accuracy needed to prevent a boundary dispute in the majority of cases. Moreover as it is recognised by the government that there are major deficiencies in the

Land Registry system, it is protected by statute and it therefore has limited liability when it comes to any negligence or maladministration claim against them. The government of the UK know that there are issues and as a result have deliberately created legislation to limit any payments that are made by the Land Registry when they make a mistake. These payments are generally miniscule and so normally do not cover all legal expenses associated with a boundary or land dispute case and in order to make a claim against the Land Registry, you must prove a loss as a result of their negligence. Conveniently for the Land Registry, by law they do not need to make a payment for their mistakes without you providing concrete evidence to show that they have made a clear mistake, In order to have any chance of getting any money at all, you will have to show why they should make a payment to you and they will normally limit this to a maximum of two and a half times the value of the land where they made their mistake. More to the point, they will use a county surveyor to look at the land value and in most cases; the surveyor will not value the land correctly. If the Land Registry do give you poor advice, or if they do not undertake the correct course of action as they are obliged to do so by legislation, or alternatively if do not provide necessary information to you even if they are obliged by law to hold this information, this is considered by both the Land Registry and the government to be maladministration and in which case there is no statutory indemnity to cover your losses due to their incompetence. This is a major issue that seems to be recurring time and time again and it needs to be challenged in a judicial review as the Land Registry must be made accountable for their mistakes.

## Cases Concerning the Land Registry

If you have a boundary or a land dispute with your neighbour the Land Registry are limited by law in what they can do to assist, even if they created the problem due to their incompetence or "maladministration " as they prefer it to be known. Although the Land Registry can undertake various actions to try and limit a land or boundary dispute, invariably the Land Registry do not get involved as it would be a major cost for them to do so. In cases where there is an issue relating to Land Registry's mistakes, you need to apply to the Land Registry to get them to agree to indemnify you for the costs of dealing with their mistake. In essence this is where the Land Registry says if you incur legal costs for a mistake on your boundary, we will pay you a maximum of two and a half times the value of the land in question where you have a dispute and even if we say we will indemnify you, there is no guarantee that they will pay any money to you due to their rules regarding loss.

# Solicitors

## Your Solicitors

When choosing a Solicitor to represent your case or position you need to make sure that they are good at what they do and that they have a recognised track record in dealing with the issue or issues that you have with your neighbour. There are a lot of Solicitors around who are generalists and they may have a very broad range of legal skills, however they may not have the depth of knowledge you may need to fight your case and as a result, although they may have dealt with an issue like yours in the past, they are not expert and so may make mistakes in representing you or in fighting your case. These mistakes are likely to be procedural or technical and although they may not be fatal in themselves, they will have a strong influence on the Judge presiding over your case. If your Solicitor does not know his or her subject, the Judge will likely view this dis-favourably. When looking for a Solicitor to represent you, make sure that they have strong references and that they have a good profile in the subject area that you are seeking their representation. There are many ways to find a Solicitor however the web is a good place to start. Look at their legal partnership and look at their case profiles. A web search will normally show what experience they have and by looking them up in Google or a similar search engine you should be able to get details of their court appearances and the cases they have been involved with. After choosing a few of the better Solicitors from the web, give each one a call to see how accessible they are. Most Solicitors will have a secretary or a personal assistant and their secretary or PA should be able to make an appointment for you to hold either a telephone conversation with the Solicitor in question or can arrange a face to face meeting with them. Most Solicitors will give you a short meeting without charge to discuss your issues and to see if they can be of assistance. At your first meeting ask as many questions as you can of the Solicitor around their past cases and knowledge to get a feel for what they are about. Consider their depth of knowledge, their past history and ask yourself if they are a person who you can work with. Try and gauge their character as you must be able to work with this person when times are both good and bad, when you disagree and do not see their point of view. A reasonable Solicitor will give you some advice for nothing, albeit on a limited basis and will tell you how they would propose to deal with your issues or case to reach a resolution. Bad Solicitors will give you very little knowledge apart from a very good appreciation of how much money they charge for their services.

## Can You Trust Solicitors?

Your Solicitor will be the prime point of contact between you and your neighbour in any dispute and as such you must be assured that they do the right thing and genuinely act on your behalf. Many Solicitors can be heavy handed in their dealings with others and although their tactics may work at times, your Solicitor is not the person who has to live next door to your neighbour when the dispute is solved and being heavy handed or uneven with your neighbour is not always the best idea, even if you are upset or angry with them. Make sure that your Solicitor does not antagonise your neighbour further by bullying them into an agreement as this will not help you in the long run.

Solicitors act under your instructions and the point to remember with Solicitors is that although they are supposed to be experts in their field, some Solicitors are not as qualified as they seem or as skilled would like you to believe so they do sometimes make serious mistakes. Always try and be sure that the advice they give you is correct by asking a few questions and by checking around with other sources of information such as the web. This is particularly important for issues and matters that will have a direct influence on the outcome of the case. As an illustration of this, the author experience of one particular Solicitor was that this Solicitor claimed to be an expert in his field, The Solicitors profile was good but he had no experience of Tribunal cases but did not mention this even when asked directly about his experience. He merely stated he was an expert in these cases and that his clients had great confidence and faith in him. His client believed him and appointed him to represent her at a Tribunal hearing.

As a result of this Solicitors inexperience the person who engaged with this particular Solicitor was left in a very difficult position with the Tribunal because they requested a stay of proceedings immediately before the trial commenced and were advised by their Solicitor that the stay would be automatically granted as a result of their request. The stay was not automatic and it certainly was not granted. This had the effect that an important part of their case was not heard or defended properly because the Solicitor in question had not prepared for the hearing or for the tribunal case even In the end this was highly prejudicial to the outcome of the case and the Solicitors client ultimately lost due to the Solicitors gross negligence. The Solicitor however did nothing about this mistake and when he was asked for a refund and compensation by his client his response was to offer five hundred pounds or the alternative was to sue him for professional negligence. To do this would take roughly one hundred thousand pounds and five to six years of court time with absolutely no guarantee of winning the case. If you have the money, it may be the right thing to do in a negligence case, however if you are like ninety six percent of the UK population, you are most unlikely to be able to sue your Solicitor for professional misconduct due to costs and the other barriers they will place in your way. If you have any doubt about your Solicitors knowledge or abilities or if you feel you are not getting good value for money, do not hesitate to fire them and get someone else. Bear in mind that if you do fire them you will incur costs with your new Solicitor as they will need to get up to speed with your case. This however may be more beneficial to you in the long run as your original reason for their employment was to win your case against your neighbour. The subsequent losses you may incur as a result of not winning your case due to mistakes could be higher and so always bear this in mind.

## Costs. Talk is Cheap, Until You Employ a Solicitor!

Solicitors are a very expensive if not over valued service. Of all the Solicitors the author has ever met or dealt with, very few, if any have been worth their asking price. Solicitors however work on the basis of a retainer and you will need to pay them in advance or on account if you wish to engage with their services. Costs vary for Solicitors depending on their experience and number of years in practice. These costs vary in range from around one hundred and seventy pounds per hour for a junior Solicitor to five to six hundred pounds for a more senior Solicitor or a partner with many years of experience. The problem with Solicitors is that even before you go to court to fight your case, they will cost you a fortune. They bill in six minute blocks and tend to charge for every letter as well as their costs. As a result, the expense of engaging with a Solicitor and the requirement of asking them for their legal opinion on a relatively straight forward issue will cost you from at least several hundred to several thousand pounds for an answer.

## Questions to Ask Your Solicitor

The questions that you need to ask your Solicitor are normally based upon your specific case or the problems you have. A good general question to ask the Solicitor is how they would deal with the matter. If they are good at what they do, they will seek to limit your costs and to deal with your problem as quickly and as efficiently as they can. The Solicitor should therefore advise along the lines of sending an initial letter to your neighbour outlining your grievance and they should be trying to seek a neighbours' agreement. If they cannot achieve an agreement then they should be stating that the next steps should be to start the mediation or alternative dispute resolution process. If this fails then they should only then consider pursuing the court process. Throughout your whole dealings however the Solicitor will be considering the impact of their actions on the court process and will not be undertaking any action that may be detrimental or prejudicial to your rights. A good Solicitor should advise you that the court process is the last place that you want to go and they should be advising you to seek to limit your costs and any exposure you may have. If the Solicitor does not do this, then walk away from them and employ another one. If they are not actively seeking to reduce your liabilities and exposure, they are likely to be only interested in money and in pursuing their careers rather than in assisting you to win your case with as little damage to you as possible.

## Your Opponents Solicitors

Your opponent's Solicitors should follow certain protocols when dealing with you and should not attempt to bully you or intimidate you in any way. Invariably they will do this at some stage however as they will generally try and scare you into making a deal. Many Solicitors will open their correspondence with you by stating a threat of some form of action against you if you do not change, modify or agree something with their client. When you first receive a letter from your opponents Solicitor try and understand what it is that they are saying rather than what it is they say. Look at the actual meaning of what they want rather than the words they have used to make their request. If there is a dispute between you and your neighbour, try and understand what the nature of the dispute is as you may have a different understanding of the matters or issues between you. Do not be pressured into acting because of their letter. If the letter is a bolt out of the blue, read it and get the appropriate advice as soon as you can. In all cases try and put yourself in your opponents' shoes and remember that you may not want the same thing as your neighbour. If you suspect that this is the case, try and explore the possibilities of mediation or negotiation that are available to you.

## SolicitorsLike to Win!

Solicitors are paid whether you win or whether you lose your case, If your Solicitor has given good advice or bad advice, it does not matter. This is what they do during the day as their job. For many Solicitors it is not their life's ambition to deal with legal work all the time and you must remember that whatever they do, they do not have to live with your neighbour. Most experienced Solicitors will have seen good cases, bad cases and downright fraudulent cases and will have dealt with them in a number of manners, via some form of agreement outside of court or via a trial in court. If you employ a Solicitor they are paid by you to put forward your case and to end the grievance with your neighbour. Many Solicitors may have started out with decent moral principles towards their jobs and towards life. They will change over time however as their experience will harden their attitude and resolve and they will likely advise you based upon a logical rather than emotional strategy to win your case. Even if your case has a poor chance of winning, it is their job to make the case to the court or to your neighbour so that you do win and have minimal damage to you. Morality and conscience do not appear to be high on some Solicitors' agenda as a result of the fact that they are employed to win and are not generally employed as a result of the merits of your case and so you must bear this in mind, particularly if you are the opposing party to a neighbour with a good legal team. You must also consider that an experienced Solicitor will not do anything unlawful or illegal in their dealings with you or their opposing parties; they will however know how to manipulate and influence the court so that it weakens or strengthens your case depending on whether they are representing you or whether they are representing the opposition. Solicitors are not concerned with you or your case if you are in opposition to them; they are only concerned with their own client and in winning as they are in business to make money and to grow. Reputation is key to this so they will do what they can to protect their reputation and track record of success

## Are Solicitors Unscrupulous?

Solicitors have several tools in their tool box that allow them to try and win their case. Their favourite tactic is to use good guy bad guy. If they are representing your neighbour, their first letter to you may be a strong one either with a veiled or a direct threat of some kind of action against you. Their next letter to you may be a reminder of their first letter and their next letter to you will likely be a friendlier letter asking you to act immediately upon the first and second letters. The reason for their tactic is that solicitors have a severe problem in so far as they need to know how you are going to react to their client's grievance or case so that they can prepare a defence or strategy to deal with you to resolve the matter. Therefore Solicitors will try a number of different approaches to get you to react and to take a stance. As far as the Solicitors are concerned, they will try and get your emotions going as they will also want to gauge how strongly you feel about something, or some point or issue. Your best bet when dealing with them, if you can afford it is to put your Solicitor in the way of the opposing party and let them deal with the opponent and the correspondence they are generating. If you cannot do this because you cannot afford it, then do not react to the letters that you receive and do not express any emotion in your correspondence that could be picked up by your opponents Solicitor that could go against you. Do not make any statements in any correspondence apportioning blame or showing anger. Try and remember that the Solicitor is seeking to get you to react so that they can plan their next move in the case. When dealing with your opponents Solicitor be polite in your dealings with them, and seek the appropriate advice from a Solicitor to represent you wherever possible. The behaviour of some Solicitors in the process of corresponding with you and in trying to gauge the strength of your feelings is sometimes highly questionable and could be seen by some to be unscrupulous actions. From the Solicitors' perspective, they just want to win so if they cannot get you to react one way, they will try another.

## The Build up to Court

As you go through the process of defending your case, your opponents Solicitor will start to gather a lot of information to use in any case against you. Any form of litigation is a very expensive lottery and as a result, the opposing party and your Solicitor, if representing you will seek to gain any advantage they can to try and further the successful conclusion of a case. Bear in mind that the justice system in the UK is more opinion than fact and as a result, it is a Judges' opinion that will likely decide the outcome of your case. If a Solicitor can influence the Judge in any way against you, they will do so as it may be beneficial to the outcome of the case. This is particularly important to remember in matters concerning costs. Your opponents Solicitors will try a number of avenues to get information. This could include everything from credit checks to the employment of a private detective. The build up to the court process is extremely important and it is the preparation as well as the presentation of the information that is central to any court case.

## Tricks SolicitorsPlay- Time Pressure

The opposing Solicitor that is representing your neighbour or the Solicitor representing you will seek to put the other party under time pressure to try and resolve the matter and to get a reaction or settlement in their clients favour as soon as possible. They will generally set some form of deadline for you to answer their letters or to agree to a demand, whether this is a meaning full or arbitrary demand. They generally do this to try and force you or the opposition into a position where you panic and agree to their demands due to the perceived pressure as it is often presented as a one off opportunity. Typical scenarios where time pressure is employed are where a Solicitor will send a letter making an offer to limit or agree something with you. They will set a time and say that after the time the offer is no longer valid and it will be withdrawn from the negotiating table. This is utter rubbish and do not be fooled by it. Solicitors have to be reasonable and the fact that they have made an offer of something themselves is a start point and not an end point so consider this and if possible, always make a counter offer to determine their position as well. Unless you are looking for something to be resolved yourself or unless it is a court imposed deadline, do not be pressured by time.

## Solicitors Will Try to Discredit You

If your opponent or their Solicitor has the opportunity to paint you in a bad light they will do so as it will help their court case. The court process is a lottery and even if your neighbour does have a strong case, they still may not win in court. In order to increase the odds of winning towards their favour, your opponents Solicitor will try and show that you have been unreasonable towards them, that you have been obstructive to any reasonable offers they have made and that you are the aggressor in the case and that their client is the victim. To do this effectively the opposing legal team will most likely make false accusations against you or alternatively will take the smallest thing and will try and blow it out of all proportion, complaining at your behaviour at each every opportunity to the court. Because Solicitors know that the court is influenced by people's behaviour and that when a Judge is deciding costs, the Judge will look closely at pre-trial and the behaviour of both you and your legal team during the trial, any points that they can raise to show that you have been unreasonable towards your neighbour goes in their favour. If your opponent does try to discredit you at any stage, gather your facts and present them back to your opponent in a clear and objective manner. If you have any evidence to show that they are the transgressors and not you, then the likelihood is that they will either stop trying this tactic or they will do it infrequently as they are likely to get nowhere and in this case it can be detrimental to their outcome. A prime example of these sorts of tactics is where the author was asked to intervene in a case where a person received a letter accusing them of damaging their neighbours watering system and of creating a general nuisance to their neighbour. When it was pointed out that during the times that this neighbour was accusing the person of carrying out these actions the accused were not actually in the country and when the author suggested that they should get a Solicitor to threaten an injunction against this neighbour, the neighbour and his Solicitor stopped this underhand tactic and ceased all accusations. Their aim was to try and get their letter on the court record so that the accused person was seen to be the bad party in the dispute and not the neighbour who was taking the case forward to court.

## Solicitors Will Sometimes Bully You

One of the things that an unscrupulous Solicitor will do is try and bully you into writing or saying something that can be used against you or that can force you into making a reaction. The Solicitors will make an inflammatory accusation that is written in their usual spineless legalese which makes you react angrily For example they will make a threat or a series of threats that will appear to affect your case; however the threat will be false. They will state that if you do not answer or cooperate they will apply to the court to have you prevented from presenting your case to the court. There are a number of ways that they behave and their aim is to get you to take a stance. Once you have done this they can make their move. The more scrupulous Solicitors generally wait to see your argument before they react, however rest assured even they will attempt tricks to get you to react and state or change your position.

## Solicitors Can Lie, Cheat and Generally Mislead You to Win

Solicitors are supposed to be bound by a code and a set of professional ethics. There are, however bad ones who will be very loose with the interpretation of these codes and ethics at times. The way these codes are written are that they are so loose that you could drive a tank through them. Bear in mind that Solicitors are paid to win their case, however right or wrong it may be; bad Solicitors will not hesitate to do things that help their cause and win quickly. To some Solicitors this means that they are prepared to lie, or in their usual manner, make an untruthful statement that cannot come back on them, or they will make a statement that is not completely true as it is a distortion of circumstances or a situation. The typical words they use are "we are instructed that you did this or you did that…."By not stating who said what and when, there is no comeback on the Solicitor. This is a deliberate tactic as they are invariably trying to do something that is beneficial to them or to their clients. Another tactics they like to use is to focus on a minute detail in part of your correspondence or they will ask a meaningless question to divert you from a real issue or problem. They will try and make a big thing out of something trivial in order for you to focus on that, rather deal with something else. They will also withhold information from you until it is beneficial for them to release it and will likely raise the matter at the last minute with you or your Solicitor. Sometimes they will raise an objection to something in your defence or in your case and try and make something of nothing in order to force a reaction or alternatively they do this to try to get you to drop a certain element of your defence or case. Do not be fooled by this and stick with what you feel is the best course of action.

## Tricks With the Trial Bundles or Evidence

If you have not managed to resolve your issues before your case comes to trial, it will be necessary to prepare trial bundles for the case. The trial bundles are the documents that assist you in the case and they are the documents that you will use to rely upon in court. It is the responsibility of the party that has brought the case to the court to prepare the trial bundles. Trial bundles are the documents and evidence that will be relied upon in the proceedings and so they must be prepared properly in advance and they must be indexed so that they are reference able and easy to review and find during the trial. Both parties must cooperate in the preparation of the bundles and both parties must agree on their content. When preparing the bundles you must give the evidence and information that was disclosed to the County Court or Tribunal in your skeleton argument or in any follow on request for the inclusion of documents that you will rely upon in County Court or in the Tribunal. If you have new evidence that you would like to include, then you must obtain permission from the court or the Adjudicator to include the documents or evidence. When you submit your documents for inclusion in the trial bundle the opposing party will either agree or disagree them and will normally include them in an index within the bundles if agreed. If you want a document included while the other party objects to its inclusion, you will need to seek the opinion and permission of the Judge or Adjudicator for them to be included in the trial bundles.

Solicitors and barristers are supposed to be exemplary in their behaviour however experience has shown that some are not. Sometimes the opposition can include documents that may have a bearing on your case within the trial bundle that you may not have seen or agreed to. When preparing and agreeing trial bundles make absolutely sure that the documents being introduced into the bundles are as per the list of disclosed documents that were listed by the opposition and that were agreed by the Judge or Adjudicator and make sure that you have seen a copy of the documents in question well before the trial. If the documents are different in any way bring it to the attention of the Judge or Adjudicator straight away. A key example of this observed by the author was in one case where there was a boundary dispute and there was very little evidence apart from historical documents to show where the real property boundaries were. Because of this lack of evidence, the aggressor in the case did not have a good argument and had little information to back their claim. When it came to trial, hidden away within their trial bundles was the official land registry copy of the title plan for their property. This document as disclosed to the person defending was just reflected as copy plan 12345, which they already had in their possession. The aggressors' copy of the same plan however had trace marks that showed new boundary lines and miraculously, they were the only people with this map. When the matter was raised to the Judge, the Judge ignored it, however the aggressor made constant references to this title plan map and it was the corner stone of their case. Its origin and authenticity was dubious, however as the defending party did not check the trial bundles, the Judge allowed it to be used.

The other tricks that barristers and Solicitors play is that they will put you on the spot during the case or any case management hearing and will ask if you have any objections to them taking a course of action or in pursuing a line of questioning in an attempt to introduce evidence in addition to the trial bundles. If you agree with them, then they will introduce the evidence and there is nothing you can do about it. If you object at any stage after this, then this will show you in a bad light. If you disagree at the outset then they will try and show you to be a bad person, generally they will do this to destroy or bring question on your character. In either case raise it to the Judges' attention that the opposition are trying to introduce new evidence without permission or agreement. If they try and make an issue of it, point out that they have not disclosed the document or that you do not know the reasons for their questions and point out that it should not be considered any way by the court without further analysis or your agreement. As an example of this, the author observed a particularly bitter neighbour dispute at a trial where the aggressor was claiming that their neighbour was always harassing, threatening and intimidating them. This was untrue and on a number of occasions the aggressor had made threats to their neighbour. At the trial, the aggressor brought in a number of character witnesses to show that she was a good person. When questioned in the trial about her behaviour she denied that she was the aggressor and said that she never swore, got angry and never made threats. Their neighbour said otherwise and had secretly recorded this person via video camera doing exactly the things that she denied she did. In the trial, the defendants' legal team asked the aggressor directly if they had ever undertaken this type of bad behaviour. The aggressor denied that they had and the defendants' legal team immediately asked if this person had any objection to the showing of a video of them that was not mentioned within the trial bundles. This person was now very much on the spot as they had denied their behaviour. If they refused or objected to the screening of the video, then they would be seen to be untruthful. If this person allowed the screening of the video, then they would be destroyed. In either event it would have a direct bearing on the case. In this particular trial, the aggressor was so arrogant that they let the video be shown. It clearly showed her doing the very thing she denied doing and as a result, this person lost their case and all costs were awarded against her.

## Be Very Careful What You Say and How You Say It!

Everything you say before and during the trial can go for you or against you in court. This means that every piece of correspondence that either you or your legal team write has a value and it will either help or hinder your case at a trial. You must consider this fact every time you write or say anything to your neighbour or their legal team as the wrong words or tone can come back to haunt you later in the trial. Do not say anything to anyone, be it in a written or spoken manner that can harm the outcome of your case. Trivial things also matter when it comes to a trial and so trust no one but your immediate family with any information that could be harmful to you. In a court case you have very few, if any friends. The author is not suggesting that you are untruthful or that you withhold any evidence. You just need to be careful as events and information are open to interpretation and if wrongly Judged or presented, information can go against you.

If you receive any letters that are asking things about your dispute or case from your neighbours' legal team or if defending themselves, your neighbour, you must answer and acknowledge these letters but give the writer of the letter no information that could be used against you in a negative way. Therefore you must always be polite and factual in your correspondence with the other party.

## Check List

You have no legal obligation to correspond with your opponents Solicitor or your neighbour, however in not doing so you could be seen to be unreasonable. Ask if your opponents Solicitors or your neighbor are being unreasonable themselves? Are they sending letters that do not relate directly to your case? If so write to them and state that you will cease all correspondence if they insist on harassing or bullying you.

Record the exact details of any tricks that they play. You may not be able to prevent their tricks, however if you come to trial or to a costs hearing and the costs Judge is made aware of their behaviour it will be highly likely that their costs will be disallowed due to their behaviour. Record all behaviour and bring it to the attention of the Judge at your earliest opportunity.

If your opponents Solicitor misbehaves at any stage, bring it to the immediate attention of the trial Judge if you are at that stage or complain to their legal practice if before. If you are not at the trial stage when the behaviour starts then when it comes to the trial stage request permission for your opponents pre-trial behaviour to be taken into account when considering costs.

If all else fails, do not get sucked into the Solicitors game as they deliberately try to provoke anger and reactions. Do not rise to it and do not take a strong stance against them as this is exactly what they want to achieve. You can generally bring their behaviour to the attention of the costs Judge after the trial and these Judges normally take a very dim view of poor behaviour. Ultimately it will cost money to the Solicitor or your opposition although this may be little comfort if you have lost your case and are facing a very large legal bill. Any saving you can claim is worth getting however so make sure you have it noted.

## Complaining About a Solicitor

You can submit your complaints about Solicitors to the Law Society or to the Solicitors Regulatory Authority after you exhausted all possibilities of trying to resolve the matter yourself with the Solicitor you have a grievance with. However be prepared to receive no result at all to your satisfaction as the Law Society and SRA (and in fact the Bar Council for the complaints about the Barristers) appear to be more interested in protecting their own people than in genuinely solving an issue with one of their members. The author knows of people who have contacted the SRA on two occasions and these people got nowhere with a legitimate compliant. Because the SRA have no jurisdiction over negligence, as that is in the hands of the insurers, they are loath to get involved even though the majority of complaints to the SRA are about negligence in the first place. The website address of the SRA is in the appendix at the end of the book.

# Barristers

Barristers are an interesting breed of people and generally come from a different background to that of normal people. They are difficult to identify with and will have very little in common with you if you have not touched upon them before, or if you have not moved in their social or business circles. Barristers are generally not easy to communicate with and unless you either speak Latin, or appreciate Shakespeare's' sonnets or some obscure form of art you have very little chance of understanding them or what they are talking about and there will be little chance of them understanding you. For any Barrister reading this who does come from a different background to the majority of Barristers', you are one of the few and should appreciate what the author is writing about.

## Duties of a Barrister

The duties of a Barrister originate from the roots of the legal system whereby a Solicitor would deal with your legal issues on a day to day matter and a Barrister would deal with issues where a specific opinion in law, articles or proceedings needed to be drawn or a representation was required in court. As the legal system has grown, the system for Barristers has remained largely the same with the exception of the recent introduction of the direct access scheme. As it stands today a Barrister can consult with a Solicitor or individual if he or she is employed by that Solicitor or individual, he or she can represent the person with the case in court, however the Barrister cannot write to the opposing party and cannot serve any court related papers or documents on the court or the opposing legal team. Therefore if you employ a Barrister, the other activities mentioned above would generally be dealt with by the Solicitor you employ or if you employ a Barrister directly, these activities must be undertaken by you.

# Contacting a Barrister

There are two ways to contact a Barrister.

1.    Via the Direct Access Scheme

2.    Via a Solicitor

## The Direct Access Scheme

Within recent years it has been recognised by the courts and the government that the costs of litigation, as well as the volume of litigation are on the increase. When this is compared with the great imbalance between the parties who can afford their own legal representation and those that cannot afford any form or minimal form of representation, the government decided to try and make the law more accessible to all parties. The result of this drive for accessibility to allow for reduced costs and to allow lay people to deal with Barristers directly was the Direct Access Scheme.

The introduction of the Direct Access Scheme means that if you need to engage with a Barrister you can now contact them directly without the need to involve a Solicitor and the Barrister can represent you directly in defined matters relating to your case. There are advantages and disadvantages with the employment of a Barrister directly. The advantage is that you can save some money by fulfilling the role of a Solicitor yourself. You can request the Barrister to undertake various activities on your behalf and under their license, they are allowed to undertake specific actions to further your case. The Barrister is able to advise and steer a course of action for you and to give you a written brief or opinions, however the scheme is not that good as the Barrister cannot do simple tasks like write letters on your behalf, or lodge documents with the court or prepare documents outside of their court engagement. The major disadvantages with the Direct Access Scheme are that the current rules prevent a Barrister from corresponding directly with the opposing party and unless you place someone between the opposition and yourself, you have a difficult road ahead of you as you must do this yourself. Barristers can represent you in court and can create opinions and guide you down most of the path that you need to take when going to trial with a case however. The majority of Barristers are not easy to get on with as they tend to tell you their opinions and in many cases these opinions may not be what you want to hear, Barristers generally try to be objective and will advise you of your chances of success in a case. If they are reasonable in their role, the Barrister should review your case looking at the strong points as well as the weak ones, and they will give you a legal opinion and guide you through the next steps. The Barristers first port of call should be towards guiding you towards mediation and a form of settlement outside of a court case. If your grievance goes to court and a trial is presented before a Judge, then the results are a lottery as to the ultimate outcome as it will be dependent on the mood and opinion of the Judge as well as dependant on the substance of the case. If your Barrister sees negative elements in your case, then the likelihood is that a Judge would see negative points as well. Therefore even if it is the last thing in the world you want to hear, a Barrister will still advise you of your chances of success or failure and so you should still listen to your Barrister and think carefully about your future course of action after he has delivered his or her opinion.

## How to Choose or Engage With a Barrister

There are several easy ways or methods you can use to engage with a Barrister. The first and easiest way is to take a look on the web. The first URL you should navigate to should be the web site of the Bar Council. The Bar Council holds a list of all current and practicing English Law Barristers in the UK and it generally gives their chamber details. The Bar Council also hold details about the specialisms of their members and so these are other search variables to consider. After looking at the Bar Council web site, or even after phoning the Bar Council so that they can advise you, look up the name of the Barrister that has been found or recommended on the web. Find their chambers and look at the details around them. Find out what their other chamber members are doing as well as considering the profile of the practice of their chambers. Look at the profile or CV if it is on the site for the Barrister and look to see if the Barrister or his chambers are doing things in the area or the subject that you need legal assistance in. Most Barristers will have a single or multiple specialism's and if they are reasonable or good at the job that they do, they will also have a track record of the cases that have been of note during their career or they will be able to demonstrate good knowledge of their chosen legal field. If you can afford the expense, try and hire a Barrister who has a track record of either writing or lecturing about the subject area where your problem exists. This person should also have full trial lifecycle experience and this should be clearly demonstrable to you. Before you engage with a Barrister, talk to the person in question over the phone or send him or her (or to their Clerk) an email with your request or questions, although Barristers tend not to give you too much free advice, try and ask some questions of them and see if you can get along with them from their answers to your question. If the Barrister is not open to a conversation, or if you feel uneasy about the Barristers' responses, go to another Barrister and try that person instead. Remember there are a good number of Barristers out there looking for employment and the direct access scheme has created an open market so there is competition. Therefore you do not have to settle for the first Barrister you see or visit.

## How a Barrister is Likely to Work Under the Direct Access Scheme

Not every Barrister works on Direct Access Scheme. If you can find a Barrister that you want to employ on the scheme, they will want an outline of the case or the problem when you first engage with him or her. They will ask for this as it will set the foundation for understanding how much effort they need to put into the work request and in how much billing they will need to ask from you. In order to get this outline the Barrister will request the following of you at a minimum.

1. They will want to spend several hours with you face to face to get an understanding of what you want from them.

2. Will want to know what the case or issue is between you and your neighbour

3. They will ask what you have done so far and what advice you have already received as well as asking you if you have been given an opinion previously or if you have employed someone in the past on your behalf.

4. The Barrister will review all relevant correspondence between you and the opposing party.

5. The Barrister will review all correspondence from the other sources involved in the case, This means looking at evidence, witness statements, title deeds, photographs, statutory declarations, and official papers etc.

6.    The Barrister will then give you a high level or outline opinion of your chances of winning or of losing your case.

Before your meeting you must prepare a folder for the Barrister to review and if not talking immediately face to face, make sure the folder has a covering letter summarising the issues, events and also give a chronology of the case. Your brief should include all the copies of evidence and the documents, official papers, correspondence, photographs etc. that are relevant to the case.

When a Barrister gives his or her opinion he or she will generally suggest a course of action for you to take. He or she will assess the case and will tell you their view on the percentage chance you have of winning the case in court. If the percentage of winning is less than sixty percent do not insist on pursuing your case straight to court without serious consideration of other methods for settlement. If your Barristers opinion is not very high or is up to sixty percent, try and engage your Barrister to assist with other methods of case settlement such as Alternative Dispute Resolution or mediation to resolve the case with minimal damage to you. If your Barrister thinks you have a weak case, they will advise you of this and will generally suggest a settlement anyway. If you have a reasonable or a strong case they will make other suggestions as a part of their delivery of their opinion. These other suggestions could include the creation of a more in depth study of the technical issues around your case and a will then seek to use this study information to give a more formal opinion as well as prepare a case for trial. Once the additional information or output from the study has been created they will generally ask you what you want to do next with your case. If you really want to go to court, then they will create the papers for you to issue to the County Court or the High Court to enable the court proceedings and process to begin. Again if your Barrister is reasonable, they will advise you to keep an open channel to the opposing party to allow for a form of settlement at any stage, preferably before it goes to court.

To summarise a reasonable Barrister should:

1.    Listen to you and what you have to say. They should hear and understand what the issue or case is without you having to constantly repeat the same points again or without interrupting you.

2. The Barrister should give a professional opinion based upon the percentage reality you have of success.

3. The Barrister should always advise you of mediation or negotiation as early as possible within the proceedings so that you can avoid unnecessary fees or stress due to the court process.

4. The Barrister should ask how you wish to proceed with your neighbour dispute and even if you insist on pursuing your case because of your subjective or negative views, they should advise you to settle the dispute as early as possible instead of escalating it into a full blown court case.

5. The Barrister should give you a more in depth written legal opinion.

6. The Barrister should prepare papers for the pending court case if these are needed.

7. A Barrister should be considerate towards your needs and should understand that the case being presented by you is rather emotional for you as it is a personal matter and not one represented through a Solicitor and you are not legally trained to understand the matters or jargon presented by a Barrister.

8. A good Barrister should inform you of what they are thinking or doing at every step especially before making major decisions that can affect the case outcome.

9. Barristers should encourage you to keep an open channel to the opposing party or their legal team to ensure that you can reach a settlement to minimise any damage to you as the case proceeds.

10. Barristers should consider your needs and protect your interests and rights at all times.

## Barristers Attitudes

Most, if not all of the Barristers that the author has come across have been very direct in the advice they have given to their clients. The majority of these Barristers had a poor bed side manner and when this is combined with their directness and overall attitude to their clients, their approach added to the communications difficulties between their clients and themselves. These Barristers will generally look at a case and come up with an answer that may or may not meet your wants and needs. Most will take a prudent approach to their opinion and so will give a pessimistic or worse case view as well as a reasonable case view. When you formally engage a Barrister they may also look to take the non-contentious route to a solution which may not always work in the long run. This is because you may end up giving away a lot more than your opponent just because your Barrister wanted to settle the dispute early or wanted to mitigate any perceived exposure you may have. The advice a Barrister will give will usually be aimed purely at the matter at hand and will hardly ever consider the edges or a broader perspective apart from the legal one. An analogy to think about is that most Barristers are like a production line surgeon dealing with cancer patients. They will listen to the patient to understand the particular problem;they will come up with a diagnosis, no matter how painful or emotionally damaging this is to you as a patient and will then seek to remove the offending cancerous lump. This removal is seldom done with an anaesthetic and is very painful and will leave a scar. After removing the lump they will tell you that it was for your own good, they will be happy with their work and then they will pop off for tea, leaving you to deal with the consequences of the surgery and will require you to apply your own dressing. For the most part a Barristers approach generally only deals with the disease and they are not trained to consider the pain and the anguish nor the symptoms of the neighbour dispute or legal problems you have. Empathy is not a word that has been observed to be in use by the Barristers the author has met nor has it been observed as being in a Barrister's vocabulary let alone as being seen in their actions. Empathy is a skill that needs to be developed by Barristers and as most deal only through Solicitors; they are very much isolated from the problems of their end clients. It is a skill and an attitude that is not taught by the universities or when undertaking their training with a chamber. Serious consideration should be given to this training however as it will make life a lot better for many people if they were to receive it. Moreover it may even see more disputes ended sooner as the human elements are considered and explored.

## Working With a BarristerThrough a Solicitor

If you engage with a Solicitor to manage your case, they will deal with the Barrister on your behalf and so the above described situation is unlikely to occur directly. Before engaging with a Barrister, the Solicitor will have a good understanding of the issues, problems and general legalities around your case and should have already advised you of the best course of action to try and limit any damage or legal action from the opposition. When a Solicitor first engages with a Barrister they will either be seeking an in depth opinion on the chances of success of your opponents case or will be seeking the preparation of a case on your behalf. When you are looking at a case, remember that barristers are not the fastest working individuals in the world and so will take their time in reaching an opinion or in preparing papers. Bear this in mind as it can take from several weeks to several months for them to give an opinion or for them to prepare papers, depending on their work load and on how much their services are in demand.

After the Barrister has prepared their opinion they will give you a percentage understanding of your chances of success or of failing in your case. Do not be surprised if the Barristers opinion differs with your Solicitor's initial assessment of your chances of success. The Barrister will have taken the time and will have looked at the issues from a matter of case law and from an in depth legal perspectives as well as their knowledge from dealing with the types of cases you are seeking an opinion upon. Good Solicitors generally have a broad depth of knowledge; however they are not specialists in some matters of law, whereas Barristers tend to be more specialised around the cases they present and defend and in their knowledge of their chosen legal subject. By working together, the Barrister and Solicitor will generally come up with a well-rounded defence or if you are taking action, case against your neighbour. If you work directly with a Barrister and choose not to employ a Solicitor, not all of the issues that you have around your case may be considered as they are specialists and not generalists and so some of the peripheral considerations may not be on their radar.

After the Barrister has finished preparing their legal opinion, your Solicitor will seek to advise you of the best course of action against your neighbour. Even if the Barristers and Solicitors opinion says that you may have a high degree of success in fighting and winning your case, you are still not guaranteed to win in court. There is absolutely no certainty in both County Court and Tribunal cases so you must always look to the County Court or Tribunal as the last and final alternative to resolving a dispute. From a legal perspective you could have a perfect case and could lose the case in the court, simply because the Judge did not like you or because it was not presented in a structured manner. Put simply the court is a lottery where the odds are not in your favour.

If you decide that you want to go ahead with a court case after receiving an opinion, then the next step you need to take is to prepare court papers. In essence this is the foundation of the legal claim that you have against your neighbour, or is the foundation for defence. The papers will give an outline of your case and will also discuss the proposed remedy that you wish to be given solve the problem between you and your neighbour. The Barrister will normally prepare these papers on your behalf and the Solicitor will lodge or issue the papers to the court once they have confirmed that you are happy to go ahead with the case. In the process of the preparation of these legal papers, the Barrister may ask to interview you, they may ask to see the area where you have the problem or may ask for further information around your case. This could include you providing photographs, letters and statements to the Barrister. The Solicitor will normally act as the intermediary between you and the Solicitor and so will generally arrange for any meeting that you need to hold with the Barrister. When you meet with the Barrister, he or she may ask you a series of penetrating and hard hitting questions around your case. These questions will need to be answered by you as they could either come up in the case or will need to be included or excluded from it. The Barrister's principle job in this situation is to prepare the best case for your defence or prosecution and to advise you on the best way to proceed so that you can win it

## Complaining About a Barrister

If you have a complaint about the behaviour of a Barrister or the service that they have given you, you can submit your complaints about them to the Bar Council Standards Board. Although this organisation is supposed to be the custodian of the standards for Barristers and is the de facto authority on their behaviour and ethics, you will most likely receive no satisfactory result as the authors experience has shown that the Bar Council aims to protect its own members or to limit their liabilities or exposure. The Bar Council will investigate any issue you have and will come to a conclusion. If this conclusion is against the Barrister, then they can force the Barrister to take a particular course of action to remedy the complaint. If you wish to contact the Bar Council, they can be contacted on the following URL *http://www.barstandardsboard.org.uk/complaintsandhearings/*

# Judges

Judges are interesting individuals that are supposed to be appointed because of their knowledge and integrity. They are also supposed to be experts in their field and should be seen to be exemplary in everything they do. Of the many Judges that the author has met both personally and professionally, these Judges may have had knowledge, but only one or two had some form of real integrity. The others the author has met have come across as opinionated, arrogant and prejudiced in their approach to many matters. The authors' observations of court cases and trials have been mixed where sometimes the outcomes have been balanced and reasoned and sometimes the Judges' opinion has been hard to understand or reason. When in court Judges have a limited period of time to gather and assess the facts of any case that is presented before them. If a Judge takes a dislike to you, their opinions can be negative towards you and so you have to be very careful not to upset the Judge and it is sad to say that this can happen in a number of ways. A fair Judge would look at the situation and would evaluate all of the evidence before them before venturing or forming an opinion, however as most Judges are recruited from the position of Barrister, they believe in a hierarchy and protocol even if they will not admit to it. In essence Barristers talk to Solicitors and Solicitors speak to the client. If you use a Barrister on the direct access scheme, then a Barrister will lower him or herself to talk to an end client and will be the key person speaking in court on your behalf. Most, if not all Judges at present have not been a part of the direct access system and so have not been employed directly by litigants and are either tied by the hierarchy that they are used to, i.e. they tend not speak to the end client as the end client is not worthy of their presence or alternatively they do not have broad life experience and so have limited knowledge of their clients wants or needs. Similarly most Judges seem tied up in protocol and do not understand in the cases of litigants in person that lay people may have not come across the court process and are not experts in the preparation or timely submission of court papers. Until such time as Judges have a broader and wider experience of people and their life in general, some Judges will be moody, opinionated, unbalanced and unjust. Again, this is a prime area to be considered when appointing and training a Judge as they need to be shown a broader perspective to be more considerate and better at their jobs. This will be beneficial where litigants are representing themselves or where balanced and unbiased viewpoints need to be given.

## Addressing a Judge

As a Judge is an officer of the court you must address the Judge respectfully. It is better to call the Judge sir or madam. When you first come across a Judge, if representing yourself you are better to introduce yourself and anyone with you formally. If you are being represented by a Barrister or other form of council, then your legal representative will introduce you and any relevant parties to the Judge. When answering a question or indeed if you are asking questions of the Judge or any party in court, try and stick to the point you are making and try and be succinct in your asking. Sadly many Judges are not patient people and so will not be too happy if you deviate or wander from the points that are relevant to your case or if you pursue a line of argument or reasoning they have already discounted or that they feel is not relevant. An interesting example was given to the author by a Barrister who was representing a client before a very senior Judge. The Judge got very impatient with the Barrister who was making a number of points. The Barrister responded to the Judges' complaint by saying that the points were relevant to the case. The Judge responded that ten weak points do not make one strong point. The Barrister was told to present his strong points and questions first and the Judge then stated he would then decide where to go from there. After presenting two points the Judge told him to stop and summarise his case. The Barrister did not win the case for his client at this trial and learnt a painful lesson from the Judge. Sadly many more Judges' are like the senior one at this particular trial and only consider the key points and not some of the other matters. Patience is not a virtue held by a number of Judges.

## Powers of a Judge

In a court the Judge controls everything associated with the proceedings and within the realms of the law can pretty much ask or demand anything of you or of any other person present as they want if it relates to the case or any matter at hand. This means that if you create a positive impression with a Judge, they will generally be reasonable in their dealings and will allow you to be heard. If you create a poor impression then they will be hard and will interpret things against you and can order that you only speak when spoken to and in the harshest of cases can make decisions without your input. The author, having observed several Judges has seen them try and assert their authority right at the beginning of a case to test each party as to their reasonableness and fairness. If a Judge does this to you, remain calm when addressed, be respectful to the Judge and to the other people around you and try to focus on the issue that the Judge has presented to you. Judges have immense powers and can decide what you can and cannot say, what you can and cannot use as evidence in a case and they will decide what points of law you can use in your prosecution or in your defence during the court proceedings. If they have a negative opinion of you, the use of this power can go against you and sadly you cannot do anything about it unless you appeal. Even if you do appeal their defence is concrete. For you to get the Judges' decision overturned you have to prove that the decision is not within their powers or you have to prove that the Judges' decision was so wrong that another reasonable person with those powers would not make the same decision. This is almost impossible to prove so very few appeals to Judge's decisions are successful. Judges are not accountable in the UK and because they are who they are, and because they know this they can use the rules either for or against you. The authors view is that Judges need to be independent to allow for the law to work properly. Everyone however must be accountable for their actions and this accountability must include Judges and any other public or civil servant.

## Annoying a Judge

Most Judges are appointed to their positions because they are senior members of the legal profession. They are selected from the ranks of senior Solicitors or Barristers and are meant to have a wide breadth of experience as well as a good depth of knowledge in key areas of the law. Some Judges do have the necessary breadth of experience from a legal perspective; however most do not have a lot of experience when it comes to dealing with real people who work five days a week or in dealing with people outside of their perceived view of their own legal world. As a result, Judges can and will form an opinion of you very quickly if you do not conform to their preconceived views of the world or if you do not follow their expected protocols or show them the level of respect they expect for their position. An example that the author came across with regard to the above was when a Judge ordered a person at a trial to employ an expert and to provide evidence from this expert. Although this in itself is not an unreasonable request, the Judge failed to take into account that it was nearly Christmas and the employment of an expert with the two weeks to go before the holidays was extremely difficult and the Judge also did not take into account the financial position of the people he was making the request to nor of the profession of the people concerned as it was their busiest time of year work wise. The end result was that the order was not completed on time and the Judge penalised that person for not complying, even though the order was unreasonable given the circumstances of the person involved. The Judge however thought differently.

The upshot of the majority of a Judges outlook is that it is very easy to annoy a Judge and as a result, even though they are supposed to be independent and neutral towards individuals and are supposed to consider the case on its merits and in accordance with the law, Judges can take individuals into account and as a result, you can be placed in an awkward position due to their bias or their poor perception of you. This is a very difficult situation to deal with and the authors' observations are that some Judges will change their decision or verdict based upon their own prejudice rather than on the facts of a case if they have been annoyed by an incident or by trial behaviour. Even though you may think that the person hearing your case is supposed to work in the favour of justice, he or she could be opinionated and so you will need to be very careful in how you address or deal with your situation in the court, particularly if you are a litigant in person or if you have limited funds available for your defence and have a legal team with no experience in the matters being tried or heard in the court.

## Case Management Meetings

If you are a litigant in person and if you are representing yourself at trial, or if you have a legal team with strong feelings, then there are chances that you or your team will have a number of disagreements with your opponents' legal team, you may also possibly have a disagreement as to the case and any evidence or procedures that may need to be followed. To deal with cases where there are any points in dispute or that need to be agreed, the concept of the case management meeting was dreamt up and instantiated for court and adjudication cases. The aim of case management meetings are to deal with any disagreements and to prepare the case for settlement. The authors' observations are that an opponents' legal team will take any and all liberties that they can get away with because you are a litigant in person or will do so if you have a legal team that they feel is inferior, they will push the boundaries as far as they can take them. They will generally bully, send inflammatory letters and make accusations or will misrepresent the truth just to try and discredit you and you case and strengthen their own case. If your position deteriorates to the point where there is either little or no trust between you and your neighbours' legal team, then the Judge hearing the County Court case or presiding over the Tribunal hearing will request a case management hearing where they will attempt to eliminate the trivial issues between you and your opponents and will seek to resolve the problems between you and the opposition. This of course is a good idea but it never happens in reality and the case management meetings are generally used to set the dates for the hearing instead. If the Judge presiding over the case management hearing is a reasonable and fair person, they will seek to get both parties to reach an amicable resolution before the case gets to trial and will point out some of the considerations for your case as you go forward. Examples of this could include suggestions as to methods of mediation or dispute resolution or they could include directions to ensure an outcome such as the appointment of an expert or to ensure the inclusion or disclosure of documents that are relevant to your case. If you are requested by a Judge to attend a case management meeting and if the Judge is not interested in discussing mediation voluntarily you should mention that you wish to settle the dispute and should request the Judge to intervene at that point to assist in the settlement of the case once for all. This may be your last chance to undertake mediation so make sure you use it and request it to be considered by the Judge. If the other side have so far been unreasonable, the fact that you have requested the Judge to consider it in his directions could force the hand of the opposition as it would be a consideration for costs if they refused mediation.

## Judges' or Adjudicators' Directions (Order) and Decisions

A Judge or Adjudicator can be requested by either party in a case to make directions (instructions for parties to undertake certain actions or provide information) at any time before or during the trial. Directions are normally issued in the form of a written statement signed by the Judge and sealed by the court and they include what is required of you, what you must do and when you must do it by. The normal start date for directions is either the date that the document is sealed, the day after the date on the direction or on a day as specified by the Judge. Failure to comply with a direction can have serious consequences on your case and can lead to sanctions or penalties if the Judge believes your non-compliance was deliberate or malicious. If you are unsure of a direction or order, seek clarification from the Judge as to what he or she requires and if necessary seek an extension to the time that has been given to allow for you to fulfil the requirements set out within the directions. When directions have been completed by the parties involved in the case the Judge normally makes a Decision which then becomes an Order and it then becomes a key element within the case. For example the Judge can decide to issue directions to you or your opposing party to disclose a document. The Judge will then decide if the document is to be included in the trial bundles. If the Judge believes it should be included they will order that it be included.

## Right of Appeal

You have the automatic right of appeal for any decisions that have been made by a Judge or an Adjudicator before, during or after a case. If you wish to appeal a decision you must ask the permission of the Judge whose decision you are appealing to see if they will allow an appeal. If they refuse your request, you can appeal this decision to the High Court. This sounds reasonable enough but the problem with the appeals process is that like the entire legal system it is weighted against you. It is highly unlikely that a Judge or an

Adjudicator will admit to making a mistake or that they have made the wrong decision and it is even more unlikely that they will reverse their decision or order. This leaves you with the only option of going to the High Court if their decision is wrong or unjust. If you do decide to go to the High court, it will cost two hundred pounds to issue the paperwork to the court for them to look at your case and before you do anything you must first request permission to appeal by writing to the court on the appropriate appeals form. This will be lodged with the court and at the same time you will need to pay the fee. Invariably the court will not question the decision of the lower court in their first reading of your appeal request and are highly likely to refuse permission to appeal. If they do this then the next step is to request an oral hearing where a Judge will listen to your grounds for appeal and will then make a Judgement as to whether your appeal has any real chances of success should a hearing be granted. If your case does have a chance of winning, then they will likely grant an appeal hearing for your appeal case to be heard. This however does not mean that you will win your appeal as the odds are stacked against you. Firstly your grounds for appeal must be rock solid and Judges and the opposing legal teams are masters at picking holes in the arguments and cases presented to them and more importantly if you do appeal a decision and get granted an appeal, there is an extremely low chance that you will be allowed to introduce any new evidence around your case to be included in the appeal. If you have lost your case or had a decision made by the lower court that is not in your favour, you may be unable to change the outcome with any new information you have acquired since the trial. You must only use the information and evidence supplied to the lower court as it was this information that was used by the lower court Judge to come to the conclusion that they did. This is not good news to you as it means that if the lower court made a decision based on past evidence and their decision was bad from an evidential point of view but right from a procedural point of view, you may still lose your appeal. Appeals are not retrials of the cases heard by the lower courts. They are a hearing to decide if the Judge or Adjudicator was right to make their decision based upon the information they had available to them at the time of the hearing. Appeals are a very costly process as they involve a lot of legal teams and for the average litigant in person, or person on a restricted or small budget the process and associated costs of appeal as well as the limited success rates of individuals in the appeal court make the appeals process yet another unworkable part of the UK legal system for people who do not make hundreds of thousands of pounds each year or who do not have large sums of money available to them to fight legal cases.

## Complaining About Judges

You can complain about the "behaviour" of a Judge if he or she has personally behaved badly towards you during a case. You cannot complain about their decision, or the way that they have handled your case or your hearing. Even if they have been harsh because they do not like you or they perceive that you are not a "good person", you will have a very difficult time in complaining about them as for the most part the Office of Judicial Complaints do not want to know. If you wish to complain about a Judges' personal behaviour and any comments they have made towards you, the Office of Judicial Complaints is the organisation that would deal with your complaint. The following URL gives you the forms and information that you need to complete to complain.

*http://www.judicialcomplaints.gov.uk/complaints/complaints_Judge.htm*

If you have an issue with the Judges "decision" and you wish to complain, there is nothing that you can do apart from appealing against the decision that has been made to either to the same Judge or to a higher court and both will cost you a lot of money to do. Sadly as previously stated, Judges are not accountable in the UK. It is sad to say that a biased and morally corrupt Judge can make a decision against you, can ruin your life and can wash his or her hands of your case and there is nothing you can do about it apart from appealing against that decision to the Judge or to a higher court. This is most likely to be refused because the Judge will either stick with their original decision or you will be referred to a higher court (The High Court) for them to decide. You can bet your life that your appeal to the High Court will be refused in the first instance and if you are lucky you may be given permission for an oral hearing to explain to the High Court Judge why you think that the Judge's decision on the lower court was at fault. The High Court however has a strong reticence to change the decision of a lower court.

Meanwhile the chances of a successful complaint about the Judges personal behaviour towards you being upheld are exceptionally slim. Therefore like the Tribunals service, the Office for Judicial Complaints is another great waste of tax payer's money and seemingly only exists to show that there is a hint of justice in the UK. The concept of "ordinary people's access to justice "is simply the biggest lie in the Judicial System".Unless you have enough money to pour into the legal profession to get them to represent you or unless your case is a criminal case where you may be entitled to receive free legal representation, then ordinary people in the UK have no access to justice. There is no help and assistance available to you. At the time of writing this book the system of legal aid was under review and due to the finances of the UK, it would seem that there will be further restrictions placed upon legal aid, thus this will place justice even further out of the hands of those that cannot afford it.

# Chapter 9

## Court Process

### Land Registry Adjudication and the Adjudicator to Her Majesty's Land Registry

*http://www.ahmlr.gov.uk/*

As an alternative to the County Court system or prior to the high court, the UK government recently decided to introduce the adjudication process as a means of dealing with the increasing number of boundary disputes and other type of civil cases in the UK. The adjudication process is relatively new to the UK and there are only a limited number of Solicitors or Barristers who have been involved with the adjudication process to a reasonable degree. The rules and procedures around the adjudication process are also evolving and so need to be revisited every time a case is brought. The adjudication process and procedures leave a lot to be desired and the guidance that is offered on the Land Registry Tribunal web site is sometimes incorrect, incomplete or misleading to lay people as well as to legal people.

The Adjudicator himself or his deputy Adjudicators are generally Barristers who have been appointed by the Ministry of Justice to oversee matters relating to land disputes and they have the appointed powers of a Judge. The Land Registry Tribunals Service is in essence a cost effective court set up by the government to deal with issues pertaining directly to land and land disputes. The adjudication process is supposed to be faster than the court process and was set up by the government to try and resolve land cases quickly, with minimum legal overhead and importantly for the government, as cheaply as possible as neighbour dispute cases are increasing not decreasing. Like all government departments or public bodies the Land Registry Tribunals Service is not without its problems. First and foremost it is understaffed and has very limited resources as a result. Secondly it is unresponsive and although it does have a governing set of principles and rules that is must adhere to, the Adjudicator or Deputy Adjudicators apply their own interpretation of these principles and objectives as they are not clear cut or decisive. The justice and the quality of service you get from the Adjudicator are therefore very much compromised as a result of this unclear interpretation.

As a new organisation it still has a long way to go to demonstrate its value to the ordinary person or to the legal system. At present the Adjudicator seems to be a clearing house for land disputes and it would appear that their measure of performance is how long the case has been on their books rather than measuring whether justice has actually been served. When the author made enquiries of the Adjudicator and their measurement metrics, he got very limited output of any meaningful information regarding performance, justice or the profiles of the people using the system. They were very good at stating how long it took to clear their cases and in detailing their case load and associated back log.

The Judges at the Land Registry Tribunal Service are like any other Judges in the UK. They are not accountable for their actions and as a result there are Judges employed there that do what they want rather than doing what they must do to serve justice. There are many areas within the Land Registry Tribunals Service that can be improved with a little thought and even common sense. The management team however seem to think otherwise and the Adjudicator to Her Majesties Land Registry appear not to be a learning organisation.

## The Land Registry Practice and Procedure Rules 2003

The Land Registry Practice and Procedure Rules are the governing principles that the Land Registry Tribunals Service are supposed to follow. These rules are a mix of CPR rules (Civil Procedure Rules) (The Rules that are used in the County Court and the High Court to make decisions and to administer the case) and their own rules. Resultantly there are differences in the way things are handled and dealt with by the Tribunal service and the way that the County Court service handles issues and process. For example the rules of evidence and disclosure are far weaker for the Land Registry Tribunal Service than they are for the courts. This can create issues around preparing and presenting a case particularly if your opposing side are playing tactical moves and are withholding evidence that could give you an advantage in your Tribunal case.

There are also particular rules within the land registry practice guide that relate specifically to the type of claim that you are making. For example if you have a boundary dispute and you are asking for a determined boundary application, then your behaviour before and during the tribunal process must be taken into account. If however your request is not for a determined boundary, then the Tribunal only needs to consider behaviour during the tribunal process and not before. This in itself is a major handicap as you can end up in an aggressive case that is not of your making where your neighbour clearly misbehaves before the trial, yet during it is well behaved. For example, take a hypothetical case example that is based upon a case that is well known to the author and assume the Land Registry made a mistake with the recording of your boundary. Suppose your neighbour was an opportunist and that your neighbour deliberately pushed his case to the court to try and make money on your land, or consider the scenario where your opposition flatly refused to negotiate prior to the hearing and has taken you to Tribunal. Even though you may have attempted to seek an amicable solution to the dispute, the Adjudicator would not take this into account if your neighbour was not seeking a determined boundary. All these issues, mistakes, and pre-action behaviour will not be considered at all by the Adjudicator and if your neighbour has altered the ground, moved the boundary, acted in an aggressive manner, committed assault or built a case so he or she can take your land against your will, this is all incidental. Put simply, if the opposition behaves well in the tribunal process, then if he or she has a good legal argument, and a good legal team, however wrong he or she is in taking their case forward, they are likely to be in a better position to win as prior behaviour is not a consideration. This is extremely bad news for you if you are in a position where the case is vexatious or not of your making and it is completely unjust as your neighbour is vindictive. Sadly the law makes no provision for all of this and of the Adjudicators the author has come across, they do not consider this either. If you have money and can fight a case, then you have a stronger possibility of winning if your past misdemeanours' are simply not considered. If you have no money and cannot fight your case with a strong legal team, you are unlikely to win substantially or to get a beneficial outcome without some form of damage to you. This is another area where the Tribunals need to change and behaviour must be a key consideration in all cases irrespective of the requested outcome.

## Tribunal Courts' Powers

The Tribunal has a lot of power and is in essence a substitute for the County Court. Tribunals mainly deal with civil law cases (Employment, Family, Land etc.). Their powers are not as broad but they can be far reaching in the area that they are empowered to make Judgement upon. As a result of this power in specific areas Tribunals can impose some far reaching actions and decisions upon you. Actions and decisions could include the redefining of your boundaries, making cost orders either in or against your favour and they have the power to impose punitive measures in the form of financial sanctions against you when the costs of adjudication are taken into account.

The Tribunal can also make orders against you and can order you to undertake or to cease certain activities. These activities could include disclosure of evidence or documents and the Tribunal can order you to comply with specific requirements that also have an effect. The consequences of not complying with the Adjudicators' orders can be broad and far reaching, however the authors' observations are that if you have the right representation you can break the rules, not disclose evidence and you can still win your case as the Adjudicator will allow it. The author has seen this happen at one hearing and the Deputy Adjudicator, by not dismissing this case outright, meant that the aggressor in the case could cheat, lie and deceive and be a winner for a good percentage of their case. Not only that, if the Judge is opinionated or weak, the aggressor can be awarded their costs and you can end up paying for them to win. Invariably if your opponents have not followed processes or directions there will be a form of a penalty, however it is unlikely that the penalty imposed by the Adjudicator will fit the crime (if they are even penalised at all!). Until such time as the rules change and stricter penalties are imposed on people for not complying with reasonable orders or for deliberately misleading a case or from withholding evidence, there is benefit for anyone with a vexatious mind set and a good legal team to pursue and win a case just out of spite. As always the legal system does not do anything to prevent this as it is the money that does the talking and not justice.

The Tribunal can make orders that are enforceable by law. These orders include cost orders, boundary determinations or awards of land if the case has involved adverse possession or a boundary rectification. The Adjudicators' powers and discretion are wide and both

Adjudicators and their deputies are not accountable for their decisions. This means that the Adjudicator can use his or her discretion generously to support one party and your only recourse of action if you are in opposition is to appeal against his or her decision. Because Adjudicators know that the odds of winning an appeal are stacked against you they wield this power unfairly like an axe. Unless the rules are reviewed and amended there is very little you can do about it. There is no doubt you can appeal against the decision to a higher court but the appeals process is costly and does not automatically stop the lower court process so you must ask for a "stay" if you want the decision of the lower court not to happen. You must apply to the Judge or to the Adjudicator to seek their "permission to stay or stop the decision or proceeding". In order to do this you simply put your points on a paper (in some cases you may complete a standard form) and state that because of the following reasons (your grounds), that you are seeking permission to stay the lower court process or decision so that you can take your case to a higher court for their decision instead. You are in essence saying to the Judge: "I do not like your decision; I want you to freeze this process and to allow me to have my case heard by another court".If you are refused a "stay" by the Judge you have only a limited time to appeal to the High Court to try and change this decision.

Similarly if you are not happy with the Judge's decision, be it a written or a verbal one, you can "appeal" to the Judge to ask them to reconsider his or her decision or if this is refused you can appeal to the High Court to get them to re-consider the Judge's decision. In any case your first action to start this process will be to apply to the initial Judge who made the decision to "seek permission to appeal".It is a very similar process as was explained in the previous paragraph. If you are granted permission to appeal then you should send your "appeal" and your reasons or grounds as to why you believe that the Judge's decision was wrong and any supporting legal case references (references from similar legal cases) and your other evidence (photographs, maps, formal correspondence etc). For you to be granted an appeal by either the lower court or the High Court you must have a good chance of winning your case in the appeal and even if the decision from the lower court was wrong or unjust, it is very difficult for a higher court Judge to countermand or change that decision. Appeals therefore are not generally successful and only a small percentage of them are successful. The estimated figure on success rate is somewhere in the region of thirty three percent. This means that roughly sixty seven percent of all High Court appeals fail. Yet again, the odds are stacked against you and if you have limited resources, this percentage chance of failure increases.

## County Court Process

The County Court process is more stringent and robust than the tribunal or adjudication process and there are better and clearer defined rules for dealing with dispute cases than in the Tribunal courts. The County Court has far too many rules however and these rules are predominantly based around the Civil Procedure Rules or CPR. There has been much criticism of the Civil Procedure Rules as they were introduced as a part of the Woolf Reforms and they fundamentally changed the legal system that had been in place for many hundreds of years. There is a view within the wider legal community that the CPR system and the Woolf reforms have failed fundamentally as they have given a great deal of added complexity and processes to the court system. From a litigants point of view these added procedures have not only increased costs and the time it takes for a case to be heard, the net result is that they have pushed the availability of justice out of the hands of those with a little money or no money at all into the hands of those with a lot of money. Most people earning a moderate income and those people who are not earning much money are simply not able to afford the fees associated with a court or Tribunal case and even though this extends to the adjudication system, this creates a massive imbalance. Resultantly it would appear that justice is just a word used by those in powers or within the legal system to justify their jobs or the exorbitant fees they charge.

The authors experience is that the Woolf Reforms where the Civil Procedure Rules were introduced are fundamentally flawed and they do not do what they were intended to do and so are desperately in need a thorough review. Take for instance the very first Rule (the king of all CPR rules) called the "Overriding Objectives". The Judge is supposedly to regard this rule above all rules to ensure impartiality, fairness, proportionally and justice in all trials that are held before them. These rules and the principles they are supposed to uphold are fantastic in theory; however in practice it allows the Judge to have a very high degree of autonomy to make a subjective decision as most outcomes are as a result of discretion. When these decisions are wrong, or where the Judge is opinionated or the prosecution of the trial has been unjust there is very little comeback on the legal system as Judges are not accountable in the UK and if you try and appeal a decision that has been made under these principles you cannot appeal the decision. You can only appeal as to whether the Judge was within his powers to make that decision and if so, did he or she omit or include something they should have or should have not within this decision making process. Due to the high degree of autonomy in decision making, it means that a Judge's decision is hard to challenge in both the lower court and in the Court of Appeal (High court) and it makes a complete mockery of justice if that Judge happens to be an opinionated twit. It throws a real problem to you if you have not won your case or if you have lost part of it and you are seeking an appeal in the high court as it is difficult to prove or disprove what the Judge was thinking at the time that they made their decision and you do not have a complete picture of the points or evidence they may or may not have taken into account in their decision making process.

In order to commence a case in the County Court you will need to create a case or a "prayer" that outlines the problem you have with your neighbour. In this document you will need to give your outline evidence as to the misbehaviour of the other party and will need to suggest a course of remedy. When you have presented this to the court, they will seal the document and will send it to the opposing party. The opposing party then has to decide if they are going to concede and settle out of court or alternatively they will need to decide whether they wish to fight their case.

If you receive a document from the court, you have only a limited time to respond and so as soon as you receive the document you must take the appropriate legal advice. Upon taking advice, you will need to present the court with your case and it will be presented in a similar format to the prayer as it will detail you grievance, your outline evidence and your required remedy.

If you decide to fight your corner, the court process will begin. If you decide not to fight your corner and to settle, you will either have to settle out of court and have the settlement recorded with the court, or alternatively the court will give an order for the prayer to be granted and any remedy that has been sought within it will be enforced by the court.

After you have issued your counter pleadings or case, you will need to wait until you receive a skeleton argument from the other side before you can present greater detail on your case. If you are forced down the court route, it is better to try and prepare your case in advance of getting your opposition's skeleton argument and if possible, try and employ an expert as soon as you can as their input and evidence will be highly beneficial to you. (Please see the chapters on witnesses and on skeleton arguments to get further information).

When the case comes to trial, it will be heard by a Judge in a similar manner to the way a Tribunal Judge would hear the case. The difference however is that the County Court process is better established and the court has greater powers. This means that if the case before them is malicious, vexatious or if the other party has misbehaved in any way, then they will be penalised for this. Moreover the court will take all behaviour into account before and during the trial. If the other party has failed to disclose any evidence, then the court has to power to order the party to disclose evidence and if it is found that the deliberate withholding of information has affected the case, then the transgressor will be penalised.

The County Court system is far better in many respects to the adjudication process and because of the rules of evidence and disclosure, it is always better to have a case heard in this court. Again, because the Judges in the County Court have a wider experience than those of the Adjudication Courts, they tend to be far more balanced and reasonable than the Judges that sit in the Tribunals.

# Appeals Process

## Lower Court or Tribunal

The decision of a Judge can be appealed after it has been given to both parties or alternatively you can appeal at any time that you are dissatisfied with a decision that has been made. There are strict time limits on when you can appeal a decision and these limits need to be checked with regard to specific rules for the court or Tribunal that is dealing with your case. The first point of appeal is to the Judge who made the decision the first case. Even if this Judge has made the wrong decision or if their decision is unfair or unreasonable, it is highly unlikely that the Judge who made the decision will overturn it. Simply put it is a rare person who will admit to a mistake; even if it is a mistake that will greatly affect your life. Although they are supposed to be of high moral character and good standing, most Judges will not admit they made an error and will refuse an appeal if they feel it is not warranted. Most do go through the process however of leaving it a few weeks before they say no just to make it appear that they have considered their decision. This on balance is very nice of them as they could have saved you the trouble in the first place.

The timing of appeals to any court needs to be carefully considered. As stated above there are strict time limits for an appeal to be requested and although there are many reasons you will need to consider when appealing to the court, time is of the essence so do not delay. Some Judges will allow an out of time appeal and as such you need to be mindful of this, particularly when in regard of the opposition. Although you may think that the court case is finally behind you, it can start up again on an appeal if the Judge has allowed it, whether it is in or out of time. This can cause you real heartache and many issues if you thought the case was all over and dealt with and you and your loved ones have tried to resume you lives.

When appealing to any court there must be good grounds for appeal and the Judge reading the appeal will ask the opposing side for their thoughts or comments on your grounds for appeal and they will generally ask for them to reply to the points you have raised within a certain time limit to enable them to appeal your request. An appeal can be made with regard to any decision given by a Judge of a lower court to a higher court at any time, however you are advised to ask the lower court for permission before you take your case higher as a number of test cases have shown that even though there were grounds for an appeal, by not requesting the lower court to have the opportunity to deal with the matter, you are increasing costs and lengthening the legal process. Therefore if your appeal fails you will need to decide whether you want to take it to the high court or whether you wish to walk away.

Most appeals do not get to an appeal hearing as they are generally settled before going to court. The costs of an appeal to the High Court are extremely high and you must bear this in mind when requesting your legal representatives to make an appeal or when doing this yourself if you are a litigant in person. It is extremely sad to say that the legal system is weighted in favour of those with money and so a usual tactic of anyone who has money and is engaged in litigation against you is to force you down the appeals process. By doing so they are entering you into a lottery that is not in your favour and they know how much you have to lose. Their principle reason for pursuing an appeal is to force you to pay more money to them. If the court rules in their favour it is likely you will end up paying their costs. High Court Judges and the judiciary as a whole know this fact, but do very little about it as their view is that they have to respond only on points of law. Morality, ethics and natural justice are things that Judges claim to take into account; however the authors' observations are that they very rarely do so or where these points are taken into account, the punishment for the transgressor very rarely fits the crime. This makes it easier for those who know the legal system to take clear advantage of it.

# High Court

## Written Appeal

When appealing to the high court the first point of approach is via a written appeal. This is written request needs to be presented to the court on a form N161 and this form details your reason for appeal. Along with this document you must also produce a skeleton argument, a very brief description of why you are requesting the appeal and this must be given to the court along withany material that you wish to be considered by the court. To lodge this form and skeleton argument with the court for their consideration, there is a fee of two hundred pounds to pay. Once this document set has been lodged and received by the court, they will seal the documents and will ask you to distribute them to the opposition in addition to the ones that you have lodged with the court. For an appeal to be read by the court and to be given to a Judge for a decision it takes around a month to three months of time depending on how busy the court is when you lodge your appeal. The chances of success in appeals to the high court are founded upon whether there has been a miscarriage of justice and whether you or your opposition have a good chance of success in overturning a decision based upon a point of law or a specific technicality. When reading an appeal the Judge reviewing will look at the position of the decision on balance and they will have access to no other material apart from the appeal document you put before them. With all written appeals there is a very good chance that it will be rejected by the Judge even if there is a good case to present before the court. If your appeal is rejected, then the next port of call is to request an oral hearing for you to present your appeal to the High Court Judge on a personal and face to face basis.

## Oral Hearings

A listing for an oral hearing normally takes around two months from the date of you requesting it to the date of the hearing taking place. When you get your hearing date you will need to rely upon the original appeal document that you sent to the court. You will also need your skeleton argument at the hearing and will also need to produce a document for the court that states in outline the points that you are going to cover orally at your appeal hearing. If you are receiving legal aid, you will also need to disclose this to the court as they need to know this. All of these documents will again need to be lodged with the appeal court and sent to your opposition prior to the hearing so that they can seal the documents and distribute them to the Judge before the hearing. It is the responsibility of the appealing party to send their appeal documents to the opposition. As a result, you can find yourself with very little time to review and respond to the court if you wish for something to be taken into account at an oral appeal hearing that is being heard for the other side.

When you have an oral hearing you will be placed in front of a single Judge who will hear your arguments as to why you should be granted an appeal and they will want to know on what grounds you are requesting your appeal. If you are appealing and are represented it is your Barrister who will be heard or if you are a litigant in person you will be asked to provide evidence and legal grounds for the appeal directly to the Judge. The opposition may or may not be present at this hearing but they usually are there to hear the proceedingsand the may also be asked to give oral evidence at the hearing. The point to remember is that if you are the person requesting the appeal, it is you that are going to be heard and not the opposition.

If the Judge finds that you do have good grounds for appeal hearing in the court, he or she will generally grant an appeal and will make directions for an appeal hearing to be heard in the High Court at a time to be agreed by both parties. Within the directions the Judge will state which grounds for appeal have been granted to you and will briefly state why the appeal has been granted. He or she will also make a request to the appellant (the person requesting the appeal) or his or her legal team to prepare a timetable for the case to be heard in the High Court. The chances of success in being granted an appeal at an oral hearing are quite high, and are estimated to be at around a sixty percent chance of success if it is presented correctly. The fact that an appeal has been granted to you however does not mean that you will win your case at the appeal hearing. It does however put tremendous pressure on your opposing party because; if you are successful in winning your appeal they will have to pay all of costs of the appeal and if the Judges' decision involves prior costs, they will have to pay them as well. The Judge can also order the other side to pay interest. All of these sums can be a huge amount of money and can be as much as one hundred thousand pounds to cover costs, damages and interest when they are all combined. Should an oral hearing be granted to the opposition it is advisable to start mediation with the opposition to see if you can reach a compromise as to costs as soon as the appeal hearing is granted to them. The longer you delay the settlement, the more costs the other side will incur and the more money you may need to pay them if they are successful.

## If an Appeal is Granted

If an appeal is granted you have a very short time to respond to the court with your view on the matter. Therefore you must know how you are going to deal with the appeal hearing in advance of receiving the notice and must have received advice before your response is give to the court and opposing party.

## Respondents Notice

Once an appeal order has been granted, you have fourteen days from the service of the order upon you to lodge your respondents notice with the appeal court on a form N164.The respondents notice should refer to the case number and the name of the Judge who has granted the appeal. The form should also detail what you want to be taken into account by the Judgeat the appeal hearing. This could include a request that the lower courts order be upheld for the same reasons as the decision was originally granted. It could be a request that the original order be upheld for a different reason than the one that was originally granted or alternatively you can make a request for a different decision to be made at the appeal hearing. With each or any one of these requests you must put your reasons in outline as to why the Judge should take your information or request into account. Similarly if you are asking for new evidence to be introduced or if you are requesting a directions order, you must also state this on the form. Once completed, the form must be lodged and sealed at the High Court who will then issue the copies to the Judge, and will seal your documents for you to issue to the relevant other parties. You must submit a minimum of three copies of the document at the time of lodging your respondents notice with the court. Do not delay in submitting the form to the court as it will go against you if the court does not receive it on time and you could find that you are not able to add any additional arguments or evidence to counter your opponents appeal if you do not meet the strict court timetable.

When you present your form to the court, you can also present a skeleton argument that outlines your case and the additional points you wish to raise. The form to use for this is the form N163. When the form N163 is presented to be sealed at the court there is a cost of two hundred pounds associated with it if it is not included in a respondents notice. Bear in mind that your opponent will also have a skeleton argument to present to the court as well. If your opponent has been granted an appeal, you will receive a copy of their argument first and you will then have twenty one days to build and present your argument to the court in order to counter their argument. If you have won an appeal hearing yourself, you or your legal team will need to present your revised skeleton argument within a reasonable timetable to the court, again this time is usually within twenty one days of the grant of the appeal unless the Judge states otherwise or unless you request permission for an extension of time and give a good reason for requesting the additional time for the preparation of your argument.

## Skeleton Argument

Once you have received your opponent's skeleton argument you will need to produce your own argument. The prime difference between this argument and any previous argument is that it will need to stick to the areas covered in your opponents appeal and will need to include any information you wish to be considered in your defence of that appeal. Some of the arguments that were discussed at the initial trial may not be included in the skeleton argument and you must bear in mind that the appeal hearing is not a retrial but a request for an outcome on a number of specific points or on a single point that is being appealed. If you are defending yourself you must try and focus on the defence of these specifics in their appeal as the outcome of the hearing will be based upon the original appeal request and the grounds that have been raised and agreed for the appeal hearing. Unless you can prove a different ground or alternatively can defeat your opponent's grounds for appeal, it is wise not to stray too far from the argument that has been presented to the Judge hearing the appeal. A point to remember in any court is that you can change your skeleton argument at any time; however there is normally a cost impact to doing this. There are also time limits to consider when changing your skeleton argument, particularly when you are close to the date of the hearing or trial as the opposition will need time to respond to it.

## Trial Bundles

It is the Appellants Solicitors' responsibility to produce the trial bundles for the appeal hearing. Before their production however you and your opponent will need to exchange a list of documents that you will be relying upon in court and that you wish to be included in the trial bundle. You will need to be mindful of this requirement as you may not be able to include any documents in the future hearing if you have not agreed them with your opponent first and you will not be able to include them if they have not been agreed by the court in advance of the hearing. If there are any documents that your opponent disagrees to or alternatively that you do not want to be included at the hearing but your opponent does, then these will need to be agreed by the Judge before the hearing if they are to be included in the trial bundles. If you do disagree greatly with your opposition, then you will need to produce your own trial bundle and will need to lodge the bundle with the court prior to the hearing so that they can be considered. When you lodge your bundle, you will need to justify why you need the documents to be included at the trial and will need to explain their relevancy to your case and you will also need to explain to the Judge why you were unable to work with the opposition to include these documents into the trial bundles that were to be produced by the other side.

# Chapter 10

## Cost Assessment Process

At the end of a court case or adjudication a verdict or decision (The Substantive Decision) will be made by the court and this will be followed by a cost decision. The Substantive Decision will tell you what the Judge has decided and if there have been costs associated with the trial, the costs decision within the Substantive Decision will tell you who will pay the costs of the trial. If you have been awarded costs at a trial, your opposition will need to pay you for all of your legal expenses associated with the trial. If you have lost your case, then generally you will have to pay all or some of your opponents' expenses that have been incurred as a result of the trial. In either event the amounts that may need to be paid are sometimes very large sums of money and if you have to pay the opposition because you have lost, it can have a major impact to your life as you will need to find the money to pay the court order within a very limited period of time, sometimes within three months of the decision being issued.

## Objections Before Awards

Before a Judge hands down a final decision on the costs of the case, he or she will seek representation from each party as to why each side should or should not pay the costs of the case. If you have not been awarded costs, you should detail why you as the losing party should recover your costs and why you should not pay the winning parties costs. After receiving the information from each party, the Judge will normally initiate the costs recovery and assessment process. At this stage the County Court Judge or Adjudicator can make a costs order or they will hand over the costs process to another Judge for them to decide exactly how much will be paid and by whom. This new Judge, the Costs Judge will then set a timetable for the exchange of a bill of costs and responses. If the costs are agreed, then the Costs Judge will sign a costs order detailing how much is to be paid by the relevant party. If costs are not agreed they will set a date for a costs hearing.

## Do Costs Follow the Event?

Traditionally the rule was that costs should follow the event has always prevailed when it comes to cost awards. This rule states that the winning party will always be able to recover their costs from the losing party in a litigation case or other form of court action. Although in some cases this may appear fair to the winning party, very often it is not fair for the court to enforce this rule. Examples of where this rule should be questioned are where costs that are unreasonably incurred have been claimed, or in vexatious cases (cases that should not have gone to court) or in cases that are totally disproportionate to the outcome. Other considerations for costs not following the event are areas such as where the winning party have not followed pre-action protocols, or have engaged in bad behaviour and have failed to consider negotiation. Where any of these areas are touched upon, there is a clear case for a reduction or elimination of costs. Lord Woolf recognised this and that the legal system was in need of reform and he made a series of recommendations to take into account the unfairness of the costs follows event rule. Resultantly the courts now view all of the above described areas more closely than before when they determine the award of costs to the successful party. In the past the winning parties were more or less assured of most of their cost recovery after successfully wining a trial, now however Judges can take many more matters into account than ever before when making awards and as a result, the legal system in relation to the proportionality and award of costs is becoming more balanced. It is still highly subjective and is open to interpretation by a Judge so even if your opponent does transgress at any stage and fails to follow the requirements set out by the court and wider society, there is still no guarantee that you will not receive a high legal bill if you lose your case. Wherever possible, you must record any of your opponent's transgressions and you should raise them with the court whenever necessary for you to do so. The most obvious place is during the costs process as your opponents' transgressions may have a direct bearing on the outcome of the costs decision.

# Cost Recovery and Assessment

## Indemnity Basis

Depending on the Judgement that has been given or jurisdiction of the court that has made the decision, the Judge making the award may give costs to you or your opponent on the standard basis or they may award costs on the indemnity basis. If the award is made on the indemnity basis then you will have to pay all of the costs that have been incurred by the opposition without assessment and the burden of proof as to what you should pay is always in the favour of the receiving party, or the person who has been awarded the costs. Indemnity is not generally used too often in court cases nowadays, however Indemnity costs can be awarded as a punitive measure against you if the Judge thinks that you have not behaved in a manner expected of you during your case hearing or if you have been vexatious in your case (have pursued the case with your neighbour out of spite).

## Standard Basis

If you have been awarded costs on the standard basis, then this means that all of the costs associated with the case will need to be assessed and agreed as a genuine cost that were incurred as a part of the trial or hearing before they are awarded to the winning party. Be aware that on the standard basis costs can be disallowed and if you have costs awarded against you, you will need to spend time going through the bill to see what you can have removed.

## Bill of Costs

The legal profession is geared up towards making the most money that it can out of the people that are using legal services and the bill of costs is another way in which both Solicitors and their associates can make even more money out of the people who have to pay the opposing parties bills. As the people paying are generally the losing party it is yet another sting in the tail for anyone who fights their corner in a court of law and loses. A Bill of Costs is a very old fashioned document that is normally completed by hand and then type written into a three column formatted document that lays out all of the costs associated with a court or legal case. The document is not only old fashioned, it is cumbersome and it needs to be signed by the solicitor who has had the bill drawn. The bill, the time taken to draw it up, the travel costs of the draftsman and of course the solicitors' costs are all chargeable. When any other organisation draws up a bill, it is seen to be a cost of business or of service. This is not the case in the legal profession. According to a Cost Judge this is not the same for the legal profession because the Solicitor who signs the bill of costs as being true could lose his or her license to be a Solicitor if the bill of costs is found to be incorrect. The author, having observed how seriously the legal regulators take their responsibilities with regard to complaints, this on the face of it is rubbish. Never the less unscrupulous Solicitors will likely act to gain as much as possible out of the process so you will need to watch what they do very carefully as some of the billing could be incorrect.

## Costs Draughtsmen

In order to determine the total bill of costs a Solicitor will look at all of his or her records regarding past billing and any outstanding payments due from their client, they will also look at payments they have made to experts and Barristers and any third party on behalf of their client and will then instruct a cost draughtsman to draw up a bill of costs based upon all of these expenses. A costs draughtsman will add all of these bills together and will index the costs by date and by values, by VAT amounts charged and will draw up a bill into a legally recognised format. If your case has been long and protracted, the costs process could take a long period of time to complete and could involve a lot of effort from the costs draughtsman in the production of the accounts. Bearing in mind these draughtsmen charge around one hundred and ten pounds to one hundred and thirty pounds per hour, the production of a bill of costs alone could run into several thousand pounds. Once completed the cost draughtsman will submit the completed bill of costs to the Solicitor who requested it to be drawn up. The Solicitor will then normally sign it and add another five hundred pounds or so to the bill because they are signing for its completeness and correctness and will have to review it. Once they have signed it, they will generally then send the bill to the opposition and will request their documented points in dispute. The points of dispute should cover all elements of the bill that you do not agree with.

## Points in Dispute

If you are the opposing party that has had the costs awarded against you, when you receive a bill of costs you will need to go through it in great detail, as there are likely to be things within the bill that do not relate directly to your case or that may not be chargeable by the opposition. There will be letters, telephone calls and expenses that will be unrelated or that that could be overinflated or added to the bill by mistake. You will need to check every letter and piece of correspondence that you have received from the opposing party to ensure that they are billing you for items that are purely related to the case between you and your neighbour and not for other things that may have happened before or after the case was concluded. Check the dates of the letters you have in your possession to ensure that they fall within any time limits set by the court and that they are inside of the court process or inside of the time or events that have been judged upon. For example with adjudication, all costs prior to or after the adjudication could not be charged at the time this book was written. Therefore make sure you know when your case began and when it ended as this information could save you a lot of money.

When you go through the bill of costs you will also need to look out for the following items as they are currently disallowed by the Courts and Tribunals so cannot be charged to you.

1.    Acknowledgements to letters that you have sent

2.    Photocopying charges

3.    Postage and courier charges (apart from fees for the trial bundles)

4.    Emails are not chargeable

5.    items that are unrelated to the case that you can show to be unrelated

6.    Items that are disproportionate to events. For example travel expenses for several hours of travel from an office only an hour from the court.

7.    Check any other item and make sure you are happy with them. If you are not happy with any item raise them anyway at the costs hearing and then explain to the court why you are unhappy with the item. They could disallow them and save you money.

## Solicitors Charging Rates

The author has seen very few Barristers or Solicitors that have been genuinely worth the extremely high fees that they charge. Their costs are normally charged to their clients based upon a fixed fee per hour of work. This fee is the broken down into six minute charging blocks that are then billed back to their clients. Because this six minute block is the lowest denominator from a billing perspective, unscrupulous Solicitors tend to charge this six minute block to their clients even if the work they undertake is for a lesser time period. This is extremely bad news to you as a client or a person who has to pay their bill as these six minute charges soon add up to a very sizeable amount. For a junior assistant or a legal executive you can look to pay around seventy pounds per hour for their time. The time of a junior Solicitor can cost you around one hundred and ten pounds per hour and a middle tier Solicitor can cost between one hundred and fifty to two hundred and twenty pounds per hour. A senior Solicitor or a practice partner can charge any fee that they want to charge or will charge anything from three hundred pounds to five hundred pounds per hour, sometimes even more if they can justify anything above this amount. They say that talk is cheap until you hire a Solicitor and this is very true. Every year a team of academics make a recommendation as to the charging rates they believe Solicitors should charge, depending on the area they reside within or the pay band and seniority they are in. The process of determining Solicitors charging rates is taken very seriously and the suggested rates are signed off by some of the senior law professors at some of the UK's most prestigious universities. These suggested charging rates are however no more than just recommendations and as such they are yet another worthless document produced by academics and legal professionals that have a vested interest in either justifying their existence or in increasing their importance. The authors observations are that Cost Judges do not take them into account at costs hearings unless there is a massive variance between the costs charged and the costs recommended. At one cost hearing the author observed a Solicitor had submitted an hourly fee that was twenty percent higher than the recommended rates for his band and grade. The costs Judge allowed his costs without question. If the Solicitor can justify the costs, then they have an opportunity to get away with them and these defeat the purpose of recommended fees.

## Barristers Charging Rates

Barristers generally work on a fee basis that are similar to the hourly rates Solicitors bill and they tend to charge at the higher end of the rates scales for juniors. If you want a Senior Barrister, it can cost up to a thousand pounds for a one hour conference. As an example of their high billing, if they work for more than one day on a trial for example they will demand a refresher fee. This fee is generally one thousand pounds plus just for them to attend the second day and to provide their opinions. They also charge for the day that they attend. The refresher is a bonus for turning up to work. The dubious pleasure of employing a Barrister to support your case will cost you many thousands of pounds and because of the way the legal system has been built, Barristers are generally the only ones who can speak in court with authority and they are also the people who prepare the papers for the court and who give specialised legal opinion. Solicitors tend to be more generalised in their knowledge and so with any serious case, you will always end up paying for the time of a Barrister as their specialist skills will be required at some stage of the court or adjudication process.

## Disbursements

Within the bill of costs you will see disbursements for expenses such as travel. When you look at your bill, you must make sure that these costs are proportionate to the events that have occurred and to the claim. For example if you receive a bill for travel expenses for a costs draughtsman and the travel claim is for a journey of several hours, yet the draughtsman has been employed to represent a firm that has its offices located only a few miles away from the court, then these expenses are an area where you can challenge costs as they are disproportionate. When looking at disbursements and expenses also look at the events that correlate to the costs being claimed. For example if there is a claim for several conferences between the Barrister and the Solicitor, then these need to be examined to determine if these conferences happened for a good reason and what their output was in the end. A prime example is where a Solicitor and Barrister hold several meetings and claim expenses for these meetings. A question to consider is whether the costs incurred were reasonable. If the work could have been completed in a short timescale or over the phone then these costs should not be charged.

## Strategies and Tactics for Reducing Costs

There are several tactics and strategies that you can employ to reduce your costs as they are assessed by a Costs Judge. Firstly you must demonstrate that you have followed all pre action protocols and the necessary legal processes and you must be able to show that you have been reasonable in your approach to the litigation between you and your neighbour. You must also demonstrate to the Costs Judge that you have been flexible throughout the trial process and that you have cooperated with everything that has been asked of you.

## Mediation

If you can show the court that you have made a suggestion of mediation or if you have been through mediation that it has failed, this will have an effect on costs. The courts now want to reduce their workload so if you can demonstrate that you have tried not to be a burden or that you have not taken the case forward to the court lightly, then the court should not penalise you for this. This should also be born in mind with your opposition. If you can show that they have not sought mediation, then this will have an effect on their costs and this should go in your favour.

## Letter: Without Prejudice Save as to Costs

If you can send a letter to your opponent making an offer on costs then this can be used when the court considers its assessment or award on costs. For example if you make an offer to your neighbour that you will accept fifty percent of the costs of the trial in order to settle and your opponent refuses, if the court awards the costs of fifty percent against you after the hearing, then you could request that your offer should be taken into consideration. The costs that were incurred after you made the offer were wasted costs and were a direct result of your opponents' refusal to settle. You could argue that any costs after your offer was made were not necessary and as such you can reasonably request that they should be borne by your opponent. You must also bear in mind that a letter that states without prejudice save as to costs can only be used after the Costs Judge has reached his decision and not before.

## Open Letters

An open letter can be a very powerful tool to fight legal costs. An open letter has no conditions attached to it. As the letter is an open to anyone to read, you can include an open letter into your correspondence or the trial bundles at any time you choose and it is extremely powerful if you make an offer on costs. By including an open letter it means that the Judge will have sight of your costs offer at the trial and during his decision making process. If your costs offer is a reasonable one, then it will most likely have a direct influence on the outcome of the Judges' costs decisions as he or she has direct evidence that you have not been unreasonable and that you have tried to settle costs before they have increased. If an open offer is made, then it is normal to lodge the funds associated with the offer within fourteen days with the court if that offer is accepted. You must bear this in mind as you must be able to pay your opponent when you make an offer. If you cannot pay immediately, then any delays in payment could be detrimental to you as it could show that you did not have the intention to honour the offer that you made and the opposition would highlight this to the Judge.

## CPR Part 36 Offers

A CPR Part 36 Offer is a way of settling a dispute with the involvement of the court. The process of issuing a Part 36 Offer is to formally register an offer to settle the dispute with the court and the court then writes to the opposition telling them of the offer lodged through the court. If a part 36 offer is accepted then it is normal for the party making the offer to lodge the money associated with the settlement with the court within fourteen days of the offer being accepted. The court will then ensure the money is forwarded to the receiving party as settlement. As with an open letter, if you make an offer and it is not accepted, and the case continues to a hearing, then when it comes to costs you can argue that your opponent did not take you up on a Part 36 Offer and that it was unreasonable for them not to have done so if your offer was a good one. After that, you can request that all costs after the offer was made were unnecessary and that they should not be paid by you.

## Tomlin Agreements

A Tomlin Agreement is where you agree to pay costs within a given framework or timescale that has been negotiated or agreed between you and your opposing party. If you agree to settle costs between you and your opposition, then you can agree a timeframe and payment terms via a Tomlin agreement. Tomlin agreements are contracts that are written between both parties to ensure that the timescale and fees to be paid are legally recognised and that the terms of payment are enforceable in court. These agreements are binding between both parties and in essence they freeze any legal process pending the final settlement that has been set out in the agreement. If you default on the agreement, the general terms of the contract allow for the resumption of legal proceedings at the point they were suspended prior to the Tomlin agreement being made. This means that any prior court activity or costs are not wasted if either party decides not to do what they have agreed to and that should there be a default, the resumption and outcome to a case can be reached quicker than if you had to start the whole legal process from the beginning. If you default on a Tomlin agreement and court action continues, then the defaulting party will normally have all costs awarded against them. The court takes a very dim view of defaults and would see any subsequent court action as wasted costs. If you are in a position where you have a Tomlin agreement and cannot afford to honour it, start communication with the other side as soon as you can and seek to limit any further costs. By doing so this will be observed by the court and you should not be penalised if there is a genuine reason for the default.

## Statutory Demands

Statutory Demands are a nasty tool used by the unscrupulous to force you into paying a bill or debt that you may have. If a costs award goes against you and you do not pay within fourteen days and your opponent is nasty, then they will most likely place a statutory demand upon you. A Statutory Demand is a piece of paper that is recognised by the courts and it is a document that says that there is an unpaid debt. The court will give a twenty one day time limit for you to pay or secure the debt or they will force you into bankruptcy. If you are struggling to pay your bills and if it is taking time, it is always best to try and come to an agreement with regard to payment with your opponent. You must also ensure that you copy the court in any correspondence. If your opponent issues a Statutory Demand and you have tried to make payment arrangements, then the court will view his actions with a great deal of disdain and they will be heavily penalised. If you wait for the statutory demand, you will be forced into the Bankruptcy Court. This is the last place you want to be because even if you can afford to pay your opponent, by being put on the court list, your other creditors will see you have been served with a demand and will issue their own demand. This means that you will not be able to defend yourself because you will have multiple demands to answer and you will probably be forced to sell your assets to pay your bills.

# Chapter 11

## If All Else Fails and You do Not Win Your Case or Part of It

All the way through this book the author has tried to explain that unless you have a lot of money, or unless you have very little to lose, then there is no such thing as justice. The trauma of going through a neighbour dispute is something that will change your life and in many ways the changes will be negative and not positive. The law does not compensate you for your time, lost sleep, the arguments you have had with your loved ones and if you have not won the costs of fighting your case, the money you will have to find and spend will be immense. If your opponent has won, then you may end up paying their costs as well and this will be an even bigger and bitter blow. The costs of losing could be immense and if you have been lucky enough to get a loan to cover the costs, you will most likely have to spend a long time working hard to pay the money back. If you have not got a loan and just have a bill that needs to be paid, then that is even worse. This is a terrible situation to be in and many people get depressed as a result. Do not however view it as the end of the world and although the position you are in may seem bad, you can get out of it and move on with your life.

## Money, Financing Your Dispute

### Resources for Raising Money - Before You Incur Costs

The biggest issue with the legal system in the UK is that it is one sided and it favours the rich. If you have money and can afford legal representation, then you are in a much better position than anyone else should a neighbour dispute ever arise with you. If you can get legal representation from the outset of the dispute, then the chances are that you can deal with your issues relatively successfully and quickly. If however you are like ninety six percent of the UK population, then you do not have spare money lying around just waiting to pay for legal expenses. Like most people you are likely to have a financial problem at some stage if you are forced into a legal action by your neighbour due to a neighbour dispute. The costs of a dispute are very great. You may have to find many different sources of money to fund or pay the outcome of a dispute. If you have just jumped to this page as you are thinking of taking action against your neighbour, the next two paragraphs are something for you to think about.

The biggest decision you will have to make in the dispute is to ask yourself, do I fight my neighbour and incur a huge financial cost, with the potential that I will never recover this money, or do I try and settle for as little loss as quickly as possible? Very often a neighbour dispute is not about who is right or who is wrong, as when the legal system is involved, it becomes a lottery whereby the side presenting the best argument has the best chance of winning. Even then, if you have a very strong case there are no guarantees that you win in court. Therefore if you value what you have in life, you must look at the situation from a logical point of view and ask yourself the questions

1.  How much can I afford to lose?

2.  How much am I likely to lose?

3.  Do I really want to spend the money to fight a battle?

With all three of the above questions there is a stark reality that you must face up to. That is that you will end up spending money in any event. How much or how little money you spend is really up to you as it is your choice whether you fight your neighbour or not. You must also realise that morality and the law are not a good mix. Even if you are right and your neighbour is wrong in their pursuit of the dispute, you have to be rational and try and negotiate or mediate with your neighbour. If you do not seek a settlement to the dispute before the legal bills start, you may find that you have to spend a lot of money to defend your position so that you do not get an even bigger bill if they start to take the matter to court. Pretty soon this process can cost you even more money and the costs of just defending yourself in court are huge. These costs can be anything from five thousand pounds to one hundred thousand in the most bitter and protracted case. The threats of such huge costs are such that you must consider ways to minimise the risks of receiving a bill of this size in the end.

# Bank Loans

Banks and building societies will loan you money for a number of things. You must bear in mind that most banks or building societies will only lend you a certain amount of money without a debenture or some form of security on your home. To qualify for a loan you must be able to prove your income and that you can afford the repayments to cover the loan. If you are using your home as security to leverage money from the bank or building society, they will want a valuation to be carried out before they lend you any money. Once the bank or building society is satisfied that you can afford your requested loan and you have proved that there is equity in your house, they will normally loan you money up to a maximum amount and will want to see some value or equity retained in your property. When asking for a loan it is very difficult to gauge how much money a neighbour dispute will cost you as there is a strong likelihood that it will carry on for several years. If the dispute does go to court and you win you case, you can assume that you will only recover a maximum of eighty percent of your costs in the best case. In the worst case you may end up paying all of your own costs plus the costs of your neighbour if they have won the legal case against you. These costs that you can expect to pay are anything up to one hundred thousand pounds. Typically a case will cost half of that amount, however you must bear in mind that you may also need to take some form of action based upon the Judges decision that you may not have budgeted for. This can also cost you money. Examples of this sort of expenditure include costs for the erection of a fence, the removal of a fence or the demolition of a building. A legal case can cost you even more money if the case goes to appeal and you lose and so you must consider these into your finances as well. When asking the banks for a loan, bear in mind that there may be a limit on how much money they can loan you and that they may not keep loaning you money time and time again. It is best therefore to go for a loan for as much money as you can afford and hold it in a savings account in the bank until you need it. The major disadvantage to this approach is that you will pay interest to the bank on your loan while the money is sitting in the bank waiting to be used to pay your legal fees. The alternative however is that you may spend the money and do not have it when you need it. Unfortunately there is no ideal solution to this dilemma so you must do what you can to save money and have the cash to pay any bills when you have to. The bills can come quite suddenly so you will need to have cash on hand to pay the amounts that are needed.

# Friends and Family

In today's society the banks and building societies are only interested in making money for themselves and they are certainly not interested in you unless you can make money for them. The banks and building societies have automated their systems to such an extent that if you do not fit into their model profile of typical customers, then they will tend not to lend you money. If they do lend you money, then the interest rates they will charge you for the loan are likely to be very high if you are outside of their model profile. For example, if you are self-employed, or are about to retire then they will see a higher risk of default with you so may not be willing to lend you money. As a result of this unwillingness and the high interest rates the banks or building societies may charge, it is better if you can ask your friends and family if they can assist you with your problem. If you cannot get a loan and if you risk losing everything then you must use all opportunities, contacts and options to try and keep what you have. When borrowing any money you must make sure that you can pay the loan back and you must also agree a timescale for the repayment of the money with the people who gave you the loan. Remember to thank them for their assistance and always pay them back as soon as you can, otherwise you will lose friends or alternatively you will fall out with your family and you could be left alone to fight the dispute with no support at all. The disagreement with your neighbour is bad enough without losing your friends or family as well.

# Selling Your Assets

There are many other ways of raising money that you could consider and this could include selling the things that you may not need any more; or alternatively you can make money by selling the things that you have that may be of value sitting around your home. Every house has things in it that are not needed by their owners and by selling some or all of these things that are not needed you can raise money. When you sell your possessions remember that the price you paid for something and the price you get when you sell the item are different and so even if you think something is valuable, it may not be as valuable as you think when you come to sell it. You must also bear in mind that when selling your unwanted items, the culture in the UK is moving towards that of the "Car Boot culture".That is to say that everyone is always looking for the lowest priced bargain they can find and they may not be too willing to pay your asking price. Always try and find the right market to sell your assets and unless you are absolutely desperate, do not sell your items for the first price that you get offered for them. This is especially true with jewellery as some dealers only buy based upon the weight of gold and not on the workmanship or on the stones that may be in your jewellery. The author knows of many jewellers who have made a fortune from buying rings with precious stones in them where they have only paid for the weight of the ring. The difference to you can be a matter of hundreds of pounds. Some jewellers also do not pay you the market price for your gold and so it is always better to visit several jewellers to try and get the best possible price that you can.

The other thing to think about is that if you really do need the money, it does not matter what it is that you are selling as you may be always able to buy it back or replace it with something similar. When selling your assets, do not sell things of sentimental value that are irreplaceable. These are family heirlooms, gifts from loved ones and things that may have another meanings, these are not worth losing as a result of a dispute. These should be the last things that you sell and even in the worst of times, they are the things that may bring you joy and comfort. Think very hard before you sell these items as there are other ways to make money. If you must sell them, then get the absolute best price that you can for them.

## Car Boot Sales

The best place to sell smaller less valuable items is the local market or a local car boot sale. Selling here could be a good way to raise money. Before you go to a car boot sale to sell your own things, go to a few sales beforehand and watch what people are buying, you may be very surprised. Get to the market or car boot sale early and see what is on offer, the best bargains always go first. Sometimes it is amazing what people will buy at these sales. A prime example is that people will always buy good food and so if you can make breakfasts, bake cakes, make sandwiches or lunches, then you may be able to make some reasonable money at the larger car boot sales doing this. Another thing to remember is that people tend to buy things for their homes and gardens so these things will sell most of the time. If you can grow seeds and cultivate plants then this can be another good source to raise money especially during the summer months. These ideas are also sustainable ideas and although they involve some hard work, they can be done time and time again to boost your income. If you only sell your unwanted items, you can only really do this once, so try and learn about what sells and try and do the same thing yourself.

## EBay

EBay has changed the way people buy things and it is easy to be a part of this new revolution. All you need to take part is a computer with Internet access. To join EBay you will need to set up an EBay account and you can do this very quickly by going to *http://www.ebay.co.uk.* If you just go to the URL and follow the instructions you will have an account in less than ten minutes. They will ask a few details and will also ask for verification of address and whether you are a person or a company. Once you have set up your EBay account you will also need to set up a PayPal account where you can accept payments from your buyers. Again EBay will assist you in doing this and they will redirect you to the PayPal site so you can register. When you go to the site, you will be asked for your personal details and will need to provide details on any credit or debit cards you want to use for payment to EBay and you will need to provide your current account details so that you can use this to receive payments for the goods that you have sold. PayPal will verify your bank details and identity by making a tiny payment into your account. When you receive this payment into your account you will need to log into your Pay Pal account and tell them exactly how much money you received. Once you have done this, you can start selling on EBay. This whole process from start to finish can take less than a week to complete, so you can be making money very quickly from doing this. When you are selling on EBay, look at what people are buying and if you can find a supply of what people are buying, then you can start selling these as well and you can again make some money.

## Ideas and knowledge

Everyone has ideas and knowledge that are of use to other people. Most people do not know the vast knowledge or experiences that they have accumulated during their lives are of use to other people. If you are in need of money and are finding it hard to get inspiration, go to a quiet area and think about what you know and what skills or knowledge you can give to other people. The chances are that your skills and knowledge have a practical value and you may be able to cash in on this. Talk to others about your knowledge and see if you can find a market for your ideas and skills. Do not be discouraged by people who do not buy into your ideas or who do not agree with them. Some people will be encouraging and others will not be of use to you at all as they will be negative or uncomplimentary. If you think about it long and hard enough then you will find a way to sell your ideas and to make some money.

## Gardening, Fruit and Vegetables

The garden can produce a wealth of produce that can feed you and your family in many different ways. Not only can you grow fruit and vegetables, you can grow plants, trees and flowers as well. All of these have a value. If you have an abundance of crops, or if you grow plants, trees and flowers, you can sell the things that you do not want and in turn make some money. At first glance this may not seem like a massive money spinner; however the fruit and vegetables that you grow yourself will taste a lot better than the supermarket produce and any excess that you can sell will most likely be enough to pay for your meat and dairy produce if you plan it correctly. If you are good at gardening and can manage the workload, you can make several hundred pounds per month during the summer months from your plants and the produce that you grow. The effort that will be involved in order to grow and nurture your plants can be therapeutic to you as it will help to take your mind off the dispute with your neighbour and will also generate some money that will likely be much needed if you have to pay for legal fees or for experts to represent your case.

## Part Time Work

If only one member of your family works, then there is an opportunity for other family members to get a part time job, or alternatively if you have spare time you can do the same. Although many people require their rest and relaxation, a part time job can be beneficial from two perspectives. Firstly it will bring in some more money that will be needed to pay your bills and you will definitely need this going forwards, secondly by getting a second job, or a part time one, it will distract you from your dispute and will give you something to occupy your mind. This is something that you will also need moving forward as it will be very hard not to think about the dispute at certain times. When considering getting a part time job, also consider the impact to your family life and regular routine. If you can find a job that does not impact upon these areas too much, then a part time job may be worth considering as a way to boost your income.

## Tax

When you are buying and selling your unwanted household items, it is unlikely that you will need to pay tax on their sale unless you make a lot of money from them. If you do start selling as a business to make money, you will need to disclose your income to the tax authorities and they will advise you of any tax you may need to pay. If you have any doubts as to tax matters, always seek the correct advice and contact the tax authorities. The last thing in the world you need if you are in a dispute with your neighbour is a big bill or an enquiry from the tax man.

## Resources to Take Your Mind Off the Dispute

Sadly any neighbour dispute will become all-consuming of both your time and your emotions and as a result you can find that the dispute takes over your life. This is bad news to you as you will find yourself very much alone on at least a few occasions. In order to escape the dispute and the problems it brings to you, try and find some resources to distract your mind off your problems. Give below are just a few resources that may help you to do this.

## Jokes & Humour

*http://www.coolfunnyjokes.com/*
*http://www.funnyandjokes.com/*

## Places to Visit

If you need a break and just have to get away for a day consider *The National Trust. They have hundreds of places that are well worth a visit.From country parks to stately homes* http://www.nationaltrust.org.uk *In Scotland the Scottish national trust also has hundreds of properties to visit* http://www.nts.org.uk/

## Places to Drink

Alcohol is not the answer to your problems; however a nice drink every now and then can help you to de stress so long as you do not drink too much. Try
http://www.thegoodpubguide.co.uk/
http://www.britishpubguide.com
http://www.pubinnguide.com
http://www.beerintheevening.com

## Music

Listening to music can be an escape for a time.
*YouTube has a vast amount of music videos and clips for you to watch and listen to. http://*www.youtube.com

# Chapter 12

## Final Thoughts

Any neighbour dispute will leave you with a legacy that will take you a long time to put behind you and forget. You will always feel bad about the dispute and elements of it. There will be certain things or events that will remind you of your dispute and they will bring back a wave of feelings or emotions. Whatever the outcome from the dispute, whether you won your case or lost it completely, whether you are in the middle of winning or losing your case with your neighbour, your best option will always be to try and limit the financial and emotional damage that the dispute will eithercause you as it progresses or if it has come to a conclusion, the damage that it may have already done.

If you are in the middle of a dispute, you should always look to a quick, peaceful and less financially damaging solution to your problems. The tools available to you are mediation; neighbour agreements and good old fashion conversation that you can use to limit the damage and to reduce the impact of the dispute.

If you have ended up in a dispute, you must remember it is not the end of the world, but a new beginning and it is one that you must take. Get yourself a hobby and ensure that you get as much quality out of life as possible. Distract yourself during the dark moments that will always be with you. As time progresses, you will find that the distractions and the quality that you seek will make life better and by doing so all of the negative can turn into a positive.

## Be Thankful for What You Have

When you are in a dispute it seems as though you are on your own as you have little or no support from friends and anyone but your immediate family. In most cases if you have gone down the path of dispute and the situation has deteriorated into a court case, you will have a lot to lose both from an emotional and financial perspective. When this happens to you take a moment and reflect upon the good things in life. Be thankful for what you have in your life and for your achievements and that of your family and do not let your dispute or the arguments with your neighbour ruin your life. Although it is difficult, try and control your thoughts so that the negative ones are not as dominant and the positive ones are foremost in your mind. If you can do this, life will be better and you will escape the dispute with your sanity and a better perspective on both life and your achievements.

It is all too easy to go into an ever repetitive spiral of depression, anger and lethargy because you have a disagreement with your neighbour that is consuming all of your thoughts, energy and emotions. You must fight hard to prevent the dispute from affecting you and your family and even if you do not win your case when it comes to court or a negotiated settlement, even if you have to pay some money, you will have retained your dignity and sanity. When you are worrying or obsessing it is very easy for you not to take care of yourself and those around you as your mind will not be thinking about certain things, particularly if you are facing financial difficulties due to your legal expenses or the Judgement from the court. If you focus on the good things and try and block out the bad, you will also find that you will eat better, sleep better and will remain relatively healthy. The way you think is a personal choice and with a bit of training you will be able to conquer even the most negative of emotions and should be able to put the dispute aside and behind you when it finally ends.

In your darkest moments, when you believe that things cannot get any worse, try and visualise a happy moment in your life, and try and think and see something that makes you smile or laugh and it will completely change your perspective on the situation, even if this is just for a moment, try it. This in turn will lead to you getting a faster recovery from your issues and will assist you overall in putting your bad experiences behind you. Whatever the outcome from your dispute, you will have to live with the decision and the consequences, even though they may not have been under your control. Simply put you will have to get on with your life. What you do and how you do it will make a massive difference to how well you cope with the challenges ahead of you and if you are not good at coping with or in managing stress, seek a councillor.

When things are bad and you are feeling low, do not lose faith in what you believe in. The legal system, your neighbours and the others that have wronged you are not representative of your values and beliefs and even if there are others do not believe in what you are doing, or in what you have done you must make sure that you hold true to your own beliefs and conscience. You must always support the people around you in both good times and bad and should always work with your family and friends to ensure that you retain some semblance of dignity, belief and most of all unity and friendship. The dispute is bad enough without it destroying your family and friends or your beliefs. If you work hard, you can overcome this.

# Appendix

## Useful Resources

## Before You Move In

http://www.upmystreet.com is a website that has lots of useful information on each area and details information about everything from shops, restaurants, schools and nursery's. The police figures and statistics for each area are also shown so you can get an idea on crime rates.

http://www.dfes.gov.uk/performancetables/ is a website that shows the performance of local schools and details how good or bad the schools are in terms of educational performance. They also detail absentee rates and this can be useful to see if children or young people are in school or whether they are not at school and so causing mischief, or if they are roaming the streets. Although not conclusive, if correlated with the crime rate, a good indication of youth issues can be obtained.

http://www.nsdatabase.co.uk/index.html is a website that shows the details of all newspapers in the UK and you can search on a county basis, it details all newspapers within the county and you can select a newspaper that covers the area where you live or where you want to live.

http://www.ordnancesurvey.co.uk/oswebsite/ is the Ordnance Survey website where you can buy all UK OS maps. It also contains useful data on interpreting and reading maps.

## After You Move In

### Aerial Photographs

http://www2.getmapping.com/ is a useful resource for both maps and Aerial Photographs

http://www.ukaerialphotos.com/ is another cheap resource
http://www.bluesky-world.com/products/ is also another supplier of
aerial pictures

# When You Have Issues (The Law Regarding Problems)

## Nuisance and Noise

*Noise Act 1996*
http://www.opsi.gov.uk/acts/acts1996/ukpga_19960037_en_1

*Noise &Statutory Nuisance Act 1993*
http://www.opsi.gov.uk/ACTS/acts1993/ukpga_19930040_en_1

*Environmental Protection Act 1990 (Pollution &Smoke)*
http://www.opsi.gov.uk/acts/acts1990/Ukpga_19900043_en_1.htm

*Clean Air Act 1993*
http://www.opsi.gov.uk/acts/acts1993/ukpga_19930011_en_1

## *Pets*

*Dogs Act 1996 (Fouling the Pavement)*
http://www.opsi.gov.uk/acts/acts1996/ukpga_19960020_en_1

## Support &Statutory Powers

### *Local Government Act 2000 (Council Powers)*
http://www.opsi.gov.uk/Acts/acts2000/ukpga_20000022_en_1

### *Crime and Disorder Act 1998 (Anti Social Behaviour)*
http://www.opsi.gov.uk/acts/acts1998/ukpga_19980037_en_1

### *Protection from Harassment Act 1997 (Harassment &Fear of Violence)*
http://www.opsi.gov.uk/acts/acts1997/ukpga_19970040_en_1

*Criminal Justice and Police Act 2001 (Disorderly Behaviour)*
http://www.opsi.gov.uk/acts/acts2001/ukpga_20010016_en_1

*Criminal Justice and Public Disorder Act 1994 (Trespass and Nuisance)*
http://www.opsi.gov.uk/acts/acts1994/ukpga_19940033_en_1

**Land &Boundary Related Matters**

*Access to Neighbouring Land Act 1992 (Cutting Your Neighbours Trees orHedges, Getting Into Their Garden)*
http://www.opsi.gov.uk/Acts/acts1992/ukpga_19920023_en_1

**Land Registration Act 2002**
http://www.legislation.gov.uk/ukpga/2002/9/contents

**Landlords**

*Housing Act 1996*
http://www.opsi.gov.uk/Acts/acts1996/ukpga_19960052_en_1

*Protection From Eviction Act 1977*
http://www.opsi.gov.uk/RevisedStatutes/Acts/ukpga/1977/cukpga_19770043_en_1

*Noise Nuisance*

Environmental Protection UK. This organisation provides a series of very useful leaflets that explain about noise problems and your rights around noise. They also provide advice around how you can deal with a noise problem
http://www.environmental-protection.org.uk

*Mediation*

There are many different sources of mediation; however the best source of mediators is Alternative Dispute Resolution now. This organisation provides a list of trained mediators and gives their contact details.
http:// www.adrnow.org.uk.

# Forms and Documents

Skeleton Arguments

http://www.hmcourts-
service.gov.uk/cms/files/SKELETON_ARGUMENT_TEMPLATE.doc

Appeals Forms & Advice

http://www.rcjadvice.org.uk/documents/Howtoappealacourtdecision.pdf

CPR Part 36

http://www.justice.gov.uk/civil/procrules_fin/contents/parts/part36.htm
Adjudicator to HMLR Forms & Guidance
http://www.ahmlr.gov.uk/formsguidance.htm

# Adjudicator to Her Majesty's Land Registry

http://www.ahmlr.gov.uk/index.htm

Forms & Guidance

http://www.ahmlr.gov.uk/formsguidance.htm

Practice & Procedure Rules

http://www.legislation.gov.uk/uksi/2008/1731/contents/made

Adjudication Appeal Process

http://www.legislation.gov.uk/uksi/2008/1730/contents/made

# Her Majesty's Courts Service

http://www.hmcourts-service.gov.uk/

# The Legal and Professional Regulators, Sources

## Royal Institute of Chartered Surveyors (RICS)

http://www.rics.org/
    The Royal Institution of Chartered Surveyors (RICS) is the
organisation that governs land surveyors in the UK. RICS are a good
source of information regarding boundary disputes and have a large
amount of information available for you to look at on line. If you get

into a boundary dispute, then they are a good first port of call for information about the nature of your dispute and as they are a membership organisation, they also list the contact details of surveyors and their respective specialities.

## Joint Surveyors

RICS run a service where they can find you a joint surveyor to survey the ground in dispute cases if you wish to do it jointly with your neighbour. Typically if you have a land dispute and a surveyor has not been appointed by either party, a joint surveyor is normally suggested by the court. In order to find a joint and independent surveyor however RICS charge for this service. More information on this service can be found on the RICS website.

## Register of Chartered Surveyors

RICS hold a register of all chartered surveyors in the UK and they can normally recommend someone to you if you have a specific need. Although RICS are supposed to be independent in their suggestions some of their staffs have made recommendations that appear to favour certain individuals. If RICS do make a recommendation, check the credentials of the person they are recommending as there are very good chances that they have been approached by your opposing party in the dispute If RICS have also been approached by them.

## Complaints About Surveyors

RICS are supposedly the governing body for surveyors in the UK and as such are supposed to be able to regulate and control surveyors who do not adhere to the rules that have been set or who misbehave in any way. The truth however is that RICS are very reluctant to deal with complaints about surveyors and very often dismiss them if they feel that your case or grounds for complaint are not strong enough, even if you may have some evidence to the contrary. In a practical sense, it is therefore very hard to get anywhere with a complaint about a surveyor with RICS.

## Citizens Advice Bureau
http://www.citizensadvice.org.uk/

The Citizens Advice Bureau (CAB) is a good source of advice and assistance on many matters regarding neighbour problems or disputes. The CAB can advise on varying areas associated with the life cycle of a neighbour issue. This advice includes disputes, credit issues and money matters as well as basic counselling on personal or emotional issues. The CAB are however a registered charity and as such cannot give legal advice to you. They do however have a number of publications, guides and leaflets that are freely available to you and that have been written by legal people. These can be useful sources of information and guidance through several stages of a dispute so they are well worth collecting and reading. Most towns have a CAB and the council can tell you where they are if you contact them. The CAB also has a specialist team that works with the High Court. This team was set up so that they could advise you of some of the administrative elements around High Court processes. If you need to use the CAB High Court Service you will need to make an appointment in advance as their hours and availability is limited. Be aware that they only work specific times and days during the week so it is best to telephone to make an appointment rather than go to their offices as they could be closed and you could have a wasted journey.

## Pro Bono Barristers
http://www.barprobono.org.uk/

The law in the UK is weighted in favour of those with money. If you are like 96% of the UK population and cannot afford huge sums on legal fees you have very few places to go to fund any legal cases that are put before the courts. Of the few sources of help, Bar Pro Bono is one of the more notable ones. Bar Pro Bono are a charity that has been set up to assist people on low income with legal issues that require a Barrister. To qualify for assistance you generally have to be on income support or on welfare or have very few savings. You can approach the charity directly but you must be sponsored by a Solicitor and if you qualify, the charity will allocate a Barrister to assist you for a maximum of three days free of charge. Bar Pro Bono do not provide Barristers that can represent you in court however. Even if you think you do not qualify for their assistance, they may still be able to help or make recommendations so they are worth looking at irrespectively. However it must be said that the author has tried to get help for a number of people and could not get any assistance from them due to the high demand and back log of cases. Do not be discouraged and keep trying.

## Pro Bono Solicitors
http://www.lawworks.org.uk/

Law Works provide a Solicitor on a pro bono basis if you are unable to afford to pay for one. Their criterion for assistance is very strict and you generally have to be on low income or income support with little or no savings. If you need their assistance, as with Bar Pro Bono, you will have to prove your income to them and they will allocate a Solicitor for a period of time to assist. Again like Bar Pro Bono, if you feel you may not qualify they can be a good source of help and can point you in the right direction. Bear in mind however that if you do not qualify, any assistance from a Solicitor or a Barrister will be chargeable.

## The Law Society
http://www.lawsociety.org.uk/home.law

The Law Society is the representative body for Solicitors in the UK. They act on behalf of Solicitors and represent their interests across a wide range of areas including lobbying the government and in defining training requirements and standards. The Law Society website is a useful source of information when you are searching for a Solicitor and the website gives a good overview of what it takes to become a Solicitor and so may give an insight into their mind-sets.

# Complaints

## The Bar Council
http://www.barcouncil.org.uk/

The Bar Council is the authority that regulates and licenses Barristers in the UK. For a Barrister to practice law, he or she must have completed a requisite amount of study and must have passed both the Bar exam and must have undertaken an apprenticeship within a Barristers chambers. Most, if not all Barristers are self-employed and they represent themselves through chambers.

A Barrister is a member of a chamber and this is your first port of call for any complaint about the Barrister. If you complain to the chamber, they are obliged to investigate the matter. If the chamber cannot deal with the issue directly, the next port of call for your complaint is the Bar Council. Once a complaint is received they will hand it to a specific person who will contact you to tell you they will be handling the complaint and then they will start to investigate the matter. The Bar Council have some strict rules as to what they will and will not investigate and if you have a personal issue with a Barrister, then the chances are that the Bar Council will not do anything about it and will not investigate the matter. If, however the Barrister has been in breach of his or her professional standards or ethics, or if he or she has been negligent or if he or she has misbehaved in any way apart from personally, then the Bar Council may be able to rectify the matter. The thing to bear in mind is that the Bar Council is run by Barristers and these Barristers will very seldom penalise someone to the level or extent that most normal people would feel is just. The author's experience of the Bar Council is very negative to the date of writing this book, this may be different for you so it is worth trying.

## The Solicitors Regulation Authority
http://www.sra.org.uk/solicitors/solicitors.page

Like barristers, Solicitors are regulated in the UK. Again like barristers, most Solicitors' offices are a partnership, so technically each Solicitor is self-employed but working within a group of other self-employed people. The complaints process against Solicitors is very similar to the complaints process of the Bar Council in so far as your first port of call to lodge your complaint is the Solicitors' offices. The Solicitors' office will normally have a person who has been appointed within the partnership to deal with complaints and as they are part of the same partnership as the Solicitor you are complaining about, they generally have a vested interest in dealing with the matters from a legal rather than a moral standpoint. So far the authors experience of Solicitors complaints procedures are that they are not weighted in any way in your favour. Solicitors will very seldom admit that they have done something wrong or that they have made a mistake and it is very seldom that they will deal with your complaint to a good degree of satisfaction.

After having dealt with the Solicitors' offices complaints process and not succeeded your next point of call is to make a complaint to the Solicitors Regulation Authority. Solicitors are a self-regulating profession and the SRA will only deal with matters of misconduct around personal areas and not professional ones. The SRA do not deal with matters such as professional negligence where the Solicitor has given incorrect advice to you or where they have conducted your case incorrectly. To deal with these matters, you must actually sue the Solicitor for professional negligence. Your chances of winning a case against a Solicitor are very remote as the insurance companies that are employed by the Solicitors have teams of people whose sole jobs are to protect the interests of Solicitors and their practice. The authors' experience of the Solicitors Regulation Authority to date is that they seem to have difficulty regulating timely correspondence so also struggle with the actual matters that they were set up to deal with.

http://www.lawsoc-ni.org/making-a-complaint/complaints-procedure/

http://www.sra.org.uk/solicitors/code-of-conduct/rule1.page

## Administrative Justice & Tribunals Council
http://www.ajtc.gov.uk/

The Administrative Justice & Tribunals Council is a Governmental Arm's Length Body that was set up to advise and guide the tribunals so that they are efficient and meet their aims and objectives around the administration of justice. This organisation absorbs several million pounds of tax payer s money each year and produces advice and guidance to the Tribunals. The organisation for all of its best efforts is useless and is a complete waste of time. Their guidance is exactly that, a guide and the Tribunals do not have to adhere to their guidance or recommendations and invariably they do not. This is because the government funds the Tribunals on a reduced budget and as a result, the Tribunals do not invest in processes and procedures unless there is a statutory obligation to do so. The Tribunals concerns are to save money and the Tribunal's council are interested in process and additional administration. Sadly the heads of the Tribunals are not interested in spending money so are at odds with this organisation.

## Independent Police Complaints Commission
www.ipcc.gov.uk/

The IPCC are the independent body that investigates any complaint raised against the police. To make a complaint about the police you can either write to the IPCC or use their web site. As with all other professional bodies or regulators, the IPCC have a vested interest in the police and they tend to air on the side of caution when it comes to decisions about police conduct rather than sticking with neutrality. Unless your compliant is serious enough to warrant it, the IPCC generally do very little to assist in dealing with your complaints against the police.

Printed in Dunstable, United Kingdom